D1695499

Aesthetic Reason
and Imaginative Freedom

SUNY series in Contemporary Continental Philosophy

Dennis J. Schmidt, editor

Aesthetic Reason and Imaginative Freedom

Friedrich Schiller and Philosophy

Edited by

María del Rosario Acosta López

and

Jeffrey L. Powell

SUNY PRESS

Published by State University of New York Press, Albany

© 2018 State University of New York

All rights reserved

Printed in the United States of America

No part of this book may be used or reproduced in any manner whatsoever without written permission. No part of this book may be stored in a retrieval system or transmitted in any form or by any means including electronic, electrostatic, magnetic tape, mechanical, photocopying, recording, or otherwise without the prior permission in writing of the publisher.

For information, contact State University of New York Press, Albany, NY
www.sunypress.edu

Library of Congress Cataloging-in-Publication Data

Names: Acosta López, María del Rosario, editor. | Powell, Jeffrey L., editor
Title: Aesthetic reason and imaginative freedom : Friedrich Schiller and philosophy /
  edited by María del Rosario Acosta López and Jeffrey L. Powell.
Description: Albany : State University of New York, 2018. | Includes bibliographical
  references and index.
Identifiers: LCCN 2018000108 | ISBN 9781438472195 (hardcover : alk. paper) |
  ISBN 9781438472218 (ebook)
Subjects: LCSH: Schiller, Friedrich, 1759–1805.
Classification: LCC B3086.S34 A63 2018 | DDC 193—dc23
LC record available at https://lccn.loc.gov/2018000108

10 9 8 7 6 5 4 3 2 1

Contents

Introduction   1
María del Rosario Acosta López and Jeffrey L. Powell

Part I: Schiller's Historico-Philosophical Significance

1. Schiller, Rousseau, and the Aesthetic Education of Man   11
   Yvonne Nilges

2. Schiller on Emotions: Problems of (In)Consistency in His Ethics   23
   Laura Anna Macor

3. Schiller's Aesthetics between Kant and Schelling   37
   Manfred Frank, translated by Christina M. Gschwandtner and Jeffrey L. Powell

4. The Violence of Reason: Schiller and Hegel on the French Revolution   59
   María del Rosario Acosta López

5. Schiller and Pessimism   83
   Frederick Beiser

Part II: Imagining Schiller Today

6. Naïve and Sentimental Character: Schiller's Poetic Phenomenology   101
   Daniel Dahlstrom

7. Schiller and the Aesthetic Promise 123
    Jacques Rancière, translated by Owen Glyn-Williams

8. On the Fate of the Aesthetic Education: Rancière, Posa, and *The Police* 137
    Christoph Menke, translated by Eliza Little

9. Kant, Schiller, and Aesthetic Transformation 153
    Jeffrey L. Powell

10. Aesthetic *Dispositifs* and Sensible Forms of Emancipation 175
    María Luciana Cadahia

Friedrich Schiller's Works Cited 193

Bibliography 195

Contributors 207

Index 211

Introduction

María del Rosario Acosta López and Jeffrey L. Powell

In recent years more and more attention has been directed toward mid- and late-eighteenth-century German thought. While Kant and Hegel have been responsible for a regular and abundant flow of secondary literature, as well as the source of new developments within philosophical scholarship, a number of other, formerly less well-known figures, have captured the attention of thinkers in the English-speaking world. German Romanticism has especially benefitted from this interest. Thanks to the intense work that has been produced in recent years in the field of German Romanticism, we can now appreciate the scholarship devoted to this period as much richer and wider than the mere discussion of taste to which more traditional approaches had tended to reduce it in the past. The many elements of German Romanticism came together to form an aesthetic whole that was indeed larger than the sum of its parts; and its parts were each already complicated enough in themselves. Those parts included, but were not limited to the political aspects and the formation of modern democracy; the metaphysical, epistemological, and practical (ethico-political) implications of the Enlightenment; the specific encounter with the classical world that served to both reinvent that world and to invent a newer Modern world; and, of course, the highlighting of the very limits of the discoveries to which those parts gave rise. In short, German Romanticism brought to light the possibility of an aesthetic approach to philosophy that was concerned with much more than the analysis of taste for which it is mostly known through its Kantian formulation, since it developed an account of aesthetic interest that, even though acutely aware of its Kantian source, went beyond that source and developed a critical apparatus directed toward its own production. Stated more simply, we can now see in German Romanticism what Foucault saw in Kant's short essay on the Enlightenment: "an attitude, an ethos, a philosophical life in which the critique of what we are is at one and the same time the historical analysis of the limits imposed on us and the experiment with the possibility of going beyond them [*de leur franchissement possible*]."[1]

One figure who seems to have become somehow lost in this discussion is Friedrich Schiller. With few exceptions, Schiller has been absent as a reference point in philosophical literature, at least for the second half of the twentieth century and now into the twenty-first century, and particularly in secondary literature in English. Indeed, the neglect of Schiller as a philosopher is a refrain that has accompanied the treatment of his work since the inception of its critical appraisal. This is not to say that Schiller has never been treated with regard to his philosophical contribution, but it is to assert that he has only rarely been subject to such treatment within the tradition of philosophical scholarship. In a lecture given at Yale in 2005, in the context of the celebration of 200 years of Schiller's death, Frederick Beiser stated that since the end of the Second World War, and in visible contrast to the role Schiller used to play in the philosophical scene at the end of nineteenth century, "the study of Schiller's philosophy has not only entered into an abrupt decline but is virtually dead."[2] This is partially due, Beiser continues, to the increasing specialization of the English-speaking academic world, where a figure such as Schiller, who moves between literature, poetry, and philosophy, does not find an adequate place and hence has mostly been relegated to literary studies. Just a quick look at the secondary bibliography on Schiller in English, even in the last ten years, confirms this observation. The two more recent compilations on Schiller published in English, Paul Kerry's 2007 volume and Jeffrey High's 2011 collection of essays,[3] come mainly from literary studies and German studies, with only one or two chapters developed from a more explicitly philosophical perspective.

Even when the philosophical discussion does turn to Schiller, the typical form of such examination is to begin by noting the absence or inadequacy of Schiller's philosophical contribution, and to then proceed either with a more historical configuration of Schiller's aesthetic writings, or an analysis exhibiting his debt to—and often misinterpretation of—Kant or his being not yet Hegel. A notable exception to this trend in the English speaking world is Frederick Beiser's 2005 book, *Schiller as Philosopher: A Re-Examination*, which is, indeed, as its title suggests, a re-examination devoted to showing the depth and originality of Schiller's philosophical contributions, connected to, but also previous to and independent from his encounter with Kant. For all of that, however,

Beiser's magisterial study has not led to the new wave in the English-speaking world of philosophical studies on Schiller that one might have expected. This is even more conspicuous when one notices the wave of recent philosophical literature on Schiller in other languages. Starting in 2005, with the 200th-year anniversary of Schiller's death, a number of publications in French, German, Italian, and Spanish, to mention just the most numerous, has been changing for the last ten years the academic discussion and approach to Schiller.[4] Just a look at the titles of some of these works reveals the shift in Schiller's scholarship, or as Valerio Rocco has also suggested, a "paradigm turn" in Schiller's studies.[5] Jeffrey High's 2004 *Schillers Rebellionskonzept und die Französische Revolution*, Gilles Darras' 2005 *L'âme suspecte. L'anthropologie littéraire dans les premiers oeuvres de Schiller*, Laura Macor's 2008 *Il giro fangoso dell'umana destinazione. Friedrich Schiller dall'illuminismo al criticism*,[6] Yvonne Nilges's 2012 *Schiller und das Recht*, and the edited collections *Schiller: estética y libertad* by María del Rosario Acosta (2008), *El pensamiento filosófico de Friedrich Schiller* by Brigitte Jirku and Julio Rodríguez (2009), *La actualidad de Friedrich Schiller. Para una crítica cultural al inicio del siglo XXI* by Horst Nitschack and Reinhard Babel (2010), *Friedrich Schiller. Der unterschätzte Theoretiker* by Georg Bollenbeck and Lothar Ehrlich (2010), and *Schiller im philosophischen Kontext* by Cordula Burtscher and Markus Hien (2011), to mention just a few, all show a very present preoccupation to vindicate Schiller as a philosopher while also demonstrating his contemporary relevance.[7]

This volume hopes to continue this trend and to give it a decisive impulse in the English-speaking world. The pertinence of Schiller's work is unquestionable, and his philosophical importance extends beyond his dramas and his aesthetic and political writings into his intense dialogue with Kant, his influence on German Romanticism and Idealism, his very unique approach to the question and practice of philosophical critique, and his preoccupation with hermeneutics and phenomenology, among other subjects. Some of the papers collected here elaborate on Schiller's relation to the philosophy of his time and show how his proposals were not a misinterpretation of Kantian philosophy—which he read rather late in his own development as a thinker—nor simply preliminary ideas that would find a more developed and rigorous exposition in later thinkers like Schelling and Hegel, but rather the original result of a mature thinker who was very much engaged with the ethico-political and aesthetico-philosophical debates of his time and who, by the time of the *Aesthetic Letters*, had already developed his own perspective and standpoint concerning the question of freedom and its relation and tension with the questions of culture, history, and the political. Some others concentrate rather on reading Schiller from today's perspective, and producing a dialogue between his own originality as a thinker and current philosophical debates.

∼

The essays largely dedicated to the engagement of Schiller's philosophical thinking with others within his own epoch comprise one of the two sections of this collection. Each of the chapters in this first section emphasizes the productive dialogue between Schiller and other thinkers of his time, rather than presenting his philosophical thought as a misinterpretation or misappropriation of the philosophers that would have influenced him. Yvonne Nilges's essay engages in a detailed account of the way Schiller's political proposals in the *Aesthetic Letters* responds to and criticizes Rousseau's political philosophy, even though references to Rousseau almost always remain implicit in Schiller's texts. Schiller's aesthetic education is related, Nilges argues, to a philosophical conception of both the political and the historical nature of the State, which attempts to reconstruct the enlightened and humanistic spirit of Rousseau's larger project of a historical transformation of the bourgeois into a *citoyen*, rather than emphasizing the concept of the general will as it is presented in Rousseau's political philosophy, and particularly in his theory of the Social Contract.

Following this same interest in rescuing Schiller as a political thinker of his time, intimately engaged in a philosophical criticism of the French Revolution, but further than this, in a philosophical critique of the possibilities and limits of the very idea of philosophy as historical critique, María del Rosario Acosta's essay develops a comparison between Schiller and Hegel's approaches to the French Revolution and its subsequent Reign of Terror. Acosta is interested in rescuing the essentially philosophical and conceptual character of Schiller's approach, which has been highlighted in the secondary literature in the case of Hegel, but almost entirely ignored when it comes to Schiller. Comparing Hegel and Schiller allows Acosta to demonstrate the originality and maturity of Schiller's critique, and the striking clarity of his diagnosis, produced almost ten years before Hegel's.

Laura Macor and Manfred Frank's contributions also demonstrate the originality of Schiller's philosophy through his engagement with Kant. Macor shows that many of the central features of Schiller's philosophical thought precede rather than result from his encounter with Kant and demonstrates that this needs to be taken into account in order to understand the nuances of Schiller's critical engagement with Kant's practical philosophy. For Macor, Schiller is much more of a Kantian than the secondary literature has been willing to recognize, and his notion of aesthetic freedom is not to be understood—as Kant himself did—as a critique of Kant's conception of autonomy as much as an endorsement of Kantian moral principles supplemented with a more complete account of moral agency. Frank's essay, in turn, argues that Schiller's engagement with Kant's *Critique of Judgment* anticipates Schelling's interpretations of Kant and also provides the "first glimmer" of the philosophy of nature that would be developed by Schelling and the Romantics.

Frederick Beiser's exploration of Schiller as a "pessimist" brings the first part of this volume to a close by showing the importance of Schiller on the philosophical developments of the nineteenth century. In his contribution, Beiser reinforces his insistence, as developed in his previous work, on the need to recognize Schiller's texts on their own merits as an important and original step in the history of philosophy, this time by investigating the connections between Schiller's work and later "pessimists" like Arthur Schopenhauer, Eduard von Hartmann, Philipp Mainländer (1841–1876), and Julius Bahnsen (1830–1881).

In this way, Beiser's essay helps to show the unexpected encounters that can still be brought to light through a rigorous engagement with the reception of Schiller in his time.

◦∾◦

There is yet another reason for the neglect of Schiller's significance for philosophy, which has to do with historical and political circumstances that are not specific to Schiller, but that certainly seem to be exaggerated concerning his work. These circumstances are particularly curious with regard to Schiller, for they concern one of the main targets of his philosophical essays. What we mean here is the use of Schiller for political purposes, and the link that has been suggested between his thought and the historical experience of the totalization and aestheticization of politics in the first half of the twentieth century, especially in the context of National Socialism. The most famous accusations come from Paul de Man, who points to the relationship between Schiller's proposal of an aesthetic state—which, according to him, is a dangerous misinterpretation and erroneous translation of Kantian aesthetics—and Goebbel's ideal of the political as a work of art.[8] One cannot ignore this side of the studies treating Schiller, but as has been the case with so many authors in the last decades, it is also a philosophical responsibility to study their limits and extent of their implications, and re-read Schiller in light of this awareness. Only then can a rigorous reading of Schiller show how aware he was of such risks, and how not only his *Aesthetic Letters*, but also his other writings on aesthetics, history, and art, are also critical elaborations of the very notion of the political and involve a redetermination of aesthetic ground that demands an alteration in what we mean by political means. On this subject, we have the historians and Germanists to thank for their careful and exacting work.[9]

One of the main interests of the present compilation is to revisit Schiller's aesthetical-political proposal from a philosophical perspective, and to put it in dialogue with contemporary approaches and criticisms to the question of the relationship between aesthetics and politics. It is this concern that guides the second part of our collection. Thus, each of the essays in this section proposes to place Schiller in conversation with contemporary philosophy. Dahlstrom's essay, which opens this part of the volume, provides a penetrating reading of Schiller's *On Naïve and Sentimental Poetry* that shows it to be a precursor to a poetic phenomenology. His analysis of the naïve and sentimental calls for a phenomenology similar to Husserl's bracketing, while showing how this kind of reflection problematizes the very distinction between them. This problematization results, for Schiller, in the synthesis of the naïve and sentimental, though one that preserves the conflict between them. Thus, Dahlstrom's reading already introduces a reading of Schiller in light of twentieth-century philosophical concerns, and in close connection to a conversation with twentieth-century philosophical thinkers.

Jacques Rancière's piece on Schiller's aesthetic promise is the first of a few contributions in this volume devoted to showing how, rather than arguing for an aestheticized politics that can then be subordinated to a specific political agenda, Schiller's proposal is a call to redirect our attention and rethink the ground of the aesthetic. This rethinking can then be taken as the first step of a re-elaboration of what we call "the political" and the very realm of its means. According to Rancière, Schiller's notion of aesthetic play, as conceptualized in his *Aesthetic Letters*, introduces an autonomy of aesthetic practice that can dissolve the hierarchical relationship between the poles of appearance and reality, and bring forth a politics of nondomination. In discussion with Rancière's reading, and critically engaging both Schiller and Rancière from the perspective opened by Schiller's *Don Carlos*, Christoph Menke questions some of the philosophical presuppositions that guide Rancière's call for a "redistribution of the sensible," pointing out the possible blind spots of such a redistribution and delineating some of the risks of a conception of the political grounded on the autonomy of the aesthetic.

Jeffrey Powell also directs his attention to Schiller's notion of play, this time, however, to treat the kind of political subjugation that is usually associated with Walter Benjamin's aestheticization of the political. Powell considers contemporary readings of Schiller's aesthetics and their relation to Kant. He highlights the dangers of an oversimplification of Schiller's aesthetics and the overestimation of Kant's aesthetics. In the end, and contrary to contemporary critical readings of Schiller (de Man being perhaps the most well-known), Powell shows that it is actually Schiller's analysis that leads to what Benjamin called political aesthetics, while Kant leads rather to an early version of Benjamin's "aestheticization of the political." Finally, Luciana Cadahia's essay helps to preserve the contemporary relevance of Schiller's political thought by reading Schiller's conception of "positivity" in the light of what Foucault calls the *dispositif*. By putting in dialogue Schiller's aesthetic conception of positivity with Deleuze and Martín-Barbero's more dialectical interpretations of Foucault's originally critical conception of the term, Cadahia's chapter shows the critical potential of Schiller's conception of positivity in the *Aesthetic Letters*. Far from considering it as a stigmatized form of power, Cadahia shows that, for Schiller, and against a more Hegelian tradition of thought, positivity as *dispositif* can become a productive form of aesthetic-political mediation.

With all these questions and circumstances in mind, it is our hope that this collection will answer the call for a renewed appreciation of Schiller's philosophical thought, which does not only mean a look into his more philosophical work, but also in the aesthetic, ethical, and epistemological reflections behind his entire intellectual production.[10]

Notes

1. Michel Foucault, "Qu'est-ce que les Lumières?" in *Dits et écrits II, 1976–1988* (Paris; Gallimard, 2001), p. 1396. In English, "What is Enlightenment?" in *The Essential Works of Michel Foucault*, volume one, *Ethics: Subjectivity and Truth*, ed. Paul Rabinow, trans. Catherine Porter (New York: The New Press, 1997), 319.

2. Frederick Beiser, "Un lamento" (*A Lament*), in *Friedrich Schiller: Estética y Libertad*, ed. M. R. Acosta (Bogotá: Universidad Nacional, 2008), p. 131. The lecture, given in Yale in 2005, was also published in its English earlier version in Paul Kerry (ed.) *Schiller; Playwright, Poet, Philosopher, Historian* (New York: Peter Lang, 2007). Paul Kerry also begins an essay that sets out to assess the reception of Schiller's political contribution by noting the neglect of Schiller for both philosophy and political thought. Besides quoting Beiser's lecture, Kerry notices the absence of Schiller in the series *Cambridge Texts in the History of Political Thought*.

3. See Paul Kerry (ed.), *Schiller; Playwright, Poet, Philosopher, Historian* (New York: Peter Lang, 2007) and *Who Is This Schiller Now?*, ed. Jeffrey L. High, Nicholas Martin, and Norbert Oellers (Rochester, NY: Camden House, 2011).

4. As Laura Macor notices in her introduction to a special issue on Friedrich Schiller in *Philosophical Readings* published in 2013, this wave was preceded by an earlier wave in the 1980s in Germany that may have played a decisive, even if quiet, role in the more recent escalation of philosophical literature on Schiller. Macor mentions, among others, papers written during the 1980s and 1990s by Hans-Jürgen Schings and Dieter Borchmeyer, and the more influential monographic study by Wolfgang Riedel, *Die Anthropologie des jungen Schiller. Zur Ideengeschichte der medizinischen Schriften und der 'Philosophischen Briefe'* (Würzburg: Königshausen & Neumann, 1985). These were all, however, still coming from the field of German studies, while the more recent wave is, as Macor also notices, more interdisciplinary in tone, and more philosophical in depth and scope. Cf. Laura Macor, "Introducing the New Schiller," *Philosophical Readings*, volume 5 (2013): 3-6.

5. Cf. Valerio Rocco Lozano, "Los cambios de paradigma de la 'Schiller-Forschung,'" *Daimon Revista Internacional de Filosofía*, 46 (2009): 205-13.

6. Translated into German and expanded in 2010, *Der morastige Zirkel der menschlichen Bestimmung. Friedrich Schillers Weg von der Aufklärung zu Kant* (Würzburg: Königshausen & Neumann).

7. Cf. for a more complete account of secondary bibliography on Schiller the very detailed list of recent publications offered by Macor in "Introducing the New Schiller," 4-5. Cf. also the very important work that the journal *Philosophical Readings* has also done in this regard, by producing in the last five years two entire special issues devoted to Schiller as a philosopher (cf. Volume 5, 2013, edited by Laura Macor and devoted to "Reading Schiller Anew" and Volume 9, 2017, edited by Laura Macor and Valerio Rocco and devoted to Friedrich Schiller and the French Revolution).

8. See Paul De Man "Kant and Schiller" in *The Aesthetic Ideology* (Minneapolis: University of Minnesota Press, 1996). For a more detailed treatment of this problem see M. R. Acosta "Making other people's feelings our own" in *Who Is This Schiller Now?*, ed. Jeffrey L. High, Nicholas Martin, and Norbert Oellers (Rochester, NY: Camden House, 2011), 187ff.

9. A fine, more recent example of this is provided by Wulf Koepke in his "The Reception of Schiller in the Twentieth Century" in *A Companion to the Works of Friedrich Schiller*, ed. Steven D. Martinson (Rochester, NY: Camden House, 2005), 271-93.

10. Editorial preparation for this volume, together with copyediting work and translation of Christoph Menke's contribution, was made possible by a grant provided by the University Research Council (URC), DePaul University, 2016-2017.

Part I

Schiller's Historico-Philosophical Significance

1

Schiller, Rousseau, and the Aesthetic Education of Man

Yvonne Nilges

Schiller considered his letters on aesthetic education (1795) to be the most significant of his theoretical writings. This is not merely due to the aesthetic substance of the letters, but just as much to what Schiller himself identified as his "political creed"[1]: the aesthetic education of man engages with contemporary constitutional law as a result of the French Revolution, most notably with Rousseau's legal and political philosophy. As early as in his lecture "The Legislation of Lycurgus and Solon," (1789) Schiller had rejected Rousseau's claim for direct democracy (without identifying Rousseau by name).[2] In the years to follow, the reign of terror in France did not cause Schiller to revoke his judgment on the general will; rather, Schiller's *Vernunftgericht* (tribunal of reason)—a term derived from Kant's ethics—is directly opposed to Rousseau's ideas on society and on the state and even is an increase from Schiller's former criticism.

To this day little is known about Schiller's reception of Rousseau. At a first glance, this seems to be surprising, but the reason for this void is certainly twofold: on the one hand, Schiller refers to Rousseau merely implicitly in virtually all of his works, and on the other, this very reference is a deeply dialectical one starting in 1789. Schiller's political attitude toward Rousseau is rooted in ambivalence, tending toward repudiation, to the effect that Schiller intricately revises Rousseau's political conceptions (as he does with Kant's ethics, which is, however, often mentioned explicitly in Schiller's works).³ On the following pages we shall for the first time trace the crucial influence the Social Contract had on Schiller and, in so doing, trace Schiller's criticism of Rousseau which takes the form of an appellate court in the legal dispute of the time.

Rousseau's theory, according to Schiller's judgment, is but a one-sided one, lending itself to excessively rigid conclusions and even to devastating consequences as the course of the French Revolution had unfortunately shown. This does not mean, however, that Schiller ignores Rousseau's good will, but he believes the *Contrat social* to be too theoretical, i.e., nothing but rational, whereas in his own view, *mundus intelligibilis* and *mundus sensibilis*, intelligibility and sensibility, must indeed be reconciled. When Schiller dedicated himself to representative democracy in 1789 thus renouncing Rousseau's *volonté générale*, this was because he did not trust the general will to be truly judicious. Chaos and riotous masses had, a few years later, actually taken possession of France. These later historical developments therefore confirm Schiller's concerns, and *On the Aesthetic Education of Man in a Series of Letters* aims to be a suggestion for improvement, at least in the first part, to which we shall now direct our attention. The Enlightenment—and Rousseau's direct democracy—has, according to Schiller, overestimated itself as a result of its drastic one-sidedness and its self-righteous apodictic statements. Thus Rousseau writes in his *Contrat social*.⁴

> Sovereignty cannot be represented for the same reason that it cannot be alienated; it consists essentially in the general will, and the will does not admit of being represented: either it is the same or it is different; there is no middle ground.

Schiller's tribunal of reason, in contrast, attempts to mediate and to communicate, thereby introducing a *renegotiation* of contemporary legal and political matters (VIII, 499). In the second of his letters Schiller thus starts by connecting the state to the sphere of art: the former, he argues, ought to be regarded as the most accomplished work of art in order to really and truly secure political freedom (VIII, 558/AL, 88). This, however, is an indirect correction of the notion of the state as asserted by Rousseau. According to the Social Contract, the state is not an artwork, but rather a *machine*—and the most accomplished legislator "the mechanic who invents the machine."⁵ The metaphors could not be more converse. Rousseau's description of the state as a machine exemplifies the enlightened mindset, such as La Mettrie's materialistic philosophy, for instance (*L'homme machine*, 1748). Yet this very reduction to one simple theoretical idea should in the following lead to what Burke, in his

Reflections on the Revolution in France (1790), had at an early point described as incomplete, i.e., as a merely geometrical and arithmetical political experiment.[6]

A machine, as an inanimate object, is insensible and cold. Therefore, when Schiller complains that the enlightenment has not lacked light but *warmth*, not a philosophical but rather an aesthetic culture (VIII, 505),[7] this too refers to Rousseau's affirmative notion of a state machinery as opposed to Schiller's own concept of the state as a perfect work of art:

> Reason has accomplished all that she can accomplish by discovering the law and establishing it. Its execution demands . . . the ardor of feeling . . . If she [truth] has hitherto displayed so little of her conquering power, this was due, not to the intellect that was powerless to unveil her, but to the heart that closed itself against her . . . since the way to the head must be opened through the heart. (VIII, 580ff./AL, 106–07)

Reason alone has accomplished everything it could achieve; the completion, however, is up to *sensitivity* as the way to the head must be opened through the heart.[8]

It is the third letter on aesthetic education where Schiller's "political creed" and Rousseau's *Contrat social* clash even more. Here Schiller introduces the word "*Notstaat*" (the state born out of need; VIII, 561/AL, 90) or, alternatively, the word "*Naturstaat*" (the state of nature; VIII, 562/AL, 91), which needs to be replaced by a true state of reason, i.e., a state of truthful liberty "*Staat der Freiheit*" (VIII, 567/AL, 95). As we can easily recognize, Schiller is again alluding to Rousseau's Social Contract (which is, in Schiller's view, to be annulled), but how exactly does he operate within Rousseau's terms, how circumspectly does he dismantle and reassemble Rousseau's diction?

To begin with, the primordial state of man (*Naturstand*) is something that Schiller was very cautious to idealize, departing from Rousseau. To Schiller, the process of civilization generally means *progression* (culture) and nothing that one should regret. Consequently, the state of man *before* civilization, which must be conceived as an unachievable role model if we follow Rousseau, becomes the opposite in Schiller's understanding. Rousseau's "*amour de soi*" that characterizes the noble savage is in fact immature narcissism in Schiller's eyes—or what Rousseau himself had called the "*amour-propre*" (which he had associated with man *after* the beginning of civilization). Schiller thus *reverses* Rousseau's judgment, interpreting civilization as a *remedy* for humankind, whereas Rousseau himself regards the process of socialization (and, stemming from this development, culture and art) as a mere sign of decay. As a result, however, this also means that Schiller's state of nature is, at the same time, not Rousseau's state of nature: to Schiller it is a purely physical state born out of need that must be overcome. While Schiller's diction therefore alludes to Rousseau, Schiller still implicitly dissociates himself from Rousseau's very ideas—despite the fact that the *connotation* of the word "*Naturstaat*" in the context of Schiller's third letter refers to the absolutist state, which both Rousseau and Schiller do repudiate. What happens in this third letter is that Schiller seemingly adopts Rousseau's vocabulary, but by combining Rousseau's cultural, aesthetic and political theories, he gives Rousseau's ideas a different color, which is actually antithetic. The very idea of an *aesthetic* education in support of political change is as much opposed to Rousseau's principles as one could possibly imagine (cf. Rousseau's *Émile, ou De l'éducation*, 1762).[9]

The aim of Schiller's aesthetic letters is to "cure" the Revolution by means of an aesthetic education: which is to lead to a true state of reason instead of a radical call for a republic that has meanwhile become distorted. Rousseau's legal and political philosophy, according to Schiller, fails to take into account that man was not yet educated enough in order to act politically mature; the enlightened education had not been a *holistic* one, just as Rousseau's own principles had been rationalistic only, neglecting sensibility. To cultivate the heart as well and, in so doing, to cultivate a sense of human *totality* is to what Schiller's appellate court aspires.

Strikingly, Schiller operates with Rousseau's "inalienable rights" by taking them in another direction. Schiller asserts that it is part of man's inalienable rights to simply annul the Social Contract and to leave the *circulus vitiosus* of apodictic theory in ideational realization. That way, man will truly come of age and learn to not rush into political caesuras for which he is not ready:

> [he] conceives, as idea, a *state of nature* [*Naturstand*] . . . attributes to himself in this idealized natural state a purpose of which in his actual natural state he was entirely ignorant, and a power of free choice of which he was at that time wholly incapable; and now proceeds exactly as if he were starting from scratch, and were, from sheer insight and free resolve, exchanging a state of complete independence for a state of social contracts. (VIII, 562/AL, 90–91)

In his fifth letter, Schiller paraphrases the problem even more pointedly: the generous moment of the French Revolution has found an unreceptive generation; the physical opportunity was there, Schiller maintains, but the moral one was not—"The *moral* possibility is lacking, and a moment so prodigal of opportunity finds a generation unprepared to receive it." (VIII, 567/AL, 96)

At one point, admittedly, even the *Contrat social* concedes that there is a time of human maturity needed before legislative effects can hope to be fruitful; Rousseau's word choice is characteristic in this context and not compatible with Schiller's own notion of liberty. Rousseau, in the said passage, speaks of oppressive "subjection" to the law and then acknowledges that this necessary subjection is not advisable at just any time: "but the maturity of a people is not always easy to recognize, and if one acts too soon the work is ruined."[10] However, this is precisely Schiller's objection. The enlightened belief in incessant progressiveness has run out of patience after all and therefore prevented man from coming to terms with himself first. Man has relied on his intellect only and neglected the cultivation of the heart, to the effect that there has been no balance that could have enabled him to act politically wiser. When Schiller thus chooses a certain phrase from Rousseau's novel *Julie ou la Nouvelle Héloïse* (1760) to be the motto serving his aesthetic letters, he expresses his surprise at the fact that in his novel, Rousseau has in fact valued a holistic approach, while in his *Social Contract*, slightly later, he has not. The phrase in question—Schiller's motto—reads "*Si c'est la raison, qui fait l'homme, c'est le sentiment, qui le conduit*" (VIII, 556). In his *Contrat social* Rousseau has become entirely abstract and therefore extreme, to the point that he supports totalitarian measures. According to Rousseau's *volonté générale*, the citizen may well be forced to succumb to the general will, "which means nothing other than he shall be forced to be free."[11] However, pressure and oppression is exactly what Schiller has been observing on the basis of the French developments; these are, like Rousseau's claims, the birth of tragedy from the spirit of pure theory.

As early as in a letter from September 18, 1787, Schiller's friend Körner had raised the question of whether a one-sided, *despotic* enlightenment was actually helpful, and although this question originally referred to the Illuminati, in Schiller's perception the parallels to Rousseau and to Rousseau's reception in the Revolution are self-evident. As a result, Schiller's demonstrative motto taken from Rousseau's *Julie* may be regarded as a dialectical effort to come to Rousseau's defense after all Schiller's tribunal of reason, matter-of-factly, can only deliver the judgment that Rousseau's political principles, with the most serious consequences, have become guilty by being caught up in abstract theory. Hence, Schiller contrasts a merely "theoretical culture" with what he defines as a "practical culture"; the latter, however, and therefore true political liberty can only be obtained with the help of an aesthetic education that cultivates man as a whole.

As shown above, Schiller's aesthetic letters have a *therapeutic* agenda, at least in the first section when Schiller is still optimistic that society must and can eventually be cured. This too implies that Schiller does appreciate Rousseau's legal reflections in spite of criticizing them. The malady of the time, Schiller hopefully asserts, is in effect a children's disease that can be defeated in the long run if only man's "alienation" can be overcome. This sounds like an anticipation of Marx's diagnostic findings, and Schiller's thoughts are indeed emphatically modern at this point. Schiller alludes to what Hegel in his philosophy of law (1821) was to explain more explicitly around three decades in the future: in modern times, man has disintegrated himself, becoming a private individual on the one hand and a political citizen on the other. He has lost his integrity as a result of losing his totality. Without describing this development in Hegel's insight, Schiller's train of thought is the same. Both Hegel and Schiller pertain to a terminological differentiation in this context that had first been made in Rousseau's *Contrat social*. Hegel refers to Rousseau more directly while Schiller's approach is—again—an indirect one; yet in both cases the crucial point is Rousseau's distinction between man as "bourgeois" and man as "*citoyen*."[12]

In a digression concerning Greek polity, Rousseau had defined this momentous difference as follows: "The true sense of this word is almost entirely effaced among the moderns; most take a city for a City, and a bourgeois for a Citizen."[13] In the years to come, Kant adopted Rousseau's disjuncture of "bourgeois" and "*citoyen*," but he also adopted Rousseau's original context.[14] Schiller, in contrast, refers to Rousseau's distinction on the basis of *man's intrinsic modern ability* (as Hegel will do so several years later). In his letters on aesthetic education, Schiller constantly engages with Rousseau's understanding of the state, but always comes to different judgments and conclusions. The French "*Déclaration des droits de l'homme et du citoyen* [!]" had turned into terror before long, and Schiller's appellate court points to the fact that man's one-sidedness also holds true for Rousseau. As with regard to Rousseau's novel *Julie* and his Social Contract that was published shortly afterwards, Schiller once more notices a strange discrepancy. Rousseau, in spite of having recognized and indeed specified the modern splitting of man so very perceptively, was at the same time too short-sighted to perceive this very splitting as a *loss*. According to Schiller, he failed to apply his own novelistic phrase to his political philosophy, just as he failed to thoroughly think out his own observations on man's dissociation and the problems that this splitting might eventually cause. The enlightened loss of totality, the diminution of sensibility in favor of pure intellect that is so typical of the time thus also applies to the *Contrat social* as a whole. Judging from Rousseau's political philosophy, Schiller comes to the conclusion that the

Social Contract has rightfully deprived the absolutist state of its legitimation. However, according to the tribunal of reason, what the Social Contract actually left was virtually void of air. Accordingly, Rousseau's jurisdiction on the state eventually led to cruel consequences when the general will had in fact been put into practice and had been enforced at all costs. The abstract philosopher, Schiller argues in his aesthetic letters, oftentimes has a cold heart as he knows well how to anatomize the circumstances, but not how to think holistically and thereby touch the soul: "the abstract thinker very often has a *cold* heart, since he dissects his impressions, and impressions can move the soul only as long as they remain whole" (VIII, 575/AL, 102). Thus according to Schiller's sixth letter Rousseau's state machinery had accordingly been *cold*.

Despite the Enlightenment, people are still barbarians (VIII, 581/AL, 106) because the Enlightenment was not complete. It was Nietzsche who, much later, agreed with Schiller. He describes the dialectic of enlightenment and its dangers more sharply and much more polemically yet the conclusion is the same. Unlike Schiller, Nietzsche in this context does refer to Rousseau explicitly:

> All the semi-insanity, histrionicism, bestial cruelty, voluptuousness, and especially sentimentality and selfintoxication, which taken together constitutes the actual substance of the Revolution and had, before the Revolution, become flesh and spirit in Rousseau—this creature then went on with perfidious enthusiasm to set the Enlightenment too on its fanatical head, which thereby itself began to glow as though in a transfigured light: the Enlightenment, which is fundamentally so alien to the Revolution and, left to itself, would have passed quietly along like a gleam in the clouds and for long been content to address itself only to the individual: so that it would have transformed the customs and institutions of nations only very slowly. Now, however, tied to a violent and impulsive companion, the Enlightenment itself became violent and impulsive. Its perilousness has thereby become almost greater than the liberating illumination it brought to the great revolutionary movement. He who grasps this will also know out of what compound it has to be extracted, of what impurity it has to be cleansed: so as then to continue the work of the Enlightenment in himself, and to strangle the Revolution at birth, to make it not happen. (Friedrich Nietzsche, *Sämtliche Werke. Kritische Studienausgabe*, Band 2, eds. Giorgio Colli and Mazzino Montinari [Munich: Walter de Gruyter 1999]: 654. In English, *Human, All Too Human: A Book for Free*

Spirits, trans. R. J. Hollingdale [New York: Cambridge University Press, 1986] 367

The French Revolution needs to be undone; to assist man in making this happen is the task of Schiller's aesthetic education. Schiller's "political creed," therefore, is to undermine the *status quo* by forming man for the state *first* before the state, in turn, can eventually be formed to suit mankind. Within the context of his appellate court Schiller, as a judge, appeals to true political freedom and passes on his legacy to a fictitious "young friend":

> The edifice of error and caprice will fall—it must fall, indeed it has already fallen—from the moment you are certain that it is on the point of giving way. But it is in man's inner being that it must give way, not just in the externals he presents to the world. It is in the modest sanctuary of your heart that you must rear victorious truth, and project it out of yourself in the form of beauty, so that not only thought can pay it hommage, but sense, too, lay loving hold on its appearance. And lest you should find yourself receiving from the world as it is the model you yourself should be providing, do not venture into its equivocal company without first being sure that you bear within your own heart an escort from the world of the ideal. (VIII, 586/AL, 110)

This is the future of the truthful state of liberty, which will then deserve its name in its entirety: as a state that is able to abstain from overhasty measurements and that emerges as a state of reason. Thus ends the first part of Schiller's aesthetic letters.

The second part, however, is more problematic from a political and legal point of view as Schiller, slowly but surely, departs from his original political concern. Aesthetics, which had so far been the means to a political end, now more and more becomes the end itself, which is due to Schiller's increasing disillusionment regarding the French Revolution. As Schiller loses his political optimism as time goes by (we must keep in mind that he wrote the letters as a work in progress and over a period of two years), he focuses on transcendental philosophy instead, initially a digression but one from which he does not return. At the end of Schiller's letters, the so-called "aesthetic state" has therefore replaced the original—political—state of reason.

Is this revaluation of all values, then, connected to Rousseau as well? Indeed it is, since Schiller, as we have already seen, holds a view on aesthetics that essentially contrasts with that of Rousseau. This is the starting point from which he now reverses Rousseau's *Discours sur l'origine et les fondements de l'inégalité parmi les hommes* (1755) at the end of his treatise shortly before introducing the term of the aesthetic state. To Rousseau, culture and art are negative manifestations and partially synonymous, whereas to Schiller, culture and art mean exactly one—the same—admirable thing. Hence, the metaphor of the aesthetic state finally results from an attempt to devise a counter concept to Rousseau again: not as much to his political and legal theory this time, but to his theory of *civilization,* which depicts culture as a symptom of decline.[16]

Still, as a compensatory equivalent to the political state of reason, Schiller's metaphor of the aesthetic state is characterized by the same constitution that Schiller had previously assigned to his state of truthful liberty: in analogical form the non-political aesthetic state is, at the end of the aesthetic letters, nonetheless a representative democracy, with only winners and no oppression whatsoever.

> *To bestow freedom by means of freedom* is the fundamental law of this kingdom. May the individual neither struggle here with the whole, nor the whole struggle with the individual. Not because the one concedes may the other be mighty; may there here be only one victor, but no defeated. (VIII, 674/AL, 176)

In the aesthetic state there is no general will to "subject" the individual (violently, if necessary); rather, according to Schiller, the will of society and the will of the individual are one because of man's final sense of balance and totality, i.e., because of the harmonious reconciliation of man and mankind.

> The dynamic state can merely make society possible, by letting one nature be curbed by another; the ethical state can merely make it (morally) necessary, by subjecting the individual will to the general; the aesthetic state alone can make it real, because it consummates the will of the whole through the nature of the individual. (Ibid.)

At the end of his aesthetic letters, Schiller thus assigns exactly the same qualities to the aesthetic state that he had previously assigned to the political state of reason. The difference is that art and aesthetics have now become an end in themselves and no longer serve a "political creed." It is remarkable, however, that although Schiller no longer believes in political improvement and has turned away from politics, his very "political creed" from the first part of the letters continues to shine through. In analogical form, Schiller's aesthetic state is still an appellate court that engages with Rousseau: "Beauty alone do we enjoy at once as individual and as genus, i.e., as *representatives* of the human genus" (VIII, 675/AL 177). The representativeness of democracy persists—not in real politics—but in the metaphor of the aesthetic state, since Schiller's renegotiation in the legal dispute of the time has now shifted to the aesthetic sphere. This is where Schiller now judges accordingly.

Notes

1. Cf. his letter to Christian Garve, January 25, 1795. Quotations from Schiller's works subsequently pertain to the following edition: Friedrich Schiller, *Werke und Briefe in zwölf Bänden*, ed. by Otto Dann et al. (Frankfurt/Main: Suhrkamp, 1988–2004 (here volume XI, page 786). The *Aesthetic Letters* are contained in volume VIII of this collection and will be referenced accordingly followed by the English page numbers in AL as stated in the bibliography.

2. Cf. Yvonne Nilges, "Schiller und die Demokratie," in *Who Is This Schiller Now? Essays on His Reception and Significance*, eds. Jeffrey L. High, Nicholas Martin and Norbert Oellers (Rochester, NY: Camden House, 2011), 205–16.

3. As for Rousseau's depreciation of the theatre, Schiller had reacted with a similar reserve as early as in 1784 (cf. "The Stage as a Moral Institution," although Rousseau is again not directly mentioned). The following remarks are mostly concerned with Schiller's *political and legal* thoughts and his reaction to Rousseau's *Contrat social* (1762).

4. *Œuvres de Jean-Jacques Rousseau* (Paris: E.A. Lequien, 1821–1823), vol. V:210 (*Du Contrat social, ou Principes du droit politique*). In English, "Of the Social Contract," in *The Social and other later political writings*, ed. and trans. Victor Gourevitch (New York: Cambridge University Press, 1997), 114. Subsequent citations will provide the French, then English, page numbers.

5. Ibid., 140/69.

6. Burke speaks of "much, but bad, metaphysics," which had emerged from French philosophers and had been conferred on the Revolution, "much, but bad, geometry; much, but false, proportionate arithmetic. [. . .] It is remarkable, that in [such] a great arrangement of mankind, not one reference whatsoever is to be found [. . .] that relates to the concerns, the actions, the passions, the interests of men. *Hominem non sapiunt*." Edmund Burke, *Reflections on the Revolution in France, and on the Proceedings of Certain Societies in London Relative to That Event. In a Letter Intended to Have Been Sent to a Gentleman in Paris* (London 1791), 268.

7. This occurs in a letter to the Duke of Augustenburg from July 13, 1793 (eds.). No corresponding English translation has been located.

8. Within this holistic context we need to place Schiller's rejection of the death penalty, an issue that Rousseau, in turn, supports: "the preservation of the state is incompatible with his own [the preservation of the criminal], one of the two has to perish, and when the guilty man is put to death, it is less as a Citizen than as an enemy. The proceedings, the judgment are the proofs and declaration that he has

broken the social treaty, and consequently is no longer a member of the State. Now, since he recognized himself as one, at the very least by residence, he must be cut off from it either by exile as a violator of the treaty, or by death as a public enemy; for such an enemy is not a moral person, but a man, and in that case killing the vanquished is by right of war." Jean-Jacques Rousseau, *Du Contrat social, ou Principes du droit politique*, 134/64–65.

9. It must be noted that Schiller, like most of his contemporaries, adhered to a misunderstanding concerning Rousseau. It was Voltaire who first suggested that Rousseau actually wanted to *return* to the state of nature, while in fact Rousseau explicitly eliminated any possibility thereof. The slogan "Revenons à la nature" ("back to nature") has been ascribed to Rousseau by mistake, also by Schiller: "Vous voyez que je n'aspire pas à nous rétablir dans nôtre bêtise, quoique je regrette fort pour ma part le peu que j'en ai perdu." Rousseau's letter to Voltaire, September 7, 1755, in: *Correspondance complète de Jean Jacques Rousseau*, Vol. 3, ed. the Institute et Musée Voltaire and the Voltaire Foundation (Geneva/Oxford 1965–1998), 164.

10. *Du Contrat social, ou Principes du droit politique*, loc. cit., 147/73.

11. Ibid., 116/53.

12. Cf. Georg Wilhelm Friedrich Hegel, *Werke*, eds. Eva Moldenhauer and Karl Markus Michel (Frankfurt/Main: Suhrkamp, 1979), VII: 343 and 348. In English, *Elements of the Philosophy of Right*, ed. Allen W. Wood, trans. H. B. Nisbet (New York: Cambridge University Press, 1991). For a further comparison between Schiller and Hegel regarding both Rousseau and the French Revolution, see also María Acosta's chapter in the present volume.

13. *Du Contrat social, ou Principes du droit politique*, loc. cit., p. 113/51.

14. Cf. Kant's treatise "On the Popular Judgment: That may be Right in Theory, but does not Hold Good in the Praxis" (1793).

15. Friedrich Nietzsche, *Sämtliche Werke. Kritische Studienausgabe in 15 Bänden*, eds. Giorgio Colli and Mazzino Montinari (Munich: Walter de Gruyter 1999) II: 654. In English, *Human, All Too Human: A Book for Free Spirits*, trans. R. J. Hollingdale (New York: Cambridge University Press, 1986), 367.

16. In his poem "The Artists" (1789) Schiller had already reversed Rousseau and declared art to be the pioneer of culture (without arriving at the climax of the aesthetic state, of course). Both the poem and "The Stage as a Moral Institution" anticipate the concept of autonomy with the sphere of art to a considerable extent. Yet in the second part of Schiller's aesthetic letters, art becomes something *exclusive*, since here art is understood not only in the context of autonomy, but also in the context of self-sufficiency, which is based on Schiller's final political disappointment. The aesthetic state is an *autarkic* state, an opposing model to the shattering political reality.

17. The final two sentences of this citation do not appear in the English translation; translation here provided by the editors of this volume.

2

Schiller on Emotions

Problems of (In)Consistency in His Ethics

Laura Anna Macor

Introduction

During the eighteenth century emotions became a central element in ethical theories. Fine and noble feelings were assumed to be capable of promoting virtue over the power of egoism and violent passions, and hence love, sympathy, or enjoyment of beauty lay at the very core of such theories as Scottish moral sense and Rousseau's philosophy. In the German-speaking world, these foreign suggestions, combined with truly local ideas—namely those of the Wolffian school—gained a central role and remained the cornerstone of ethics until Kant's revolution,[1] the novelty of which consisted precisely in its break with these models and in its exclusion of emotions as foundational elements.

Schiller's attitude toward emotions has always been a matter of debate because of its apparent ambiguity: on the one hand, he follows Kant in abandoning the sentimental view endorsed in his youth, and on the other, he explicitly questions Kant's overlooking of the role emotions play in moral life. The charge of inconsistency thus seems unavoidable, and it is not surprising that this has occasionally been tackled in scholarship.[2] Over recent decades, however, a new perspective has started to emerge, according to which Schiller's philosophical insight is seen as being far from naïve and hence deserving closer attention and serious consideration.[3]

This paper aims to lend stronger arguments to this new interpretation by dealing with Schiller's assessment of both the limitations (§2) and the usefulness (§3) of emotions in moral life. The endorsement of Kant's foundation of morals represents only one side of Schiller's moral theory; the other gives a more complete account of moral agency without being detrimental to the purity of the moral law which Schiller shares with Kant. This consistency with Kantian principles will be proved by an excursus devoted to Kant's assessments of virtue, taste, and the joyful fulfilment of duty (§4). In this way, Schiller's philosophical importance will become evident not only for historians of philosophy but also for contemporary ethical theorists interested in finding a connection between duty and nature (§5).

The Limitations of Emotions

Schiller dealt with the non-empirical grounding of morals in his essays of the 1790s following Kant's foundation of ethics. He ordered the *Critique of Practical Reason* on November 28, 1791, and then focused his attention on Kantian philosophy almost exclusively until 1795.

In 1793 he devoted several reflections to Kantian ethics and thereby professed himself explicitly a Kantian. On February 8 he writes to his friend Christian Gottfried Körner that "[p]ractical reason abstracts from all knowledge and has to do only with the determination of the will, with inner actions,"[4] because "[p]ractical reason and determination of the will from mere reason, are one and the same" (KB 181/KL 150). Consequently, the "*form* of practical reason is the immediate relation of the will to the representations of reason, that is, to the *exclusion of every external* principle of determination; for a will which is not determined purely by the form of practical reason is determined from outside, by what is material and heteronomous" (KB 181/KL 150). To accomplish a "moral action" means therefore "to be determined by mere form, and autonomously" (KB 181/KL 151). Thus, a rational being has to act "on the basis of *pure reason* if it is to show self-determination" (KB 182/KL 151). On February 18 a clear endorsement follows what might otherwise have seemed a mere resume of the Kantian arguments: to Schiller, "*no* mortal" is said to have spoken "a greater word than this Kantian word, which also encapsulates his whole philosophy: determine yourself from within yourself" (KB 191/KL 153). Accordingly, a Kantian credo is to be found in the letter of December 3 to the Prince of Augustenburg, when Schiller admits "to think[ing] in a wholly

Kantian way in the chief point of ethics," namely in attributing moral worth only to those "actions to which we are determined exclusively by respect [*Achtung*] for the law of reason and not by any drives [*Antriebe*], however refined they might be, or however impressive names they might carry." Schiller claims to share "with the most rigid moralists" the conviction "that virtue must simply rest on itself and must not be referred to any other purpose but itself." He "fully subscribe[s] in this aspect to the principles of Kant" and believes that "it is good [. . .] what happens merely because it is good" (NA, XXVI 322).⁵

Between February and December 1793 Schiller composed several philosophical essays in which he dealt comprehensively with Kantian ethics. In *On Grace and Dignity*, "ethical behaviour is not about the *legality* of the deeds but only about the *dutiful nature* of the attitude," and the "part played by inclination in a free action demonstrates nothing about the purely dutiful nature of this action," because the will ought to "pursue [only] the *law*, and never the *impulse*."⁶ It is a merit of "the immortal author of the *Critique*" if "pleasure" has ceased to be "the reason for acting rationally" (AuW 282/GD 148), and Schiller declares he "would hardly think that one would not rather give up one's whole humanity than accept a different result from reason about this situation" (AuW 284/GD 150). In *On the Danger of Aesthetic Manners*, which belongs in this period although it was published two years later, Schiller insists on similar Kantian assertions by claiming that "respect is a feeling that can be felt only for the law and for what corresponds to it," and "requires for absolute obedience" (NA, XXI 24).⁷ In *The Moral Utility of Aesthetic Manners*, which is the published version of the December 3 letter to the Prince of Augustenburg, he says that "the morality of an interior action depends upon the *immediate determination of the will by the law of reason*" (NA, XXI 29).

In 1794, Schiller confirmed his philosophical argumentation by commenting on a review of his early lyric *Resignation* (published in 1786). During his first stay in Swabia after he had fled from there in his youth, Schiller read the comment of the Stuttgart banker, Gottlieb Heinrich Rapp, on the abovementioned lyric and wrote a short essay aimed at explaining his moral convictions, particularly in relation to religion. Virtue must not be accomplished because we hope to be rewarded "in the afterlife," since virtue has an "*inner* necessity" and "our moral duties" compel us "not in the way a contract would do but rather absolutely," independently of the expectation of "future goods" (NA, XXII 178).

In short, Schiller rejects any empirical or religious foundation of ethics and sustains Kant's view of pure practical reason.⁸ From Schiller's point of view, the moral agent must accomplish her actions because of their intrinsic goodness, i.e., because they respond to the moral law without any thought of reward, either in this life or in the next. No natural feeling can thereby play a role since it is contingent, casual, and misleading.

As a matter of fact, "*a good heart*" which possesses merely the "*virtue born of temperament*," performs what is right simply because (and only if) "justice is, luckily, situated on the side of inclination," but will surely follow "the natural instinct" whenever this accidental chance no longer occurs. "[W]hen a sacrifice is necessary, it will be made by the ethical and not the sensuous" (AuW 284/GD 158). Even "*love*," which is an "ennobled affect" and the most "fruitful" one "in impressions corresponding to the true dignity of man," is only a source of self-deception by virtue of which we think we are acting selflessly (and hence morally), whereas in actual fact we are merely pursuing our own self-interest. To prove this assertion, Schiller suggests that "a loved object [. . .] is unhappy, and unhappy because of us, and that it depends only on ourselves to make it happy by sacrificing a few moral scruples" (NA, XXI, 24). A series of false questions then arises:

> Shall we let this loved being suffer for the pleasure of keeping our conscience pure? Is this resistance required by this generous, devoted affection, always ready to forget itself for its object? I grant it is going against conscience to have recourse to this immoral means to solace the being we love; but can we be said to *love* if in the presence of this being and of its sorrow we continue to think of ourselves? Are we not more taken up with ourselves than with it, since we prefer to see it unhappy, rather than consent to be so ourselves by the reproaches of our conscience? (NA, XXI 25)

Schiller defines these as the "sophistic" arguments through which love can make conscience an object of contempt because of its supposed selfishness and lead us to see "moral dignity as a *component of our happiness*" (NA, XXI 25). It comes in no way as a surprise that "love" is considered "at the same time the most magnanimous and the most selfish thing in nature" since, on the one hand, "it receives nothing from its object but gives it everything," but on the other, "it is always its own self that it seeks and appreciates in its object" (AuW 304/GD 166).

If one recalls the fact that Schiller based his early ethics on love, one becomes immediately aware of the degree of Schiller's agreement with Kant.[9] Yet Schiller is not willing to exclude emotions from moral life completely and acknowledges that they are of some use in promoting virtue.

The Usefulness of Emotions

In the same essays in which he claims identification with Kant, Schiller unexpectedly expresses grave doubts about the sterility and emptiness of Kant's ethics, as if it provided us with merely theoretical knowledge lacking all engagement with the concrete. In general, he reproaches Kant with being wholly unaware of the importance that feelings and emotions play in moral life, especially with regard to the realization of the moral law.

In "On Grace and Dignity" Schiller says that he aims to "assert the demands of the sensuous in the realm of appearance and in the actual fulfilment of ethical obligations, which are *completely* rejected in the sphere of pure reason and moral legislation." In doing so, he hopes he does not become a "*latitudinarian*" (AuW 283/GD 149).[10] However, he goes even further by stating that "virtue is nothing other than 'an inclination for duty'" and that "humans not only *may*, but *should* combine enjoyment with duty; they should obey their reason with joy" (AuW 283/GD 149). It is not simply by chance that after these assessments Schiller expressly charges Kant with having delivered a moral theory wherein "the idea of *duty* is presented with a severity that repels all graces and might tempt a weak intellect to seek moral perfection by taking the path of a somber and monkish asceticism" (AuW 283/GD 150).

In *The Moral Utility of Aesthetic Manners* Schiller deals with the "great influence a vivid and pure sentiment of beauty exerts on moral life" and makes the claim that "taste contributes to virtue" (NA, XXI 28, 28–29). In fact, the culture of sensibility diminishes the power of instinct and thus permits morality to be exerted even in the presence of a weak will, which would otherwise have followed its own impulses. The merit of taste is therefore to "banish from the soul all those material inclinations and rough desires which often oppose in a so obstinate and impetuous way the realization of good," and to substitute for them "more noble and gentle inclinations referring to order, harmony and perfection." In this way, in ordaining "actions of order, harmony and perfection, reason will find not only no opposition but rather the most lively concurrence of the inclination" (NA, XXI 32).

From here it is just a short step to the notorious slogan of the letters on the *Aesthetic Education of Man*, according to which "the development of man's capacity for feeling is [. . .] the more urgent need of our age,"[11] since "it will always argue a still defective education if the moral character is able to assert itself only by sacrificing the natural" (ÄB 316–317/AL 19).

These assertions are, to say the least, somewhat disconcerting when compared with those related in §2, and they have led in the past to accusations of inconsistency on account of, first, Schiller's alleged philosophical incompetence and, second, his seemingly purely poetical attitude. However, the stress that Schiller placed on feelings and emotions is wholly consistent with his "Kantian identity" and, moreover, his aim was in fact to raise Kant's moral theory to a higher level. The following explains exactly how.

Schiller himself was concerned with eliminating all suspicion of inconsistency since he was well aware of the apparently paradoxical nature that his claim for reconsidering emotions might seem to hold—a circumstance which has never been taken into account to the extent that it deserves. In the essay *The Moral Utility of Aesthetic Manners*, which in its theme ought to be the text that most explicitly readmits sensibility as an identifying factor into morality, Schiller, on the contrary, repeatedly warns readers against the risk that aesthetics poses to the purity of morals. Throughout the entire text he alternates his defence of the education of sensibility with an apparently contradictory relativization of it. In point of fact, Schiller declares that "it is not at least [his] opinion that the participation of good taste in an action can make this action a moral one," because "taste can be *favourable* to morality in the conduct" but "never *produce* anything moral" (NA, XXI 28). The "victory of taste over brutish affections is by no means a moral action," since taste "governs the soul only by the attraction of pleasure, of a nobler type indeed, because its principle is reason, but still, as long as the will is determined by pleasure, there is not yet morality" (NA, XXI 31, 32). In short, taste is "supremely favourable to the *legality* of our conduct" (NA, XXI 35).

What role, then, should emotions and their education play? How may they improve morality if they are in principle incapable of producing anything moral? There are two sides to Schiller's proposal, so it needs to be analyzed in two steps.

First, Schiller conceives of culture as a factor that improves morality since it removes the obstacles to the realization of the moral law, namely sensible drives and raw desires. Hence, there are "two different ways of favouring morality [. . .]: either we must strengthen the side of reason and the power of the good will, so that no temptation can overcome it; or we must break the force of temptation, in order that the reason and the will, although both weaker, should yet be in a state to surmount it." Taste pursues the second task and aims at undermining "the inner natural enemy of morality," i.e., "the sensuous instinct." Undoubtedly, Schiller himself admits that it might seem that "morality gains nothing by this second proceeding, because it happens without any modification of the will, whose nature alone gives to actions their moral character" (NA, XXI 30). However, he explains that, precisely as in the case of "external *physical* freedom," my "inner and *moral* freedom" can also be due to the absence of "a principle distinct from my reason, as soon as this principle is recognized as a force which could have constrained my independence" (NA, XXI 28), or more explicitly, "an action does not cease to be free because the man who could have opposed it, fortunately remains quiet, as soon as we know that the agent followed her own will alone without considering any other; in the same way an interior action does not yet lose the characteristic of being a moral action because all those temptations are fortunately missing which could have reversed it, once it is admitted that the agent followed only the statement of her reason with exclusion of any external incentives" (NA, XXI 29). Therefore, "all which neutralizes the resistance offered to the law of duty by the inclination really favours morality," above all good taste (NA, XXI 30).

Second, Schiller sees in the education of emotions an important supplement to Kant's pure moral theory insofar as it refers to the moral agent and not to the single moral action. A single action is moral only if it is accomplished for the sake of the law regardless of the inner disposition of the man accomplishing it. That is to say that the action is and remains a moral one, whether the moral agent performs it reluctantly or joyfully. Conversely, the "ethical perfection of the human being" depends specifically upon the "part played by the inclination in moral actions" because the "human being is not destined to perform individual ethical actions but to be an ethical being" (AuW 283/GD 149), and "the excellence of man does not absolutely consist in the larger *sum of single moral-rigoristic* actions, but in the greater conformity of his entire natural disposition with the moral law" (NA, XXI 34). This means that man's vocation is to develop and educate his sensibility in order to achieve the habit of performing his duty with joy and effortlessly, as a "person does not make a good impression on me if [s]he can trust the voice of impulse so little as to feel obliged [every time] to test its tone against that of moral principles" (AuW 287/GD 152).

Accordingly, the moral agent faces two possible ways of accomplishing a moral action, the latter being an action exclusively performed out of respect for the law: either with pleasure or not. Schiller considers several situations in order to clarify his intention to rehabilitate the emotions from a moral perspective; one of these scenarios suits the present purpose best. It is the "adaptation" of the parable of the good Samaritan, found in Schiller's letters to Körner on February 18 and 19, 1793.

Let us suppose, Schiller writes to his friend, that a man who has been robbed and wounded is lying in the street and urgently needs help. Among those who happen to go past, two deserve closer attention in this paper: the third, who is willing to help the man after having been engaged in an inner struggle and having overcome his own contrary desires, and the fifth (and last) who helps the man spontaneously and without any effort. According to Schiller the former action is "*purely moral* (but also no more than that), because it occurred against the interests of the senses, out of pure respect for the law" (KB 196/KL 158), whereas the latter is "*beautiful*" (KB 197/KL 158). Following Schiller's own argument, a moral action, "if it is not at once related to taste," cannot be beautiful since violence against nature is too evident to avoid the impression of "heteronomy in the appearance" (KB 195/KL 156, trans. modified).[12] In contrast, a moral action performed gracefully does not lead one to think of the imperative underlying it and therefore *seems* to be performed out of instinct. Yet, this does not mean that the "beautiful" moral agent acts according to duty as part of her nature, but that she has internalized the demands of the moral law so well that she no longer feels any constraint and hence fulfils them with pleasure. Schiller is quite clear on this point:

> Thus, a moral action would be a beautiful action only if it *appears* [*aussieht wie*] as an immediate outcome of nature. [. . .] Our sensory nature must thus *appear* free, where morality is concerned, *although it is really not free*, and it must *appear* [*das Ansehen haben*] as if [*als wenn*] nature were merely fulfilling the commission of our drives by subjugating itself to the mastery of the pure will, at the expense of its own drives. (KB 198/KL 159, all emphases added)

As a matter of fact, the last passerby in Schiller's version of the parable explicitly says that he has the "duty [*schuldig sein*]" of helping the injured man (KB 287/KL 157), but fulfils this duty "*without solicitation*, without considering the action" (unlike the traveller performing a purely moral action), and "disregarding the cost to himself;" in so doing, he demonstrates an ease "*as if* [*als wenn*] it had been the mere instinct which had acted through him" (KB 287/KL 159, second emphasis added, trans. modified). In the same way, the beautiful soul in *Grace and Dignity* acts with an ease "*as if* [*als wenn*]" its actions were "simply [. . .] the actions of its inner instinct"; it even performs "humankind's most exacting duties" letting them "*appear[] to the eye* [*in die Augen fallen*] *as* [*wie*] a free operation of this impulse" (AuW 287/GD 152, all emphases added, trans. modified),[13] and owes to grace "the *appearance* of free will [*Schein von Freiwilligkeit*]" issuing from its own nature while carrying out "the commands of the mind" (AuW 297/GD 160, emphasis added).[14]

In short, the difference between the two mentioned passersby in Schiller's parable concerns neither the action to be performed (which is the same) nor the incentive underlying this action (which is in both cases respect for the law). It has rather to do with the manner in which the two agents obey the demands of pure practical reason: the latter does it immediately on the grounds of an inner moral disposition, the former after a strong and difficult inner struggle. The action has in both cases the same moral worth, the person accomplishing it does not. On the one hand, we have a moral person; on the other, an agent performing a moral action. The education of sensibility and taste provides its positive contribution to morality (alongside the negative one, which consists in banishing inner obstacles in order to follow the moral law), precisely in the preparation of the soul to achieve moral status. From this perspective, the role that emotions and feelings play in moral life does not pertain to the realization of a single moral action but to the character of the moral agent, who can perform the same action with or without pleasure without damaging its purely moral nature. Schiller says that a man who risks his own life in order to save that of others "out of pure respect for the prescription of reason," but who possesses at the same time a fine taste on account of which "he performs *with* inclination [*Neigung*] what without this tender sensibility to beauty he would have had to do *against* inclination [*Neigung*]," is not only not performing a less moral action but is rather an "infinitely more suitable subject for virtue" (NA, XXI 34). Consequently, it is "the character as a whole" that is moral in the beautiful soul (AuW 287/GD 152), and only in this sense can one say that "*duty has become its nature*" (KB 198/KL 150).

To sum up, inclinations and feelings have no role in determining the moral quality of a single action, but "only" in determining the moral character of the person accomplishing it. Man's purpose lies precisely in becoming a moral being.

A Kantian Excursus

In rehabilitating the role of emotions in moral life, Schiller does not, therefore, contradict his endorsement of Kant's pure foundation of ethics, since he is trying rather to give a more complete account of moral agency by supplementing—as far as character is concerned—the narrow view focused on single moral actions with a broader one. While this might be clear from a theoretical standpoint, a historical confirmation cannot fail to be welcome, particularly because it comes from Kant himself. In point of fact, across his own works Kant also deals more or less comprehensively with the "negative" role played by culture, the joyful accomplishment of duty and the problem of virtue.

In the *Critique of the Power of Judgment* (1790), Kant defines the "culture of training (discipline)" as "negative," since it "consists in the liberation of the will from the despotism of the desires" which would otherwise make us "incapable of choosing for ourselves:"[15] "[b]eautiful arts and sciences, which by means of a universally communicable pleasure and an elegance and refinement make human beings, if not morally better, at least better mannered for society, very much reduce the tyranny of sensible tendencies, and prepare humans for a sovereignty in which reason alone shall have power."[16]

In the second edition of his *Religion within the Boundaries of Mere Reason* (1794) Kant replies to Schiller's criticism in *Grace and Dignity* and, in spite of his own warning against the risks of combining aesthetics and morals, he ends up agreeing with his purported rival as far as "the *aesthetic* constitution, the *temperament* so to speak *of virtue*" is concerned: a "slavish frame of mind" reveals "a hidden *hatred* of the law, whereas a heart joyous in the *compliance* with its duty [. . .] is the sign of genuineness in virtuous disposition." This "joyous frame of mind" is necessary in order to be "certain of having *gained* also a *love* for the good, i.e., of having incorporated the good into one's maxim."[17] Furthermore, in the *Critique of Practical Reason* (1788) Kant already saw in the "love for the law [. . .] the constant though unattainable goal of his [man's] striving," for "through increasing facility in satisfying" duty, "the most reverential dread changes into liking and respect into love."[18]

So far so good with Kant's writings of the early 1790s, these being writings which Schiller knew and must thus have considered while developing his own theory of emotions. However, one should not omit to mention the *Metaphysics of Morals* (1797), which provides a further insight into Kant's own preoccupation with moral feelings. In this later work, when discussing the necessity for an "Ethical Ascetics," Kant stresses the need to have a "*cheerful*" frame of mind in "fulfilling [one's] duties," since "what is not done with pleasure but merely as compulsory service has no inner worth for one who attends to his duty in this way."[19] Moreover, it is only in the cultivation of "the compassionate natural (aesthetic) feelings in us" that man can "do what the representation of duty alone might not accomplish."[20]

Evidently, Schiller's attention to emotions and feelings is to be seen as proof of both his competence as an interpreter of Kant (in that he understands what he can add to Kant's theory without contesting its foundations) and his autonomy as a thinker (in that he is not afraid to outline an original theory of virtue). Above all, his approach must finally be acknowledged as being wholly consistent with his parallel appraisal of Kant's pure foundation of morality.

Conclusion

Schiller's theory of moral emotions is a clear example of how an ethics with pure motivational features can be raised to a higher level where moral feelings may also play a role, since attributing morality only to those actions which are performed exclusively for the sake of duty in no way implies that emotions are to be banished. On the contrary, they must remain within the field of ethics since ethics deals with human beings, i.e., with mixed beings who are both rational and sensible. It is in this sense that Schiller draws attention to the fact that the "things that one must necessarily separate in philosophy are not consequently always separated in reality as well" (AuW 266/GD 136), because "[h]uman nature is a more coherent whole in reality than a philosopher, who can only achieve results through separation, is permitted to reveal" (AuW 286/GD 152).

Moreover, Schiller's account of moral agency can be seen as an entirely new approach in the history of ethics thanks to its programmatic connection to beauty, its reference to the beautiful soul and the stress it puts on the "as if" dimension, which is why both historians of philosophy and contemporary ethical theorists should take note of Schiller's ideas.

Notes

1. Cf. H.-J. Schings, *Der mitleidigste Mensch ist der beste Mensch. Poetik des Mitleids von Lessing bis Büchner* (München: Beck, 1980.) W. Riedel, *Um ein Naturprinzip der Sittlichkeit. Motive der Mitleidsdiskussion im 18. Jahrhundert*, in *Ethik und Ästhetik des Mitleids*, eds. N. Gülcher and I. van der Lühe (Freiburg/Br.-Berlin: Rombach, 2007), 15–31. M.-G. Dehrmann, *Moralische Empfindung, Vernunft, Offenbarung. Das Problem der Moralbegründung bei Gellert, Spalding, Chladenius und Mendelssohn*, in *Gellert und die empfindsame Aufklärung. Vermittlungs-, Austausch- und Rezeptionsprozesse in Wissenschaft, Kunst und Kultur*, eds. S. Schönborn and V. Viehöver (Berlin: Schmidt Verlag, 2009), 53–65.

2. Cf. L. Sharpe, *Schiller's Aesthetic Essays: Two Centuries of Criticism* (Columbia, SC: Camden House, 1995), 66; J. Heinz, "*'Philosophischpoetische Visionen.' Schiller als philosophischer Dilettant*," in *Dilettantismus um 1800*, eds. S. Blechschmidt and A. Heinz (Heidelberg: Winter Verlag, 2007), 185–204.

3. Cf. A. Quero Sánchez, *Der Einfluß der Kantischen Philosophie auf Schiller und der fragmentarische Zustand des "Geistersehers" und der "Philosophischen Briefe,"* Literaturwissenschaftliches Jahrbuch, NF, no 45 (2004): 71–98; F. Beiser, *Schiller as Philosopher. A Re-Examination* (Oxford: Oxford University Press, 2005); M. del Rosario Acosta López ed., *Friedrich Schiller: estética y libertad* (Bogotá: Universidad Nacional de Colombia. Faculdad de Ciencias Humanas, 2008); B. E. Jirku and J. Rodríguez Gonzáles eds., *El pensamiento filosófico de Friedrich Schiller* (València: Universitat de València, 2009); V. Rocco Lozano, *Los cambios de paradigma de la "Schiller-Forschung,"* in Daimon. Revista Internacional de Filosofía, 46 (2009), 205–13; L. A. Macor, *Der morastige Zirkel der menschlichen Bestimmung. Friedrich Schillers Weg von der Aufklärung zu Kant, von der Verfasserin aus dem Italienischen übersetzt, auf den neuesten Stand gebracht und erweitert* (Würzburg: Königshausen & Neumann, 2010); C. Burtscher and M. Hien, eds., *Schiller im philosophischen Kontext* (Würzburg: Königshausen & Neumann, 2011).

4. *Schillers Werke: Nationalausgabe,* i.A. des Goethe- und Schiller-Archivs, des Schiller-Nationalmuseums und der Deutschen Akademie, ed. Julius Petersen et al. (Weimar: Hermann Böhlaus Nachfolger, 1943–2010), vol. XXVI, 181. Given that Schiller's letters to Körner of January–February 1793 articulate reflections on beauty originally designed to be published in a treatise entitled "Kallias oder über Schönheit," they are often referred to as "Kallias Briefe," which is why from now they will be cited as KB, followed by the reference in the English translation. Cf. "*Kallias* or Concerning Beauty: Letters to Gottfried Körner," in *Classic and Romantic German Aesthetics,* ed. Jay M. Bernstein (Cambridge: Cambridge University Press, 2003), 150. From here referred to as KL. The *Nationalausgabe* will in turn be referred to as NA.

5. Where no corresponding English edition is provided, the translation is by the author (eds.). On Schiller's letters to his Maecenas and their being undeservedly neglected by scholars see W. Riedel, "Philosophie des Schönen als politische Anthropologie. Schillers 'Augustenburger Briefe' und die 'Briefe über die ästhetische Erziehung des Menschen,'" *Philosophical Readings,* no 5 (2013) Special Issue: *Reading Schiller. Ethics, Aesthetics, and Religion,* ed. L.A. Macor, 118–71.

6. "Über Anmuth und Würde," NA, vol. XX: 283, 282. From now on AuW, in text citations, followed by the reference to the English translation in *Schiller's "On Grace and Dignity" in Its Cultural Context. Essays and a New Translation,* eds. J. V. Curran and C. Fricker (Rochester, NY: Camden House, 2005), 149. From now on GD.

7. This essay was later included in "On the Necessary Limits in the Use of Beautiful Forms," which is why in the NA it is published as part of the latter.

8. Schiller distances himself from religious ethics not only in the abovementioned lyric *Resignation* but also in his *Philosophical Letters* (also published in 1786), where he becomes aware of the fact that the hope for a divine reward or the fear of a divine punishment leads to the very opposite of morality. In the *Philosophical Dialogue* of the *Ghost-Seer* (1789) he therefore tries to give a fully worldly and non-egotistical account of morality. On all these aspects see: W. Riedel, *Die Anthropologie des jungen*

Schiller. *Zur Ideengeschichte der medizinischen Schriften und der "Philosophischen Briefe,"* (Würzburg: Königshausen & Neumann, 1985), 239–48; W. Riedel, *Abschied von der Ewigkeit ["Resignation"]*, in *Gedichte von Friedrich Schiller. Interpretationen,* ed. N. Oellers (Stuttgart: Reclam, 1996), 51–63; L. A. Macor, *Der morastige Zirkel,* 59–68; C. Burtscher, *"Die gesunde und schöne Natur braucht [. . .] keine Gottheit. Schillers Weg von der Religionskritik zur Ästhetik,"* in: *Schiller im philosophischen Kontext,* 80–91; 83–86; C. Burtscher, *Glaube und Furcht. Religion und Religionskritik bei Schiller* (Würzburg: Königshausen & Neumann, 2014).

    9. Schiller had already seen the inadequacy of love as a moral principle in his early writings, i.e., before reading Kant. In *The Robbers* (1781) he reveals the egotistical core of the ethics of love by letting both Karl and Franz Moor react vindictively to their father's supposed lack of love; in his letter to Reinwald of April 14, 1783, he defines love as "a *happy illusion*" (NA, XXIII, 79); in the *Philosophical Letters,* finally, love becomes just another name for interested virtue. In all these cases, altruistic love is irreversibly undermined. In this regard, I take the liberty of referring to my own studies: Macor, *Der morastige Zirkel,* 57–71; L. A. Macor, *Die Moralphilosophie des jungen Schiller. Ein "Kantianer ante litteram,"* in J. L. High, N. Martin, and N. Oellers (eds.), *Who Is This Schiller Now? Essays on His Reception and Significance* (Rochester, NY: Camden House, 2011), 99–115; L. A. Macor, *The Bankruptcy of Love: Schiller's Early Ethics,* Publications of the English Goethe Society 86 (2017), 1, 29–41.

    10. The key-term "latitudinarian" comes from the first edition (1793) of Kant's *Religion within the Boundaries of Mere Reason,* in I. Kant, *Gesammelte Schriften,* ed. by the *Königlich Preußische Akademie der Wissenschaften,* Berlin: de Gruyter, VI:1900ff. (from now on GS followed by volume and page number); *Religion within the Boundaries of Mere Reason And Other Writings,* eds. A. Wood and G. di Giovanni (Cambridge: Cambridge University Press, 1998), 48. The term "latitudinarianism" goes back to the British debates of the seventeenth century on religion, theology and orthodoxy, cf. M. I. J. Griffin, *Latitudinarianism in the Seventeenth-Century Church of England,* annotated by R. H. Popkin and ed. by L. Freedman (Leiden: Brill, 1992).

    11. NA, XX 332; *On the Aesthetic Education of Man. In a Series of Letters,* ed. and trans. with an Introduction, Commentary and Glossary of Terms by E. M. Wilkinson and L. A. Willoughby (Oxford: Clarendon Press, 1967), 53. From now on the German and English editions will be referred to as ÄB and AL, respectively.

    12. This is not the place to discuss Schiller's definition of beauty as "freedom in appearance," for which I refer to Beiser, *Schiller as Philosopher,* 62–74; W. Riedel, "Theorie der Übertragung. Empirische Psychologie und Ästhetik der schönen Natur bei Schiller," in *Kunst und Wissen. Beziehungen zwischen Ästhetik und Erkenntnistheorie im 18. und 19. Jahrhundert,* eds. A. Bauereisen, S. Pabst and A. Vesper (Würzburg: Königshausen & Neumann, 2009), 121–38; J. Robert, *Vor der Klassik. Die Ästhetik Schillers zwischen Karlsschule und Kant-Rezeption* (New York: de Gruyter, 2011), 363–72.

    13. In this passage Schiller uses almost the same expressions and the same syntactical structure as in the February 19 letter to Körner.

14. Therefore, Katerina Deligiorgi ("The Proper Telos of Life: Schiller, Kant and Having Autonomy as an End," *Inquiry*, 5:54 (2011): 494–511, 500) is quite right in saying that "necessitation is primarily a technical term not a description of an emotion." On this point, see also Beiser, *Schiller as Philosopher*, 82–83.

15. GS, vol. V, 432; *Critique of the Power of Judgment*, ed. P. Guyer, trans. P. Guyer and E. Matthews (Cambridge: Cambridge University Press, 2000), 299.

16. Ibid. 433; 301.

17. GS, vol. VI, 23n; 49n.

18. GS, vol. V, 84; *Critique of Practical Reason*, trans. Mary Gregory, introduction A. Reath (Cambridge: Cambridge University Press, 1997), 72.

19. GS, vol. VI, 484; *The Metaphysics of Morals*, trans. M. Gregor (Cambridge: Cambridge University Press, 1996), 227.

20. Ibid., 457; 205. On the proximity of Kant and Schiller on this point see also: M. del Rosario Acosta López, "¿Una superación estética del deber? La crítica de Schiller a Kant," *Episteme*, 28 no. 2 (2008): 1–24: 5n. For Kant's theory of virtue see: R. B. Louden, "Moralische Stärke: Tugend als eine Pflicht gegen sich selbst," in *Moralische Motivation. Kant und die Alternativen*, eds. H. Klemme, M. Kühn, and D. Schöneker (Hamburg: Meiner, 2006), 79–95; and A. M. Baxley, *Kant's Theory of Virtue. The Value of Autocracy* (Cambridge: Cambridge University Press, 2010).

3

Schiller's Aesthetics between Kant and Schelling

MANFRED FRANK

TRANSLATED BY CHRISTINA M. GSCHWANDTNER
AND JEFFREY L. POWELL

I.

In the year 1792 Schiller interrupted his work with a break for reflection. This break was the result of his desire to engage with Kant's *Critique of Judgment* in a fundamental fashion. In this Schiller may well have experienced what Schelling, his junior compatriot (by 16 years), describes as a "supernova"-type effect of Kantian criticism on the German mind (to Hegel on Jan. 6, 1795):

> When a great man appears and sets a new meteoric pace, high above the heads of other people, how fearful does the great crowd of measured and comfortable people who walk the middle road become. Who wants to bury in the dust of ancient times, when the current of his time sweeps him up and away time and again. Currently I live and weave in philosophy. Philosophy is not yet at its end. Kant has provided the results, but the premises are still missing. And who can understand results without premises? (Mat. 118f.)[1]

With this Schelling expresses an opinion that was widely shared: *Juvat vivere, juvat philosophari*, if one has the great luck to be a contemporary of the greatest and most revolutionary Western thinker. This opportunity was not to be squandered through dull disregard. Yet, Kant's consequences were generally regarded as insufficiently grounded and therefore incomprehensible. One sought their grounds of explanation that would render them comprehensible. Among the most important of those who attempted this from the end of the 1780s onward was Schiller's Jena colleague Karl Leonhard Reinhold. What is the driving thought in Kant's critical project? Among his lecture notes is found the brief explanation: "The year [of] '69 gave me great light."[2]

There has been much speculation about what this means. My hypothesis is: it consists in the insight that pure reason cannot come to valid insights in its reasoning and only those propositions are valid that can be controlled through experience of the senses. This is precisely why Kant's chief work is called *Critique of pure reason* and not "defense" of pure reason.

The expression "pure" always sounds good in the context of German philosophy. Yet that is not self-evidently the case for Kant. For him only those insights are "pure" which we reach without any cooperation of the senses, e.g., René Descartes's ontological proof for the existence of God or the totality of Western metaphysical claims.[3] This is why Kant's *Critique* was regarded by many contemporaries as the work of a gigantic guillotine: set up in order to take a knife to the demands of various claims for validity on the basis of pure reason in the same way as the guillotine of the French Revolution beheaded unfounded claims of governance "by divine right."

In order to aim this instrument of execution at pure reason Kant had to accept an important theoretical presupposition. Sensibility and understanding must be perceived as fundamentally distinct faculties [*Vermögen*]. And that is exactly what Kant assumes. One speaks of his "two-stem-theory" in regard to human cognition. Like all dualistic positions it had to withstand sharp criticism, raised especially by Salomon Maimon, Friedrich Schiller, and representatives of the emerging German Idealism. Why Kant held such an uncomfortable position only becomes clear when one begins to wonder about the *function* of this separation. For by it Kant intended to respond to a position that assumed a monism of sense and understanding. In Kant's view this position does not withstand a critique of pure reason.

This critique was directed first and foremost against the so-called school philosophy, whose representatives following Leibniz were Christian Wolff and his students. They were of the opinion that a continuum extended between sensibility and understanding. Accordingly, sensory experiences are confused concepts, while concepts are clear or ideally plainly evident intuitions. Aesthetics also found its place in this development: Intuitions that we call "beautiful" really do give us something to cognize, yet they do so in an elementary, but nonconceptual and hence confused, manner ("cognitio inferior"). Of course part of their charm, their "je ne sais quoi" ["I don't know what"; Leibniz's, *Discours de Métaphysique*][4] consists precisely in the fact that they stimulate the mind [*Geist*] without definitely acquiring a concept for themselves. Schiller's *Philosophical Letters* (from 1786) with their enthusiasm for the inner connection between sense and understanding, spirit and nature, like his vehemently anti-materialistic 1779 dissertation (*Philosophy of Physiology*) already, are also deeply shaped by Leibniz's and Wolff's doctrine of "all-unity."

Yet this monistic vision had a price that Kant was decidedly not willing to pay. In the illuminating year of 1769 he had noted that the boundary between confusion and clarity does not run between the faculties of intuition and thought, but cuts through them both: There are very clear intuitions and very confused thoughts/concepts (Refl. Nr. 204, AA XV: 79).

Let us assume that sensibility and understanding are in essential points identical as Leibniz and Wolff believed. Nevertheless one would not be able to inform sensibility about its identity with the understanding (and the reverse) out of one's own capacities, but only from the perspective of an "infinite spirit." Such a spirit is indeed assumed by Leibniz and Wolff as God or the central monad. An infinite spirit "intuits intellectually." This means that all veridical thoughts present themselves to him immediately in sensory fulfillment. Our understanding, in contrast, is empty; it requires sensory or informational data; no cognition can be achieved without its input. In the words of Novalis: "here we see that the 'I' is basically nothing—everything must be *given* to it."[5] The categories shaped by the "I" he calls "compartments without content. They are absolute correlates—they want to be filled."[6] The idea of an intuitive understanding (an *intellectus archetypus* as the schools said) meets its demise under the blows of a critique of pure reason—just as the traditional God falls by the blows of the critique of the proofs of God's existence. Kant devotes a whole paragraph in the *Critique of Judgment* (§77) to the distinction between our finite ("discursive") understanding and an infinite or intuitive understanding designed only as an opposing agenda.

This book, Kant's so-called third *Critique*, wants to solve a "great difficulty . . . a problem that nature has tangled in such a way"[7] that it resists his efforts of thinking like no other. Let us formulate it as a question: how can the unity of reason be derived from a basic principle which does not only not hinder but makes comprehensible the differentiation of its functions as faculty of the categories, on one hand, and of the ideas on the other? The principle of understanding, the pure cogito and its spontaneity, is not at the same time the principle of practice, and yet it would be unbearable for the systematic composition of philosophy to have to leave the "gap" open between description and prescription, theory and practice, nature and freedom (or however one wants to articulate it). Another impeding dualism is added to this, namely between sensibility and understanding, which roughly corresponds to that between lower and higher faculties of desire in the realm of practical philosophy. The integration of the power of imagination into the economy of theoretical philosophy is also equally as unsatisfying.

The *Critique of Judgement* seeks to respond to these questions. The powers of judgment and of the imagination are presented as especially promising candidates for closing the abyss: the power of imagination because it mediates with the conditions of the synthesis of the understanding the intuitively given, and the (reflective) power of judgment because it searches the concept of reason for concrete objects that would also still be capable of explaining their apparent contingency.

Thus the powers of imagination and judgment become "mediating links" between sensibility and understanding on the one hand and between understanding and reason on the other. Yet, due to its reflexivity, the power of judgment has more staying power. It applies configurations of intuition that have already been worked on by the understanding (via the power of imagination) to reason. Why to reason? Because the sought-after concept cannot belong to the understanding since such a concept would join intuitions together into a cognition. When I judge the beauty of (a configuration of) a representation, the judgment does not relate the representation(s) to a concept of the understanding, but to the subjective feeling and mood, which modulates the harmony of the strings of my soul. Certainly the power of judgment is also served by the categories of the understanding—the "Analytic of the Beautiful" indeed follows their table—it applies them yet it does not have any concepts at its disposal that would belong to it specifically. The concepts that it produces are indeterminate or empty, they bestow nothing to cognize, writes Kant. They provide a rule for application that does not guarantee any sort of objectivity. It is subjective; the power of judgment validates itself and is capable of nothing else, because for want of a jury its judgments must otherwise remain eternally suspended. Yet everything happens as if judgments of feeling were not merely individual, as if it were reasonable to assume universal reliability for them. This is due to the fact that what does not arise from private motivation also does not require private reasons for its validity.

I said that the power of judgment validates itself and that it has this in common with practical reason. Practical reason also does not take orders from sensibility or from the understanding. It freely and sovereignly imprints its law on sensibility. Kant refers to an agreement between the structure of the judgment of taste and that of action directed toward the good. The judgment of taste, he says, is "related" to moral interest[8] (e.g., KU 114/127, 169/167ff.). Of what exactly does the bond of this analogy consist? In both cases freedom assigns its dominion to the phenomena of the sensible world. But the analogy goes no further. For in the case of aesthetic judgment, freedom is at stake only in an improper sense, namely as the categorical/conceptual independence which allows the power of imagination to let the faculties of cognition play, while in the case of moral judgment pure freedom comes into play and binds the play of the powers of cognition or the faculty of desire strictly through its law. After all, the "free play of the power of imagination" serves as a symbol for the "free lawfulness" of practical reason—with the well-known difference that the power of imagination mandates without concepts (only in agreement with the aesthetic imperatives of feeling) and is itself passive, e.g.(belongs to sensibility). Kant notes that "intellectual is that for which the concept is an activity" (Refl. Nr. 4182, AA XVIII: 447). In this sense the power of imagination *does* nothing. In contrast freedom proceeds in conformity with law (and therefore claims universal a priori agreement). Yet symbolic presentations—different from schemata—are only incomplete conceptual representations.[9] The power of imagination can present pure freedom only indirectly in accordance with an analogy brought to light by reflection. All the same this analogy reaches so far that it represents one imperfection through another: The intuitive lack of fulfillment of the moral idea ("unpresentability") is mirrored in a certain fashion by the conceptual unsaturatedness of the aesthetic idea, of its "inexponibility" (KU 192/181ff. [=§49], 239/214ff. [= Comment I to §57]),—and the external analogy of the two relationships is discovered through reflection. Hence the conceptual inexhaustibility of the beautiful becomes a symbol for the unpresentability according to intuition and the effusiveness of freedom.

II.

It is precisely this analogy and its theoretical difficulty, which it indicates more than solves, that gave rise to Friedrich Schiller's aesthetic reflections. Between 1792 and 1796 he interrupts his poetic production, surely with the intention of coming to a deeper self-understanding through theoretical reflection on the essence of the beautiful. From the beginning it is his main concern to find an exit from what he judges to be the destructive consequences of Kantian dualism. In this he allows himself to be guided by the analogy between aesthetic and moral judgment as if by a compass. An analogy cannot replace the unity that is missing; relations of similarity remain ultimately arbitrary and lack the guidance of a coherent principle. Yet does it make sense to ground aesthetics in a principle which can be no other than that of philosophy itself? A principle could not be anchored in a merely subjective reflection, as in the *Critique of Judgment*, but must be rooted in an objective criterion. And this is precisely the declared intention of the Kallias letters (*Kallias oder über die Schönheit*). Their concern is "to posit objectively a concept of beauty and to legitimate it from the nature of reason in completely a priori fashion."[10] And in fact—the entire first half of Gadamer's *Truth and Method*[11] makes us emphatically aware of this—Kant pays for the justification of aesthetics with a radical subjectivization of the phenomenon of beauty. Not what corresponds to reality is beautiful, but only what corresponds to a reflection of the soul [*Gemüt*] on its feeling when occasioned by a certain configuration of intuitions. In his own copy of the *Critique of Judgment* Schiller underlined in the first sentence of the first paragraph the expression "feels itself": "the feeling of pleasure or displeasure which does not designate anything in the object but where *the subject feels itself* inasmuch as it is affected by the presentation."[12]

Accordingly, the feeling of aesthetic satisfaction is a kind of *self-feeling*. No contribution is made in it to the cognizing determination of an *object*. It is Schiller's ambition to overcome this subjective restriction that impairs Kant's undertaking, in view of an *objective* grounding of the phenomenon of the beautiful. In this he allows himself to be guided by the idea of the symbol and the analogy implied in it, which he immediately emphasizes. According to the two expressions of reason as theoretical and practical, there are two types of analogy through which the aesthetic judgment can become an indirect mirror image—a *Mimema*—of reason. By "form of reason" Schiller understands the "manner" in which reason presents its "power of association" externally. Reason is essentially a faculty of synthesis, of association, and it can exercise this faculty in various ways; Schiller denotes the different ways of synthesis as "forms" (following the terminology of Karl Leonhard Reinhold). According to this way of employing the word [forms] one will designate "material" what presents itself as the sensory content of reason for the purpose of the unification under concepts. Since there are two kinds of matter in the world (sensible representations and actions of the will), there must also be two corresponding ways of their synthetic unification: the forms of the understanding (what Kant calls the categories) and the forms of (practical) reason. When reason combines representations into cognitions, one speaks of the forms of theoretical reason; when it connects representations to the will to form an action, then one thus has to do with the form of practical reason. Yet, in both cases a "correspondence" takes place between reason (theoretical or practical) and representations on the one hand or, on the other hand, actions of the will. In other words, matter and form, sensory content and action of reason agree. Stated differently, matter and form, sensible content and the activity of reason are attuned together. This correspondence between the form of reason and the synthesis of representation or will can be either necessary or accidental. It is necessary when the concept (of the understanding or of reason) imprints matter (in accordance with intuition or volition) forcefully with its law. Yet it is possible—and this is a consideration that could not be further from Kant's mind—that reason finds itself simply "surprised" by the fact that the matter (of representations or volitions) submits *voluntarily* to the form that understanding or reason provides: "Here reason thus finds a correspondence with its form; there it is surprised when it finds it."[13]

One would be able to speak with Kant (who certainly anticipated this possibility) of a "favor of nature," for sensibility and the faculty of desire indeed belong to our natural condition. And if our nature submits voluntarily to the demands of reason, then it favors its application *sua sponte* (KU 303/260, ftn., cf. 15/52ff.). The violent subjection of nature by reason gives way to a state of nonviolent agreement.

Schiller now considers four respective ways of unifying the matter and form of reason according to the various possibilities of combination. First is that of theoretical reason, which connects representations together. If this connection occurs with necessity, i.e., according to an a priori concept that subordinates the matter of representations to its form (the categories), the result is thus an (objective) *cognition*. Conversely, when the representations are voluntarily joined as it were to the concept, the resulting judgment is *teleological* (i.e., that the intuitions are arranged in such a way that they are *as if* mandated by a pure concept). Third, on the part of practical reason there are connections not among representations but between representations and will; the result of this is not cognition but *action*. Now this action can again be either necessary (this is the case when the synthesis is formed according to the order of the pure moral law) or accidental, and then *beauty* develops. Beauty thus consists in Schiller's eyes in a free—hence voluntary—agreement between the synthesis of representation and will and the demands of the moral law. Certainly this [law] need no longer behave in a domineering fashion, since the representing action submits voluntarily, out of benevolence, to its imperatives. I have already pointed out that Schiller conveys by "analogy" (an expression one can occasionally also find in Kant) what Kant called "symbol."[14] Thus Schiller also now says that the submission of the synthesis of representation and will to the moral law is an event that is unintentional and not premeditated, is not the realization of the morally good but only its analogy. All the ways in which the sensory and the reasonable agree without necessity are such analogies, such indirect reproductions of morality, about which we know that it is not capable of direct presentation. Yet is a relationship of analogy sufficient for the grounding of the discussion concerning an *objective* presentation of reason in appearance?

It is clear that Schiller's reasoning relies on the theoretical grounding of Kant's critique. Yet we do not want to overlook that he adds several not insignificant modifications, which already anticipate Hölderlin's version of a "favor of nature" (celebrated in the metric form of the *Hyperion*) and thereby provide the first glimmer of a philosophy of nature to be created by Schelling and the Romantics. Indeed, the presupposition of an "insight into the suprasensible substrate of nature and its identity with what causality makes possible in the world through freedom"[15] is not at all foreign to Kant. But this is just a necessary *presupposition* to make thinkable the combination of the mechanical path of nature with the demands of the moral law. The idea of an, as it were, *primordial* agreement between nature and reason, as Schiller and Schelling would like, is completely foreign to Kant (how could a being whose freedom has been taken from him incline "voluntarily" toward its opposite?); he also would not have accepted that one could call the beautiful an *actually* accomplished appearance of freedom. Yet Schiller claims precisely this without hesitation: "Beauty *is* freedom in the appearance."[16] In order to appear, freedom would have to objectify itself entirely, would have to assume the form of an object; in Kant's view, this could happen at best symbolically, for symbols are not objects and their interpretation yields no cognition. The restriction of the *as if* is no longer necessary for Schiller. The beautiful *can* present itself *as if* a concept of reason wanted to announce itself in it from afar. To turn this subordinate clause into an assertion is to be guilty of romantic enthusiasm.

Schiller is quite aware of the boldness of this consequence and defends it vis-à-vis Gottfried Körner:

> I imagine you *will be surprised* not to find beauty under the rubric
> of theoretical reason and that this will worry you a great deal. But
> I cannot help you, beauty can certainly not be found in theoretical

reason since it is independent of concepts; and since beauty must still be counted in the *family of reason*, and practical reason is all there is besides theoretical reason, we will have to search and find beauty there. You will, I think, see from the following that this relationship will not cause you any problems.[17]

Now one will object that even Kant himself—as always more careful and without confusing regulative with constitutive principles—regarded the beautiful as a symbol of the moral (hence of practical reason).[18] Of what, then, does the decisive difference between him and Schiller consist?

Indeed the "analytic of the beautiful" has oriented itself according to the guidance of the four categories, and these categories do not determine the realm of action but that of cognition. The contemplation of the beautiful from the viewpoint of the pure concepts of the understanding assumes that the observed phenomenon consequently belongs to theoretical reason. Yet, Kant did believe the beautiful capable of symbolizing the morally good. Schiller would say that, in order to symbolize practical reason, Kant's power of imagination remains nevertheless a phenomenon of theoretical reason. That it is free can be said of the power of imagination and its play only in an improper sense—yet exactly this improper (as it were theoretical) freedom, according to an external analogy discovered by reflection, becomes a symbol of the authentic, practical freedom. In contrast, Schiller defends a position according to which beauty transcends the capacity of the faculty of cognition and can only experience its grounding from the side of practical reason. His notes in the margins of his own copy of the *Critique of Judgment* beautifully show what reasons he believed to be on his side for this. The four basic qualities of the beautiful—its universality, its disinterestedness, its inwardness (by this Schiller means the fact that beauty moves the deepest part of our being), and its fullness of sense (its conceptual inexhaustability)[19]—these four basic characteristics of the beautiful all become comprehensible when one assumes practical reason as its principle: Moral judgment demands universality by right: it is free of all individual interest, hence articulates no private desire; it concerns me in my inmost being as reasonably acting person; and finally only an idea of pure practical reason could be inexhaustibly rich in meaning, it would be absurd to say the same thing of a concept of the understanding in view of its sensible realization (for this and for the following, see Henrich, 1967).[20] It was above all the final characteristic, the fullness of meaning, of which Schiller—as Schelling after him (e.g., SW I/3, 619f.)[21] and also the Romantics—took advantage for his claim that the beautiful is an appearance of practical and not of theoretical reason. The following line of argumentation roughly underlies this: freedom, the essence of human reality, is of itself inaccessible to human cognition. It can never become object because it lacks sensibility, and it also cannot be schematized because no configuration of the power of imagination would be adequate to it. In this way it slips from the grasp of theoretical reason. In order to function as symbol (or analogy, as Schiller preferred to say) of freedom (attributed to it by Kant), the beautiful cannot be an appearance of the theoretical. It is rather a symbol of what cannot be represented solely by means of thought. The inner circling of Kantian philosophy, which is condemned to failure, the circularity, which consists in grounding the essence of practice and hence the unity of reason theoretically—this circle is broken open. The problem, to which he was able to respond only aporetically, is resolved and reconciled through the fact of beauty. It is intuitive not conceptual (since no concept could accord with the idea of practical reason, yet intuition through its fullness of sense can serve as a symbolic substitute for the conceptual unrepresentability of freedom). In precisely this sense it can be believed that Schiller could have shown an *objective* principle for beauty. Admittedly this allegedly objective principle assumes the transcendental subject as its criterion of verification, and it is also correct that the play of the liberated power of imagination remains a phenomenon of subjectivity. Schiller concedes that the power of imagination is a subjective capacity, but it is activated by an intention that is not subjective but objective and aims at the objectification of its otherwise merely internal and subjective state.

Yet, one will object, is not the liberation of the beautiful from under the thumb of theory paid for by a different one-sidedness, namely its subjection under the dominion of freedom? In other words: how is one to think the act of the reification of the power of imagination of which Schiller speaks?

Schiller replies that this is because within the beautiful occurs a self-presentation of the practical in the theoretical-sensible. Through this self-presentation, theory itself as a whole becomes a form of reflection, a form of self-presentation of the practical. In his 1794 discussion of Friedrich Matthisson's poems (*Über Matthisons Gedichte*) this expression appears for the first time.

> In souls that are active and have awakened to the feeling of their moral worth, reason never watches the play of the imagination in idle fashion; without ceasing it is diligent to shape this accidental game to accord with its own process. If now among these appearances one offers itself which can be treated according to its own (practical) rules, then this appearance becomes a symbol of its

own actions, the dead letter of nature becomes a living spiritual language, and the outer and inner eye read the same script of the appearances in quite a different manner.²²

The image, which the beautiful reflects for us, is no longer merely the theoretical analogy of the practical, but unveils itself as sensory *self-*presentation of reason, which itself transcends the contrast between theory and practice. If one speaks with Schiller of a *self-*presentation of reason, then one has conceded that the sensory is no longer as for Kant the pole opposing the intelligible. No, the sensory is *the same as* the spiritual [*Geistige*], the other of reason itself, its own (no longer indirect, analogical or incomplete, but adequate) image. Thus the beautiful is transformed from a symbol/analogy of (either theoretical or practical) reason into a site in which the proper principle of theory and practice itself is revealed. If one contemplates a real work of art, Schiller assures us, one sees an "*aesthetic idea,*" that is, one looks "as into a bottomless depth" (Ibid., 1026). Yet the sight does not scare us, it draws us to it, for the spirit that speaks to us from this bottomless depth is even more related to us. The riddle of our absolutely unique "stupefaction" before the beautiful is not explained by the strangeness of what is seen, but—to the contrary—by the experience of a deep unity of being, which looks at us out of the abyss as something familiar, something lost and found again. It is we ourselves who seemed so mysteriously foreign to us, and we react to the resolution of what was foreign with aesthetic satisfaction. Novalis says: "The art *of estranging* in an *agreeable* manner, to make an object foreign and yet familiar and attractive, that is romantic poetics" (NS III:68 (5), Nr. 668). On the other hand, since what looks at us in such an entirely mysterious manner in the work of art, is the "supersensible ground of the unity of nature and of reason" (cf. KU, XX/14–15, LVI/30–31, §59, 258/228ff., §67, 304/260–61, 352/293–94, 358/297–98, passim), which is neither presentable in intuition nor exponible in concepts (cf. KU 238/213–14ff.), the estranged can never be completely resolved into familiarity, the incommensurability of the absolute is never entirely resolved into self-consciousness. Thus Hardenberg-Novalis adds: "From the unreachable, according to its character, no reaching can be thought. [Therefore] . . . the highest works of art [are] simply *unaccommodating*—They are ideals which can—and *should*—delight us only by approximation—they are aesthetic imperatives."²³

Schiller counsels us to understand the shock that the experience of the beautiful inflicts on us as the effect of a revelation. The image offered by the senses reveals to us—in an entirely objectivized manner—the hidden interiority of our mind [*Gemüts*]. At its most basic level the beautiful has to be more than a humanly undifferentiated modification of cognition. If the human being is to feel itself called by the experience of beauty—Novalis called this an aesthetic imperative—if it is true that the human being is affected in most inwardly by beauty and in a deeper fashion than by some other experience, then it suggests itself to an aesthetician trained in the Kantian manner to search for the reason for the possibility of this experience in the moral—for it is the deepest depth of the mind [*Gemütes*]. Schiller simply cannot find a different solution for the profound impact from the experience of the beautiful than to assume that the sensory refers through it to the moral. In aesthetic satisfaction we have the experience of a *re*cognition; and what we there re-cognize with surprise and an agreeable estranging, must already be something cognized—how else could we respond with joyful consent? Our soul, Schiller says, seeks and finds *itself* in the appearance of the beautiful; but from this it follows that the beautiful, in its sensibility, is a monogram of our soul, as Schelling will say, a "tangled trace" of the soul (SW I/3, 611).

Such a thought would no longer be possible to justify on the basis of the Kantian approach, which assumes two completely irreducible sources for our cognition. Thus in *Anmut und Würde* (from 1793) Schiller posits the innovative thesis that a *bond of love* mediates between the two cognitive stems, which also spans the abyss between understanding and reason. For in love reigns (and this is what turns it into the paradigm for aesthetic experience) a decisive, centrifugal, even selfless tendency, which has little in common with what Kant called a "lower faculty of desire." In love a being transcends the sphere of its individuality, whose center of gravity seems to lie outside itself. As one said at that time, someone who is "on fire" with love for another, seeks his self-worth outside himself, attempts to win back his own being in heightened fashion from where his beloved is. The one who loves, Schiller says, does not desire the other as one desires a thing, but values him, as one respects a person. Hence love appeals—in contrast to Kant's theoretical approach—to a principle that is superior to the dichotomy between sensibility and reason, equiprimordially encloses the two poles of the relation, self and other-than-self, sensibility and reason, as the beginning of Hölderlin's hymn *Farewell* expresses in the poignant words:

> So we wanted to part? Thought it both good and wise?
> Why, then, why did the act shock us as murder would?
> Oh, ourselves we know little,
>   For within us a god commands.[24]

The decision to separate is drastically compared to murder in this verse; and this is because the other, if I really love him, is not really another, but myself in the position of the other. In this way love opens to what is more than I and you as Hölderlin says in the allusion to Ovid's "*est Deus in nobis.*" There is in us, above us, a god, who reigns through us unknowingly and forms the inseparable and unpresentable unity of which the opposition of self and other is only an imperfect and deficient expression.

Schiller applies precisely this structure to the relation that exists between the sensible and the intelligible in the phenomenon of the beautiful. I will cite the three decisive passages, in which Schiller discusses this relationship. The first is found in a 1792 Jena lecture on aesthetics and is titled "Relationship of the Beautiful to Reason." It is at the same time a good illustration of the rhetorical force and explanatory power through which Schiller sought to outdo Kant's convoluted style:

> The circumstance that the beautiful is only *felt*, not really cognized, makes the derivation of the beautiful from a priori principles doubtful. It appears that we have to be content with a pluralistic validity of judgment about beauty. We either *watch* or *contemplate* events of nature; *contemplation* alone is appropriate for beauty. The *senses* provide the manifold; *reason provides the form.* Reason connects the presentations to *cognition* or to *action*. There is *theoretical* and *practical* reason. Freedom of appearances is the object of *aesthetic evaluation.* Freedom of a thing in appearance is its self-determination, inasmuch as it falls under the senses. The aesthetic evaluation excludes all consideration of objective purposiveness and regularity and applies solely to appearance; a purpose and a rule can never appear. A form appears *free* when it declares itself and does not force the understanding to search for a reason outside of it. The moral is in *accordance* with reason, the beautiful is similar to reason. The former arouses *respect*, a feeling that develops through the comparison of sensibility with reason. Freedom in appearance does not only awaken desire in regard to the object, but also *inclination* for it; this inclination of reason to unify with the sensible is named *love*. We do not really regard the beautiful with *respect*, but with *love*; except for *human* beauty which however includes the expression of *morality* as object of respect.—If we are also to love what is worthy of respect, then we must have reached it or it

must be reachable for us. Love is an enjoyment while that is not the case for respect: in the latter case there is strain, in the former letting go.—The enjoyment of the beautiful hence arises out of the noticed analogy with reason and is tied to love.[25]

The second citation is from *Anmut und Würde*, which was produced a year later. It treats grace as a subcategory of the beautiful, namely as freedom in an appearance which is moving:

> In grace, as in the beautiful in general, reason sees its claims fulfilled in sensibility, and surprisingly one of its ideas meets it in appearance. This unexpected confluence of nature's arbitrariness with reason's necessity gives rise to a feeling of gay acclamation (*delight*), which lightens the senses, but is invigorating and engaging for spirit, and an attraction of the sensory object must ensue. This attraction we call satisfaction—*love*; a feeling that cannot be separated from grace and beauty.[26]

In this passage, as already in the previous one, the concept of "love" is first invoked in order to explain the "joyful shock" which the encounter with the beautiful calls forth, and also to justify the desire that seizes the soul in order to linger before it. Subsequently, another motive steps into the foreground: the Platonic yearning to loose oneself in the beloved other; or instead to join and dissolve with the other into that already mentioned "*Deus in nobis*." I quote *Anmut und Würde* again:

> About respect one can say that it *bows* before its object; about love that it *inclines toward* its [object]; about desire that it *hurls itself upon* its [object]. In the case of respect reason is the object and sensory nature the subject. In the case of love, the object is sensory and moral nature the subject. In the case of desire object and subject are sensory. Love alone is hence a free sensation, for its pure source flows forth from the seat of freedom, from our divine nature. It is not the small and lowly which measures itself here with the great and high, not the senses which look up dizzily to the law of reason; [but] it is the *absolutely great* itself, what has been imitated in charm and beauty and is satisfied in morality. It is the lawgiver as such, *God* in us, who plays with his own image in the world of the senses. Therefore the soul [*Gemüt*] is released in love, while

it is tightened in respect. For here [in the case of love] nothing sets boundaries for it, since the absolutely great has nothing above it and sensibility, from which alone a restriction could be derived here, agrees in the case of charm and beauty with the ideas of the mind. Love is a descending, while respect is an ascending. Therefore a bad person cannot love, even if compelled to respect; hence the good person can respect little of what he does not simultaneously surround with love. The pure spirit can only love, not respect; the senses can only respect, but not love.[27]

These textual excerpts could give one the impression that Schiller is already moving in a more or less sovereign fashion on the basis of speculative idealism, for instance that of Hegel, whose dialectic similarly proceeds from the experience of the self-enriching self-externalization that is love. Hegel even admitted that he had Schiller to thank for this theme. In the development of Schiller's own ideas, however, themes enter that prohibit an idealist reading. In fact, Schiller understands by "love" rather generally a (freely entered) union of sense and reason. The formulation appears harmless in the case of the description of the phenomenon of the beautiful. For freedom, as representation of a pure concept of reason, should here mirror itself in its appearance as sensory representation. Furthermore, if the act of objectification appears as a process of making sensible, then Schiller's talk about a predilection of reason towards the sensible seems reasonably plausible. This interpretation hits only *one* aspect of love. By "love" we usually mean a co-substantial relationship between beings who are treated equally in terms of rank and autonomy. In Schelling's finer formulation: "This is the secret of love that it unites those who could each be for themselves and yet are not, and cannot be without the other" (SW I/7, 408; cf. 174).

Now one cannot speak of such an equality-in-worth between sensibility and reason, at least not as long as the Kantian "boundary line" remains unviolated of which Hölderlin spoke in a letter to Neuffer on October 10, 1794, with a critical view to Schiller's Kantianism. Even more, Schiller attributes an *inclination* to reason, an affection, which according to Kant can belong only to the apparatus of sensibility.

How could Schiller have missed this contradiction? The answer to this question can only be given in view of the particular indecisiveness of his thinking between Kantianism and an idealism that was for him still unreachable. This indecisiveness is expressed in the fact that he formulates the idea of the self-objectification of reason for the most part in a language that remains faithful to Kant's basic approach. Yet from that approach sensibility can be conceived as a form of the externalization of the intelligible only with the greatest qualifications and with many reservations. The searching and helpless references to a "supersensible ground of unity for nature and freedom" certainly point in the same direction in which Schiller is moving. Yet his progress is more rhetorical than reflective. Schiller remains a Kantian.

In conclusion, this is what I want to show more fully. According to Kant sensibility is the manner in which we receptively comport ourselves to the world. As understanding beings we are spontaneous, as free rational beings we are active. Schiller adopted this dualism of faculties as the scheme even for his conception of spirit [*Geist*]. This becomes especially noticeable in his moral-philosophical reasoning, where he leaves no doubt that sensory boundaries must be transgressed for the sake of morality—a relationship demanding respect, not love. Even in his aesthetic sketches he never questioned the basic position of the sensible-rational dualism and consequently the bold demand for a self-objectification of reason within sense loses all comprehensibility. For "self-objectification" means that it is not something other than reason, but *reason itself* that comprehends itself in sense. Now for Kant sensibility is surely the other of reason, but in no way its own other. It could consequently at best mirror itself in sense; the mirror image will never permit sense to emerge as the other of reason itself. Sense remains foreign and external to reason in an insurmountable fashion, for sense is grounded in a cognitive stem that is completely removed from reason's dominion.

To make Schiller's project comprehensible one would need a completely new foundation for his theory of cognition, especially a *revolutionizing of his conception of freedom*. Without giving it much attention, Schiller employs this expression in at least four distinct senses. First there is *the freedom proper to nature* in the sense of the ancient Greeks; the freedom of *phyein*, of the unrestrained self-unfolding ability for instance of plants (but also of the human as a natural being) from its seed in accordance with its inner blueprint, what Aristotle calls "entelechy." This is an idea completely foreign to Kant. Schiller also speaks of the *freedom of the power of imagination*, for which Kant allows repeated appearances in the "analytic of the beautiful," yet which he assigns to the (fundamentally passive) ability for intuition. For Schiller this freedom sometimes melts with natural freedom, since in his view (which is again more Aristotelian) the power of imagination belongs to the natural condition of humans not to their intellectual faculties. Third, there is for Schiller *freedom as moral self-determination*—different from the two preceding versions—which depicts not a theoretical, but a decidedly practical capacity thus also not one that could be described as natural. In Kant's work, the freedom of the power of imagination maintains at best a relation of similarity with practical freedom (an analogy, which admittedly also includes certain products of nature, called organisms). Yet similarity is not identity; and the talk about the self-presentation of reason in the sensible cannot rely on this for it claims identity. Schiller was conscious of this, even if not sufficiently clearly. This is why he assumes the existence of a fourth freedom that could be named "*synthetic freedom*." It consists in the voluntary agreement, in a happy state of balanced weight or indifference between sensibility and morality, as if nature voluntarily submitted to the order demanded of it by morality. It does not have the character of a principle, but only of a synthesis; for instead of regulating the union of opposites from above, it must be content with reflecting a harmonious relationship between the two. It is the pole of indifference, not the principle of identity of sense and reason, the point, at which the poles limit their counteraction as it were to "*zero*"[28] (Schiller, 1992, 636/AL 147). Only with respect to this fourth type of freedom does it make some sense to say that it harbors the possibility of a *self*-mirroring of freedom in what is not freedom, but in what is sensibility. If we look more closely, however, we realize that this is not completely accurate. For it is possible that freedom looks at its own image in sensibility; yet that does not validate that sensibility—the mirror—is itself completely the objectification of freedom. And it would have to be so, if one wants to speak justifiably of a self-objectification of freedom in and as sense. Hence the beautiful soul, which Schiller regards as the ideal condition of reconciliation between morality and sensibility, remains limited to a quantitative balance between faculties, which are not themselves identified through some inner bond; and the talk about loving self-reference remains unproven rhetoric. Thus Schiller deprives his insuperable Kantianism of the fruits of a truly new approach, to which he points only in the form of prospects and wishes.

Yet by turning the critical point into something positive, one sees at the same time in what this new approach would have to consist. The middle or "zero" condition between sense and reason, of which Schiller speaks in his 1795 *Aesthetic Letters*, would require a founding in the identity of the two, and with regard to this identity one would have to show that beauty is its most perfect expression. A principle that is simultaneously the root of reality and ideality, would make the formulation that reason encounters *itself* in the other of reason comprehensible. Such an absolute identity of the real and the ideal, of nature and of spirit, was assumed first by Schelling, at about the same time as Schiller, as the necessary presupposition of both relations and their play of oppositions. If the existence of this identity could be proven, one could finally do without the Kantian "as if" which Schiller was only able to overcome rhetorically. This is what the so-called Oldest System-Program of German Idealism (whose author may well have been Schelling) does in an almost triumphant tone:

> And at the very end the idea that unifies all, the idea of *beauty*, the word taken in its higher Platonic sense. For I am convinced that the supreme act of reason, because it embraces all ideas, is an aesthetic act; and that *only in beauty* are *truth and goodness* akin.—The philosopher must possess as much aesthetic force as the poet. Those human beings who are devoid of aesthetic sense are our pedantic philosophers. The philosophy of spirit is an aesthetic philosophy. One can in no way be inspired—one can't even ruminate on historical matters in an inspired way—without aesthetic sense. Here it should become obvious to us precisely what is defective in those human beings who understand no ideas—and who concede forthrightly enough that everything becomes obscure to them the moment it involves something more than tables and indices.
>
> Poesy will thereby attain a higher dignity; in the end she will again become what she was in the beginning—*the instructress of {history} humanity*; for there will no longer be any philosophy, any history; the poetic art alone will survive all other sciences and arts. (Mat. 111)[29]

III.

This (or something like this) is what Schiller's surpassing by bold idealistic speculation could look like. But sheer boldness is not per se a philosophical virtue. Thus we should soberly ask ourselves at the end of our passage through Schiller's aesthetic reflections whether we really want to take the outcome of an absolute (supposedly graspable in thought) as a fitting alternative to that offered by Schiller's failure. My recommendation is an emphatic "no."

This is also what the early Romantics did after they had flirted for a while with the basic thought of an absolute idealism, among them especially Schiller's great admirer Friedrich von Hardenberg-Novalis. His Jena friend, Karl Forberg, derisively noted with regard to Fichte's absolute-idealist liquidation of Kantian criticism that he would rather fail with Kant than triumph with

Fichte. Hence I ask both myself and you whether we would not rather fail with Schiller than triumph with Schelling.

For much speaks against the assumption of an *existential* absolute. First of all, Kant's standing objection against the possibility of an "intellectual intuition" or an "infinite understanding." Ours is limited and works with concepts. Concepts are tools through which we *determine* something given (in addition to the concept) and determining means: to set limits (*omnis determinatio est negatio*). If we were to seek the given in a bewilderment of the mind, which is explained through its imperfection, or were we to take it for the unconscious creation of an *intellectus archetypus*, we would thus fall precisely back into the very Leibnizianism against which Kant's entire critical project stands opposed. One can take German Idealism as such a re-Leibniziation of Kant. The aging Kant watched, with growing resignation, while some of his most talented philosophical students took the path into absolute idealism.

Certainly, there was something right in the intention to surpass Kant. Did not Kant himself point in the direction of a ground of unity that would abolish [*aufhöbe*] all the dualisms of his philosophy? Reinhold was thought to have discovered such a foundation for Kantian philosophy. His argument was that something like it must be assumed. For if we define "knowledge" as "justified true belief" there must be at least one proposition that is self-evident. Only such knowledge could be called "absolute" according to the meaning of the word for absolute is only one thing, *quod est omnibus relationibus absolutum*. Yet if the foundation of knowledge were to consist of an uninterrupted reference of one proposition to another grounding it, then the chain of justifications would run to infinity and all knowledge would be relative.

Yet this argument, which seemed to have found its fulfillment in Fichte's foundationalism, soon gave rise to doubts among Reinhold's students, among them Novalis. These doubts developed in three directions. First, it was contested that a system of convictions could be based on any evidence at all since evidence amounts to private experiences of consciousness. Second, inter-subjective consensus formation cannot be explained by appeal to evidence. Yet such consensus does form a criterion for what we call knowledge. Furthermore, after closer analysis evidence cannot be clearly distinguished from "claims" (sometimes they are also called "remarks") "of common understanding." Even these claims can generally only be grounded on so-called intuitions, that is to say, we believe in them. Propositions of belief have a character similar to Euclidian axioms (and *Axioma* do mean something which is *believed*). Could they be proven, they would thus immediately lose their status of highest principles, for a proposition that finds its basis in a different one, is not the highest. Yet in this way the grounding of knowledge becomes an article of faith. Novalis will state: "It is the product of the power of imagination, in which we *believe*, without being able to perceive it in its and our nature" (for this text one and two). The most serious and most successful objection was the third. Reinhold's highest proposition does not really stand on its own. Rather he assumes for its justification several other propositions, which supposedly follow from it.

This would be a ruinous consequence for foundationalism. Novalis, for example, saw it in that way. He noted: "From what cannot be reached, according to its character, no attainment can be thought" (NS III, 685, Nr. 67). This means that to think an "I" as absolute would mean to contradict itself, inasmuch as the thought "I" is supposed to have a *determined* content. His friend Friedrich Schlegel firmly holds: "*Cognition* indicates already a *conditioned* knowledge. The non-recognition of the absolute is hence an identical triviality."[30] Both draw the consequence from this that only art is able to posit it [the absolute] before our eyes in a *mediating* fashion—symbolically, or as the Romantics preferred to say, allegorically—what neither intuition nor concept are capable of grasping for themselves alone. The inexhaustible meaningfulness of the aesthetic formation would show the conceptual unconquerability of the absolute *as such*. "When the character of the given problem is insoluable," concludes Novalis, "then we solve the same thing, when we present its insolubility [as such]" (op. cit., 376, Nr. 612). Basically this was precisely the suggestion of Kant's third *Critique*, and Schiller was guided by a good spirit when he did not transgress the "Kantian boundary line"—although admittedly this was precisely his intention. In his (presumably) later essay *On the Sublime* (first printing 1801) he revoked his idealist aspirations and turned back to Kant.

He thus stands closer to us than the Schelling of the phase of identity-philosophy, who was time and again tempted by self-critical early Romantic tendencies, until they finally drove him to give up absolute idealism. Above all Schiller's aesthetics are nearer to us than that of Hegel, who could no longer recognize aesthetic formation as the expression of the "true interests" of humanity; reflection—absolute comprehension—having supposedly outstripped the fine arts.[31] Today we no longer believe either in absolute reasons of assurance for our existence or in the deduction of our knowledge from an absolute identity or an absolute I. Yet, in no way do we regard art as the witness of antiquity, but as one of the timelessly valid manners of human self-understanding. In this way Schiller has remained our contemporary.

Notes

1. Friedrich Wilhelm Joseph Schelling, *Materialen zu Schellings philosophisches Anfängen*, ed. M. Frank (Frankfurt am Main: Suhrkamp, 1975), 118f.
2. Kants gesammelte Schriften, Königlichen Preußischen (later Deutschen) Akademie der Wissenschaften (ed.), 1900– , Berlin: Georg Reimer. Hereafter noted in text by Refl. Nr. followed by reflection number, volume number, and page number. This was written looking back on the years 1776–1778 (Refl. Nr. 5037, AA XVIII:69; the remark stands within a context of notes about that year where Reinhold tries to work through his own intellectual development reflectively, mostly in regard to the preface of Baumgarten's *Metaphysica*, here: XXXVI). Cf. also text 6.
3. To be exact, one should add that there are some *a priori* cognitions which Kant does not call pure such as those relating to the law of causality, for change implies existence (Immanuel Kant, *Critique of Pure Reason*, trans. Norman Kemp Smith (NY: Palgrave Macmillan, 2007) (43) and existence can only be recognized through perception (hence empirically) (242ff.). Therefore relations within the world of appearances that concern existence (like the question: is a or b the cause of c?) cannot be anticipated via pure reason (201ff.). There are hence non-pure synthetic judgments which are nevertheless called a priori (Konrad Cramer, *Nicht-reine synthetische Urteile a priori der Transzendentalphilosophie Immanuel* Kants (Heidelberg: Carl Winter, 1985)).
4. Gottfried Wilhelm Leibniz, Philosophische Schriften, vol. 1 (Frankfurt am Main, 1986–1990), 124. In English: "Discourse on Metaphysics" in Philosophical Papers and Letters, ed. and trans. Leroy E. Loemker (Boston: D. Reidel Publishing Co., 1976), 318–19.
5. Novalis, *Schriften*, vol. II, eds. Richard Samuel, Hans-Joachim Mähl, and Gerhard Schulz (Stuttgart: Kohlhammer, 1965), 273.
6. Ibid., 250.
7. Immanuel Kant, *Kritik der Urteilskraft*, ed. Wilhelm Weischedel (Frankfurt am Main: Suhrkamp, 1996). In English: *Critique of Judgment*, trans. Werner S. Pluhar (Indianapolis, IN: Hackett Publishing Co., 1987).
8. E.g. Kant, *Kritik der Urteilskraft*, 114, 169 (127, 167 in the English translation).
9. Ibid., §59.
10. Friedrich Schiller, *Theoretische Schriften*, eds., Rolf-Peter Janz with assistance from Hans Richard Brittmacher, Gerd Kleiner, and Fabian Störmer (Frankfurt am Main: Deutscher Klassiker Verlag, 1992), 176.
11. Hans Georg Gadamer, *Wahrheit und Methode: Grundzüge einer philosophischen Hermeneutik*, 2nd revised edition (Tübingen: Mohr-Siebeck, 1965). In English: *Truth and Method*, trans. J. Weinsheimer and D. G. Marshall (NY: Crossroad, 1989).
12. Jens Kulenkampf, *Materialien zu Kants "Kritik der Urteilskraft"* (Frankfurt am Main: Suhrkamp, 1974) 129.
13. Friedrich Schiller, *Theoretische Schriften*, 281.

14. Kant, *Kritik der Urteilskraft*, §59.
15. Ibid., 421, Remark.
16. Schiller, Friedrich, "Aus Vorlesungen zur Ästhetik" in *Theoretische Schriften*, ed. Rolf-Peter Janz (Frankfurt am Main: Deutscher Klassiker Verlag, 2008) 1069.
17. Schiller, Friedrich, "Kallias, oder Über doe Schönheit," in *Theoretische Schriften*, ed. Rolf-Peter Janz (Frankfurt am Main: Deutscher Klassiker Verlag, 2008) 282–83. The translation of this passage has been taken from Friedrich Schiller, "Kallias or Concerning Beauty: Letters to Gottfried Körner" trans. Stefan Bird-Pollan, in *Classic and Romantic German Aesthetics*, ed. J. M. Bernstein (New York: Cambridge University Press, 2003), 150. Italics sic. Hereafter referred to as KL.
18. Kant, *Kritik der Urteilskraft*, §59.
19. Ibid., 192 (In the English translation, 181ff).
20. Dieter Henrich, "Der Begriff der Schönheit in Schillers Ästhetik" in *Zeitschrift für philosophische Forschung*, VI (Frankfurt am Main: Vittorio Klosterman, 1957) 527–47.
21. Friedrich Wilhelm Joseph Schelling, *Sämmtliche Werke*, Division I, volume 3, ed. K. F. A. Schelling (Stuttgart: J. G. Cotta, 1856–64), 619ff. A nice formulation of this conviction is found in the late work. Schelling claims that the artistically beautiful is similar to a fairytale (like those of Goethe) in that its real charm consists in "feigning a meaning or showing one as from afar, but which would withdraw from us; we would be forced to pursue it, without ever being able to reach it" (Ibid., II/1, 12f.).
22. Schiller, Friedrich, "Über Matthissons Gedichte," in *Theoretische Schriften*, ed. Rolf-Peter Janz (Frankfurt am Main: Deutscher Klassiker Verlag, 2008), 1025.
23. Novalis, *Schriften*, vol. III, 413.
24. Friedrich Hölderlin, "Farewell," in *Poems and Fragments*, trans. Michael Hamburger (London: Anvil Press Poetry Ltd., 2004), 205.
25. "Aus Vorlesungen zur Ästhetik," 1072–73.
26. Schiller, Friedrich, "Über Anmut und Würde," in *Theoretische Schriften*, ed. Rolf-Peter Janz (Frankfurt am Main: Deutscher Klassiker Verlag, 2008) 387.
27. Ibid., 388–89.
28. Schiller, Friedrich, "Über die Ästhetische Erziehung des Menschen in einer Reihe von Briefen," in *Theoretische Schriften*, ed. Rolf-Peter Janz (Frankfurt am Main: Deutscher Klassiker Verlag, 2008) 635–36. Frank is citing a different source for the German edition of the "Aesthetic Letters." See bibliography for reference AL in English. Here the English page number is 147; hereafter cited in the body of the text with the German pagination followed by AL and corresponding English pagination.
29. The translation of this passage is taken from David Farrell Krell, *The Tragic Absolute: German Idealism and the Languishing God* (Bloomington and Indianapolis: Indiana University Pres, 2005), 24–25.
30. Friedrich Schlegel, *Kritische Ausgabe seiner Werke*, vol. XVIII, ed. Ernst Behler (München: Ferdinand Schöningh, 1975), 511, number 64.
31. Georg Wilhelm Friedrich Hegel, *Ästhetik*, with an introductory essay by Georg Lukács, ed. Friedrich Bassenge (Berlin: Aufbau-Verlag, 1955), 56ff.

4

The Violence of Reason
Schiller and Hegel on the French Revolution[1]

María del Rosario Acosta López

Preliminary Remarks: A Vindication of Modern Reason

Before dealing directly with the subject of this paper, I would like to begin with a series of preliminary remarks that will help to clarify the interests motivating my comparative reading of Schiller and Hegel in this chapter. Thus, I will first identify the conceptual framework underlying my approach to both authors from the standpoint of the present. This in turn will enable me to clarify the proposed method of reading their philosophical responses to the French Revolution. Last but not least, this will make it possible to explain the particular significance of such responses for the main goal of this collection, which inspires the argument of this chapter, i.e., the reinstatement of Friedrich Schiller as a philosophically relevant thinker.

Let me start by focusing briefly on the idea of the "violence of reason" that appears in the title of this article. This will allow me to lay out my position with respect to what it means to "do" history of philosophy in the present, particularly the history of modern philosophy. Within the current of thought that has become increasingly critical of the Western liberal tradition, partly as a result of Heidegger's critical reading of the history of metaphysics, there is a tendency in contemporary political philosophy to connect—perhaps too closely—the profoundly violent developments of twentieth-century historico-political events to the project of the Enlightenment and its modern conception of reason. Thus we find authors such as Jean Luc Nancy, Giorgio Agamben, and Roberto Esposito, to name just a few, calling our attention to the urgent need for a critique of modern Western metaphysics as the first necessary step toward a profound critique of the political today. Such a critique is oriented toward elucidating the kinds of violence that result from this modern framework, and which still underlie and operate within our contemporary conceptions of the political. This line of thought presents the project of a radical critique of modern reason as a task that can no longer be postponed. If the aim is to interrupt, undo, and resist the kinds of violence connected to modern metaphysics that have led to a totalitarian understanding of the political in the West, modern Western philosophy must be completely deconstructed in order to suspend the kinds of violence entailed in its commitment to the "sovereignty" of reason.[2]

It is precisely considering this context, and without dismissing its importance in orienting those doing philosophy today, that I would insist on the importance of finding a contemporary path for modern thought and the Enlightenment project.[3] We must remain alert to the possible risks and dangers involved in a certain (modern) conception of the political that is reflected in at least some of the multiple faces of violence in the present. Nonetheless, it is also important to ask whether the violence of twentieth-century totalitarianisms, which is also latent in one form or another in our current forms of democracy, is not in fact to a certain extent the result of a *betrayal of the modern project*, i.e., the result of a betrayal *of*—and not only the betrayal *by*— "enlightened reason."

It is true, of course, that modern reason may entail the risk of its own betrayal. It was the modern thinkers themselves who first began to make this evident. They were indeed the first to warn us of the dangers intrinsic to a certain propensity of reason—as Kant describes it—for forgetting its own limitations and betraying itself in the form of dogmatism and fanaticism. However, the project of modern philosophy is also the answer to this propensity. Its claim is precisely the need to make us aware of such a tendency of reason and of the multiple faces it can adopt when translated into the practical realm. The goal is to alert us to all the signs and the places where it may be happening, and thus to the fact that reason *also* produces its own kinds of violence, which may even be some of the worst.

Neither Schiller nor Hegel is unaware of this. Their answer to this problem, however, is neither a renunciation of nor a resistance to reason. On the contrary, both authors believe that reason itself also possesses the resources for understanding that—even though we are not beyond violence (the modern thinkers were not naïvely optimistic about this possibility, and Hegel was even less so)—we can at least resist its constant threat and criticize and permanently denounce its use. Both Schiller's and Hegel's criticisms of the violence resulting from the French Revolution are especially paradigmatic of this sort of critique of reason by reason itself with a view to making it more plural, broad, and, if possible, less dogmatic and violent. This is a process that can neither be concluded nor understood in progressive terms. It is rather the responsibility of thought each time to its own present.

This leads me directly to my second remark. It is common to find accounts in the secondary literature relating German philosophy's critiques of the French Revolution to the origins of a reactionary conservative line of thought that would later take hold in Germany. The clearest tendency therein would be a commitment to recovering the medieval religious and political traditions as inspiration for resisting the democratic political inclination of the French revolutionary project.[4] It is also true that both Schiller's and Hegel's critiques of the French Revolution would become points of reference and sources of inspiration for said reactionary-conservative thought, and that Hegel himself—especially in his later years—would be interpreted in close connection with a conservative stance.[5] Nonetheless, my interest in gathering both thinkers' criticisms of the political events of the day is by no means to reinforce said viewpoint. For the time being, a discussion of the reactionary character of their critiques will have to be thus left aside.

On the contrary, I believe that both Schiller's and Hegel's diagnoses of the terror resulting from the French Revolution very clearly illustrate the risks entailed precisely when *thought ceases to be revolutionary*. As I would like to show, according to both authors this happens when thought ceases to move and truly engage *with* reality, abstracting itself in a radically violent way from the singular, losing all *real* connection with concrete circumstances, and thus creating an insurmountable breach between theory and action. For both Schiller and Hegel, the *violence of reason* thus has to do rather with the violence of a unilateral theoretical approach that, due to its empty universality, finds itself somehow impotent and disempowered in stepping into action.[6] As we shall see, there is a leap that ends up being covered by and encompassed within the worst kind of violence since it acts with the absolute conviction of its own legitimacy but with the self-inflicted impotence caused by having emptied itself of all concreteness.

What I want to point out is the clarity and lucidity with which both Schiller and Hegel diagnose and comprehend the Reign of Terror in France as a historical manifestation of this phenomenon. That is as a historical event closely and perhaps even necessarily connected to its theoretical formulations. In other words, the Reign of Terror would, at least to a certain extent, be the result of a philosophical and theoretical approach that represents a latent danger in the Enlightenment project. I am thus interested in the lucidness both thinkers show when pointing out the direct effects that the modern commitment to a certain kind of thought can produce in reality, and thus the radical responsibility that this implies for philosophical thinking in turn.

For the same reason, I would like to insist once again that in the opinion of both these authors, revolutionary thought is not simply a mere "revolution in thought" (the famous phrase that Marx coined years later, but which already resonated earlier and would lead many German thinkers to view the French Revolution from the comfortable position of the spectator).[7] In contrast with this, I am using the term "revolutionary thinking" here to refer to a mode of philosophical thinking that knows itself to be fully involved in its own historical reality. Hence it is one that cannot be conceived of as opposed to but rather as directly engaged in transforming the historical world. This is a philosophical approach that to be consequent with itself and with a critique of the dogmatism of abstract reason seeks to confront and inhabit the contradictions of its present reality. The task is to set these contradictions in motion instead of merely showing their unsustainability *from a neutral theoretical distance*. I believe this to be the case with both Schiller and Hegel, and their analyses of the French Revolution are a suitable occasion to highlight this mode of philosophical procedure. In both cases, we have the opportunity to follow them in their direct involvement in their concrete historical present. Hence, we find here a very opportune example of the *critical* potential underlying modern thought, its commitment to a critique of the present, and the tasks and responsibility for philosophy that consequently follow from it.

Finally, my last remark is related to a concern I share with others who seek to study Schiller from a philosophical perspective: the same concern that has motivated this volume altogether. My interest in connecting Schiller's critique of the French Revolution to Hegel's analysis of the same phenomenon does not stem from any intention to portray Schiller only as an *important forerunner* of Hegel's philosophy. To make this the ultimate goal of the comparison would mean falling into line with the tendency that has predominated in philosophical studies of Schiller throughout the past century and has only just begun to change in recent years. I am referring here to the tendency to attribute philosophical value to his thought *only* as a reader of Kant (and one whose reading is usually deemed defective and inadequate in studies aimed at showing how he overlooked, misinterpreted, and even dangerously translated concepts of Kantian philosophy in his aesthetic-political proposal).[8] The other prevailing attitude has been to hail him as an important predecessor of the thinkers associated with German Idealism and/or Romanticism.[9]

The relationship I want to propose between Schiller and Hegel does not fit into this prevailing tradition in the literature. I do not wish to trace back to Schiller elements that Hegel would later recover. Nor do I think that such elements only acquired their final philosophical form and cogency in Hegel. On the contrary, I am interested in showing precisely how Schiller's critique of the French Revolution in his *Letters on the Aesthetic Education of Man*, written between 1793 and 1795, stands on its own in its lucidity and philosophical cogency at the side of, and on *par* with, Hegel's well-known reading of the Reign of Terror in the *Phenomenology of Spirit*. By comparing these two texts, the structure of their arguments, and the spirit that nourishes and activates the critique in each case, I wish to show the profound philosophical value of Schiller's arguments. I also hope to show how Schiller's very clear critical diagnosis of the phenomenon of terror is quite close to Hegel's argument, which was published more than ten years later in the section devoted to the French Revolution and the Reign of Terror in the *Phenomenology of Spirit*. This will also confirm Schiller's work as an important forerunner of Hegel's critique of modernity. Nonetheless, the central argument of my paper is not historical in this sense, but rather philosophical; namely, I am not interested in showing where and how Schiller's arguments would or would not have been recovered later by Hegel.[10]

In what follows I am going to focus exclusively on the two texts mentioned above: *Letters on the Aesthetic Education of Man*, specifically the first seven letters where Schiller presents a diagnosis of his historical present and the section of the Spirit chapter in Hegel's *Phenomenology of Spirit* titled "Absolute Freedom and Terror." This is the section that comes just after the Enlightenment's conception of the world and before the critique of Kantian moral philosophy.[11] I will propose a parallel follow-up on the general structure of the argument in each case. I am interested in detailing two aspects of the reading that Schiller and Hegel propose of the French Revolution. In the first section, I highlight the conceptual framework and type of philosophical thinking they undertake and that gives rise in both cases to the very particular *construction* of their critique. In the second section of the paper, I combine this approach with a follow-up on the *general structure* of the argument that each author raises around the (philosophical) reasons that led the Revolution of 1789 to become the Jacobin dictatorship of 1793. I will have to leave aside, however, the many nuances and subtleties of their arguments in order to be able to present the points on which both authors' philosophical diagnoses coincide.

Neither will I be able to carry out two additional steps that I would have liked to explore in greater detail but which I can only mention here. One is the connection in both cases between the criticism of the French Revolution and the critique of Kant's practical philosophy. For now it will suffice to caution that, although they sometimes appear together in Schiller's exposition and have often been confused in careless readings of Hegel, they constitute two very different arguments that should be studied separately. This is due to the fact that what is at stake in both cases and for both thinkers is precisely the philosophical statute of morality along with complex and not directly connected relations between the moral and the political.

Nor will I be able to explore the response that both Schiller and Hegel propose as an alternative to and an interruption of the kinds of violence the Revolution had mobilized historically as the catalyst of the abstractions of Enlightenment. In the case of Schiller, the philosophical and political proposal that arises from his critiques of the French Revolution has to do with the need for an aesthetic education in response to the violent immediacy of the revolution. In the case of Hegel, it is related to the crucial (and similar) place that civil society should occupy within the political arena as a necessary moment of mediation, i.e., of the training and education of the individual for citizenship.[12]

Toward an Understanding of the Historical Present:
A Renewal of Philosophical Critique

The critiques of the French Revolution in Schiller and Hegel are linked to an interest in performing a philosophical diagnosis of their own present. For both authors it is evident that in the case of the political events in France, as Schiller wrote to the Prince of Augustenburg, "the very fate of mankind is being debated" (AL 89).[13] However, neither one considers that a philosophical analysis of their historical present could be limited to the "political scene" alone (AL 89). On the contrary, both their analyses of the French Revolution are oriented by an interest in understanding the "world" in which such an event had taken place. This means, on one hand, an understanding of the contradictions and conditions of an era that had made such a historic event possible. On the other hand, it also means an understanding of how these contradictions had become more radical and thenceforth more visible in said historical manifestation. The *event* to be understood, therefore, is not strictly the historical developments in France, but rather what Schiller describes in the *Letters* as the great process that "is being brought before the tribunal of pure reason itself" (AL 89), namely, the coincidence of a political revolution with a revolution in thought—the Enlightenment. Such a coincidence required a much more careful philosophical analysis.

However, such analysis, according to both authors, cannot be taken up from the perspective of a philosophical conception that aims to carry out what Hegel describes as the task of "explanation," i.e., a view that reflects on and judges its object from an "outside" without engaging it fully from within. On the contrary, Schiller and Hegel are not only profoundly aware of the historicity of their own theoretical view, it is also clear that for both philosophical activity has to be closely intertwined with said historicity. Thus, both authors are interested in distancing themselves from the kind of philosophical approaches for which "explanation" is the prioritized mode of procedure. Explanation is more a matter of the understanding than of reason. Unlike reason, understanding needs to separate and dissect its object in order to analyze it from an outside perspective, thereby losing sight of the whole. Although this kind of analysis is a necessary and useful moment as both recognize, it cannot be the last step in the broader task demanded by a thorough philosophical approach. This is because "the all-dividing understanding [*Verstand*]," Schiller writes, "must first destroy the object of inner sense in order to make it its own" (AL 87). In the attempt to give an explanation, the object escapes our comprehension; "in dissolving the essential amalgam of its elements we find we have dissolved its very being" (AL 88). In a similar way, in the Preface to the *Phenomenology* Hegel warns that with this sort of method, "the living essence of what is at stake has been omitted or concealed"[14] By reducing scientific rigor to a mere schematic formalism, knowledge understood merely as explanation runs the risk of being "reduced to a lifeless schema, to a mere façade . . . a tabular chart."[15]

Both authors emphasize the risks involved in seeking to approach the study of experience from a strictly analytical, external perspective. They both consider that such an approach imposes "violence to what is sensuous."[16] That statement is Hegel's, but it also reflects perfectly the starting point of Schiller's analysis. The problem of sticking exclusively to the perspective of understanding is that by expelling sensibility from the realm of reason, the possibilities of the latter are entirely falsified. Sensibility, Schiller argues, has always been given naturally to reason as a necessary starting point.[17] Therefore the abstraction that understanding must avail itself of in order to do its work of analysis cannot be the ultimate goal of philosophical criticism. Hegel insists that the form of the judgment pertaining to explanation immobilizes the object of experience and imposes on it "the mere semblance of conceptual thought."[18] As long as the philosopher, Schiller writes, must "lay hold of the fleeting phenomenon" by binding it "in the fetters of rule," he or she will always end up "tearing its fair body to pieces by reducing it to concepts, preserving its living spirit in a sorry skeleton of words" (AL 88). Just "like a skeleton with small bits of paper stuck all over it," Hegel writes, "where there are only bones with the flesh and blood stripped off of them."[19]

For these reasons, an *enlargement of the philosophical outlook* is very much needed. An enlargement but not a *change* of outlook since for both Schiller and Hegel it is important to preserve continuity with the critical project of the Enlightenment and to seek the means to carry it to fruition. This is an outlook which, without renouncing understanding, much less the possibility of criticism, must be capable of rising to a viewpoint that Schiller will describe in the *Letters* as "a complete anthropological view, where content counts no less than form" (AL 93). The point is, Hegel writes, to "descend entirely into the content and move itself by its own nature."[20] Only then can "the rigorous exertion of the concept"[21] be assumed, namely, the possibility of penetrating into the movement of the phenomena, understanding truth as the very process that "creates its own moments and passes through them all."[22] Truth here results from a direct involvement with the contradictions inherent to the real, unlike an activity of thought that limits itself to avoiding contradiction, confusing it with falsehood and error. Thus, Schiller proclaims, in a gesture that could easily be Hegel's,[23] "as long as philosophy has to make its prime business the provision of safeguards against error, truth will be bound to have its martyrs" (AL 103).

This enlarged outlook, which for Hegel will be the achievement of reason's full potential for knowledge, is closely related in Schiller's case to what he calls "the aesthetic path" in his *Letters* and other writings from the same period.[24] Hence, for Schiller, the aesthetic perspective is not only limited to his well-known proposal of an aesthetic education for politics, namely an education *in* sensibility that can make the latter a natural (in the sense of a "second nature") participant in the deliberations of practical reason. Although this is the most commented upon version of Schiller's proposal, it is necessary to bear in mind that his reflections on an aesthetic perspective extend far beyond the aesthetic free (harmonious) play of the faculties and the practical experience resulting from it, to the much broader levels of thought and language. The aesthetic path for Schiller is thus, first and foremost, *the configuration of an alternative mode of philosophical approach*. The integration of sensibility into rational activity is directly related to a way of conceiving the experience of thought as profoundly involved in and entangled with sensible bodily experience.

In this sense, Schiller is also very close to a critique of the "epistemological" turn in modern philosophy of the type Hegel develops in detail throughout his corpus. He is also much closer to a conception of the experience of philosophical consciousness of the kind Hegel denominates "phenomenological." Furthermore, in Schiller's case, as in Hegel's, this is all connected to a profound reflection on the nature and character of *philosophical language*. Writing becomes therefore for both authors a main subject of reflection (or self-reflection one should say), together with the question about the limits and possibilities of a language that, while inevitably propositional in structure, must seek to overcome its exclusively referential nature in the very experience of its own exposition. This is what Hegel describes in the *Phenomenology* in relation to his proposal of speculative thought as the plasticity of an adequate philosophical exposition.[25] It is also closely connected to what Schiller determines as the goal of true philosophic writing, perfectly exemplified for him in the figure of the *darstellende Schriftsteller*; namely the ideal of a writer who, without sacrificing the clarity and rigorousness of his or her presentation, elevates language to be the very experience of thought and not just its mere communication.[26]

Although I cannot develop any of this in detail here, I would nonetheless like to insist that neither Schiller's nor Hegel's reading of the French Revolution can be studied in isolation from a much broader philosophical project, which both would attempt to implement in their own historical present. Moreover, they both seem to be equally aware that at least two steps are necessary in order to carry out this task. In the first place, they must distance themselves from a certain philosophical approach that limits reason, as they both describe it, to *mere* understanding and explanation. In the second place, it is consequently necessary to produce or even invent a different, broader type of philosophical understanding that imposes less violence on the sensible realm.

The close relationship between these two needs is paradigmatically revealed in their critiques of the French Revolution, along with the very particular type of violence that both authors believe results from a certain philosophical and theoretical outlook of the world. That is to say: *the causes both authors credit for the violent development of events in the case of the French Revolution are closely related to the philosophical approach from which they would both consequently seek to distance themselves*. The Revolution is thus a historical sign of the urgent need to enlarge our philosophical outlook, but this urgency only becomes visible with a thorough understanding of the event that presupposes it in advance.

I believe this to be the hermeneutic circle within which both Schiller and Hegel's criticism takes place, one I will now proceed to explore in some detail.

From the French Revolution to the Reign of Terror: The Violence Inherent to the Revolutionary Project

For both Schiller and Hegel, the diagnosis of the French Revolution is closely related to a critical reading of Rousseau, who they consider to be one of the theoretical harbingers of the revolutionary ideals set in motion in France in 1789. Moreover, as I have mentioned above, neither of their critiques departs from the historical events in order to detect possible links to their theoretical antecedents. What is distinctive in Schiller and Hegel's critiques is that they arise from Rousseau's thinking itself as representative of the Enlightenment, specifically in relation to the concepts developed in the latter's theory of the social contract. According to both authors, there is a foreshadowing in Rousseau's very conception of the general will, as well as in its theoretical and conceptual assumptions, of something that is almost inevitably connected to the violent development of the Jacobin dictatorship of 1793. From this point of view, the Reign of Terror is not simply a contingent development of the Revolution. It is rather *a result tightly related to the implementation of the Revolution's theoretical foundations* (and, as we have seen, of a certain theoretical *attitude* related to them).

Insofar as Rousseau considers the general will to be a *postulate* rather than a *result* as we shall see, Schiller and Hegel will find in this absence of mediation between theory and practice, between the ideal of reason and the historical conditions of the reality where it is to be implemented, the main reason for its violent fate. Since singularity must be completely denied and abstracted in the very concept of the general will, the latter will have to resort arbitrarily to an accidental content in its step into practice. Both authors show that this arbitrariness brings into question the necessity as well as the legitimacy of the general will since it eventually ends up materializing as a contingent unity of particular wills: a type of unity that Rousseau himself recognizes as problematic and markedly totalitarian. Thus, as Hegel affirms at the end of his review of this figure of consciousness in the *Phenomenology*, Rousseau's enlightened ideal of the general will "finds its reality to be totally other than what its concept of itself was."[27] The general will finds that its only possible reality is the imposition of the will as "the will of all." Regardless of whether or not this is a valid criticism, faithful to the spirit of Rousseau's proposal, this is in fact the reading that both Schiller and Hegel propose in connection to and as an essential antecedent of the French Revolution. I will therefore set aside the concrete details of Rousseau's argument to concentrate instead on the dangers that both authors perceive at the very heart of his theory of the general will.

ROUSSEAU'S ENLIGHTENED STEP

Both Schiller and Hegel begin by vindicating the importance of the step Rousseau has taken with his *concept* of the general will. Schiller highlights it as the very philosophical step that makes it possible to decisively move from a state of necessity (Hobbesian we might think) to the idea of a "moral" state. In his third *Letter*, for instance, where Schiller is continually tacitly referring to both the *Discourse on Inequality* and the *Social Contract*, he writes:

> And thus in his maturity he [human being] retrieves by means of a fiction the childhood of the race; he conceives, as *idea*, a state of nature, a state not indeed given to him by any experience, but a necessary result of what reason destined him to be; attributes to himself in this idealized natural state a purpose of which in his actual natural state he was entirely ignorant, and a power of free choice of which he was at the same time wholly incapable; and now proceeds exactly as if he were starting from scratch, and were, from sheer insight and free resolve, exchanging a state of complete independence for a state of social contracts. (AL 90–91, my emphasis)

For Schiller, Rousseau's gesture is valuable in that it manages to relate the possibility of the contract to that of the universality of reason beyond an instrumental rationality that would ultimately lead only to a notion of contract as negotiation (and thus as the sum) of individual interests. Rousseau's contractual state *elevates the subject to a universal standpoint that serves as a guarantee for the rational autonomy of its decision.*

Hence, Rousseau's notion of a general will is not, as Hegel also clarifies, "the empty thought of the will, which is posited as lying in a tacit or in a represented consent."[28] It is not therefore the result of each individual giving up his or her authority and autonomy in exchange for the (empty) representation of the law.[29] It is rather, Hegel points out, "a *real* universal will, the will of all individuals as such" so that "what emerges as an activity of the whole is the *immediate* and conscious activity on the part of each."[30] This operation proper to the general will is thus not, at least not in its philosophical conceptualization, one that merely results from the abstraction of all particularities. It is rather the (immediate) elevation of each individual will to the *real* universal will. The principle that gives its foundation to Rousseau's general will has therefore rational value, and this elevation to a real universality is, as Schiller also points out, reason's (self-)positing. This is the premise and the starting point of the social contract and, in any event, an important antecedent for what in Schiller and Hegel's eyes will be one of Kant's greatest achievements: the moral concept of a categorical imperative.

CRITICISM OF THE THEORETICAL ATTITUDE: THE RISKS IMPLICIT IN THE THEORY

Now one should also consider, as both Schiller and Hegel do, the implicit risks (not only the achievements) that come with Rousseau's notion of the general will. If one goes back to the quotes cited above, the notions of "idea" in the case of Schiller and of "immediacy" in the case of Hegel are already a clue toward their critique. To illustrate this, let us consider the following. According to Schiller, for an idea like that of the moral State to be possible at all, there must have been a historical process of radical separation of the powers or drives that mobilize human nature towards culture. The sensible drive is thus severed from the formal drive, eventually producing "one-sidedness in the exercise of his [human being's] powers" (AL 103). Each one of these powers or drives is thus developed to the highest degree. This occurs nonetheless at the cost of completely losing sight of the relationship of each drive to, and of its necessary dependence on, the other. Form appears thus as *pure form*, devoid of content. Matter in turn unfolds as *pure contingency*, independent from all form. This is all connected to Schiller's well-known diagnosis of Modernity:

> Only by concentrating the whole energy of our mind into a single focal point, contracting our whole being into a single power, do we, as it were, lend wings to this individual power and lead it, by artificial means, far beyond the limits that nature seems to have assigned to it . . . It is beyond question that human powers would never have produced . . . a critique of pure reason, unless, in the individuals called to perform such feats, reason had separated itself off, *disentangled itself as it were from all matter*, and by *the most intense effort of abstraction* armed their eyes with glass for peering into the absolute. (AL 103, emphasis mine)

The universality of reason and the ideas it produces as the basis of its practical determination, are thus guaranteed, at least in their first formulation and historical experience, by this *radical disconnection and abstraction* from all matter.

Hegel describes in a very similar way the oppositions resulting from the divisions proper to the world of the "Enlightenment," intrinsically connected to a type of consciousness he describes as "pure insight," a consciousness that experiences itself no longer as a "singular self," but rather as a "universal subject." This mode of awareness is marked by a tendency to understand itself in terms of absolute antagonisms. Enlightened consciousness, he writes, "completely separates its positive from its negative essence," opposing "pure thought" to "pure matter."[31] Such is the main feature of Hegel's diagnosis of the Enlightenment in the *Phenomenology*, namely, the philosophical and historical moment in which "at the pinnacle of the concept, the oppositions themselves have begun to stand out." "The next stage," Hegel writes, "will be for them to totally collapse, and the Enlightenment shall then experience the fruits of its deeds."[32]

The core of the problem is that in taking these oppositions to their limit, consciousness has gained its universality in an *abstract* way. It thinks of itself as "pure thought," in Hegel's terms, or as "pure form" immediately devoid of all content, as Schiller puts it. Anything that resists this empty universality, anything coming from the standpoint of the *singularity of historical and concrete existence* is therefore perceived as *nothing* by such a consciousness. Consciousness experiences reality therefore as pure *negativity*, and is thereby radically opposed to the only legitimate viewpoint this consciousness admits as its own, namely, the "purity" of the concept, the pure form of reason. This abstraction does not prevent said consciousness, however, from experiencing its relationship to any content in an *immediate*, and automatically legitimate, way. If the concrete, singular, real is *nothing vis-à-vis* the potency of the concept, then nothing prevents the latter from conceiving of itself as the immediate essence of the real. "Its knowing concept," Hegel writes, "is the essence of all actuality."[33] Reality is for this form of consciousness nothing other than what the concept determines it *should* be.

This is why Hegel names this moment of consciousness "Absolute Freedom," a notion that Hegel relates directly to the unavoidable historical fate of Rousseau's idea of the general will. Given that in its pure "absolute" form this moment of consciousness recognizes nothing other than its own self-posited concept, "the world is quite simply its will, and this will is the universal will."[34] Schiller also speaks in this context of a "spirit of speculation" that "in its striving after inalienable possessions in the realm of ideas, could do no other than become stranger to the world of sense, and lose sight of matter for the sake of form" (AL 101). In this way, Schiller continues, this spirit has "stood too high to discern the particular" (AL 101). Since it is completely devoid of matter, there is nothing that appears before it as resisting its impulse to "give form." This is an immediate, pure form, which this spirit conceives of the same way as an artisan relates to his work material. Schiller writes, "when the artisan lays hands upon the formless mass in order to shape it to his ends, he has no scruple in doing it violence; for the natural material he is working with merits no respect for itself" (AL 94). Thus, Hegel argues, in its behavior as absolute freedom, "consciousness does not begin its movement in it *as something alien* from which it principally returns into itself; rather, in its eyes the object *is* consciousness itself."[35] Consciousness in this case "lets nothing break loose so that it would become a free-standing object confronting it."[36]

We meet here a type of formal, abstract attitude, for which reality's singularity is not even a means for achieving the ideal end. Violence here is not even the result of an instrumental application of reason; individuals are not even in this case means for the realization of an ideal and purely conceived end. For there is no mediation whatsoever, but rather an *immediate* negation of all resistance on the part of matter, on the part of the existing historical reality. This theoretical attitude leads ultimately, as both authors clearly see, to the worst of all kinds of violence, namely a completely annihilating violence, a violence that will no longer be used as a means, but solely and exclusively as an *end* in itself. As Hegel writes: "This undivided substance of absolute freedom elevates itself to the throne of the world without any power capable of resisting it."[37]

Nevertheless, this step from a "theoretical" to an actual annihilating violence—or, from "disappearance" [*Verschwinden*] to "terror" and "destruction," as Hegel differentiates them in these passages in the *Phenomenology*[38]—is not at all self-evident. In order to understand why the immediate step into action implies violence, and precisely this type of annihilating violence, it is necessary to trace the very phenomenological path of this mode of consciousness. For Hegel, as for Schiller, this path is carried out in a paradigmatic way by the French Revolution's historical development. And so it is that we move from theory—the modern attitude and ideal of the Enlightenment—to its implementation. We move on to examine why this theoretical attitude is also necessarily and already an implementation, an abstraction that cannot remain solely as a mere disposition of thought.[39] As Schiller warns us in his *Letters*, "the damaging effects that the turn that spirit [*Geistesrichtung*] thus took were not confined to knowledge . . . it affected feeling and action no less" (AL 101–02).

FROM ACTION TO TERROR: THE CURSE OF THE REVOLUTION

Schiller and Hegel both prove that the Revolution as well as its denouement in terror are an essential part of the experience the Enlightenment had to undergo, announced in advance, as we have suggested, by the risks implicit in its theoretical configuration. A mode of consciousness absolutely convinced of the legitimacy of its ideal necessarily entails the imperative of its step into *praxis*. This is because its will, as we have already seen, does not think of itself as either singular or as contingent, but rather as universal and, as such, necessary (and necessarily practical). Thus, Schiller writes, this speculative spirit is "tempted to model the actual world on a world conceivable by the mind, and to exalt the subjective conditions of its faculty of representation [*Vorstellungskraft*] into *laws constitutive* of existence" (AL 101). The step into *praxis* is therefore not just any step, but one that also has some very particular characteristics. It is a consciousness (or a theoretical attitude) that, as shown above, acts *in the name of* universality, and therefore its action is also immediately universal action (i.e., law):

> However, this individual consciousness is in the same way immediately conscious of itself as the universal will. In its eyes, it is conscious that its object is a law given by itself and is a work carried out by itself, and *in making the transition into activity and into creating objectivity, it is thus not making anything which is individual; it is merely making laws and state-actions.*[40]

This figure of consciousness, Hegel continues, does "not let itself be deceived about the actuality of giving itself the law and its accomplishing the universal itself and not merely some individual piece of work."[41] Its action is therefore understood immediately as "universal work," or more precisely, as the immediately practical realization of the universal will.

Both authors' critical diagnoses are definitive in respect to this point: every "work" that presents itself as the "work of universality," without any mediation and, therefore, without any consideration of the limits and contingencies that singular (finite) reality necessarily imposes upon it, can only be carried out dogmatically. Its action will therefore necessarily reveal itself as a *violent imposition* on, *and destruction* of, any singular reality. Schiller writes:

> But physical man does in fact exist, whereas the existence of moral man is as yet only a supposition [*problematisch*]. If, then, reason

> does away with the natural state (as she of necessity must if she would put her own in its place), she jeopardizes the physical man who actually exists for the sake of a moral man who is as yet only supposed, risks the very existence of society for a merely hypothetical (even though morally necessary) ideal of society. She takes from man something he actually possesses, and without which he possesses nothing, and refers him instead to something that he could and should possess . . . Before he has had time to cleave unto the law with the full force of his moral will, she would have drawn from under his feet the ladder of nature. What we must chiefly bear in mind, then, is that physical society in time must never for a moment cease to exist while moral society as idea is in the process of being formed; that for the sake of man's moral dignity, his actual existence must never be jeopardized. (AL 91–92)

This is the violence of the *idea* of the moral State, or better yet, this is the moral State conceived (immediately) as a universal and legitimate idea (very different from a moral State that, instead of being simply posited in advance, can develop as the result of an aesthetically mediated process).[42] It is, therefore, the violence of an abstract version of reason. As Hegel will understand it, it is the fanatic and "terrorist" somber companion of Rousseau's Enlightened project: a subjectivity that conceives of itself immediately as the work of universal freedom. Since this action is undertaken in the name of an idea that, as Schiller points out, is so far only a supposition, the consequences are clear: no reality can ever entirely and satisfactorily correspond to its demands. As Hegel remarks in the *Phenomenology*: "the individual self-consciousness does not find itself [*sich nicht findet*] in this universal work of absolute freedom as existing substance," neither does it identify or recognize itself therefore "in the real deeds and individual actions of the will of absolute freedom."[43] In its constant search for ways to turn reality into a perfect reflection of the idea, consciousness as absolute freedom needs to radically negate all singularity since nothing singular can perfectly correspond to the purity of the ideal posited by reason.

Nevertheless, this mode of consciousness clings to, and is entirely convinced of, the legitimacy of its ideal. Its continuous effort to impose itself denies everything that attempts to resist it. This is why, Hegel insists, the figure of absolute freedom cannot achieve any positive work, "universal freedom can thus produce neither a positive work nor a positive deed, and there remains for it merely the negative act. It is merely the fury of disappearing."[44] It is thus an inevitably annihilating will: every individual *disappears* in the face of the universality of the idea. Once this is translated into action, and more precisely, once this is translated into State action, carried out in the name of this supposed (posited) universality, terror turns out to be the ultimate result:

> The sole work and deed of universal freedom is thus death, namely, a death which has no inner amplitude and no inner fulfillment, since what is negated is the unfulfilled empty "point" of the absolutely free self. It is therefore the coldest, emptiest death of all, having no more meaning than chopping off a head of cabbage or swallowing a mouthful of water.[45]

Terror, the "fury of destruction" as Hegel calls it in the *Philosophy of Right*,[46] is therefore the last stage of the experience undertaken by the Rousseauian Enlightened project.[47] It is the inevitable destiny, according to Schiller, of the Rousseauian idea of the general will. In this context, Schiller reminds us: "We know that the modes of determination of the human will must always remain contingent, and that it is only in absolute being that physical necessity coincides with moral necessity" (AL 92). For this same reason, he warns us, in the attempt to step into practice, i.e., in the attempt to immediately harmonize "man existing in time" with "man as idea," "the ideal man" ends up "suppressing empirical man." Along with this the State ends up entirely suppressing individuals (cf. AE IV 93), and the totalitarian will ends up suppressing the Rousseauian idea of the general will: "Thus little by little the concrete life of the individual is destroyed in order that the abstract idea of the whole may drag out its sorry existence" (AL 101).

This is therefore a kind of violence that results, as Schiller describes it, from the seldom recognized "egoism of our reason" (AL 123). If reason is stripped of all sensibility, he warns us, it can become much more violent than a sensibility blindly driven by its own impulses. For Schiller this is the unilateral limit-case of the *barbarian* who, in the rush to escape from arbitrariness (from the selfish drives of the so-called state of necessity) ends up rather perpetuating it in the most dangerous way. This is because the conviction of his own universal legitimate claims renders him incapable of recognizing the one-sidedness and singularity of his will.

Hegel's account of the violence of absolute freedom as the fury of destruction seems to recall Schiller's description of the abstract thinker's "cold heart," whose "imagination, imprisoned within the unvarying confines of his own calling, is incapable of extending itself to appreciate other ways of seeing and knowing" (AL 102). Reason without imagination is a cold, empty reason, incapable of being "outside of one's own self," turned completely in "upon itself" (cf. AL 203). Only sensibility can radically expose us to others. It alone prepares us "to receive into ourselves, faithfully and truthfully, natures unlike ours" (AL 124). This also clarifies why, according to Schiller, it is the aesthetic path that is capable of interrupting the circle of violence in which the revolution is inevitably trapped. Aesthetics is precisely what allows us to expand our gaze. It seems to be the outlook that, instead of moving precipitously toward the exclusion of all that is strange and toward the negation of everything that resists our comprehension, would be capable of undertaking the experience of this strangeness, thereby making it the very point of departure for our experience of freedom.

For understanding this with the detail and depth it deserves, we would have to delve into the mysterious paths of the beautiful and the sublime, something we cannot undertake here. Let it suffice for now to remind the reader that, for Schiller as much as for Hegel, interrupting cycles of violence is always closely related to the question of never renouncing the revolutionary character of thought. This means a revolution that, more than confronting the violence that provides the basis for all law, would instead seek to render this violence "superfluous," and "inoperative,"[48] through an understanding of the political that starts by questioning its own constituent categories that comes from the very heart of our Modern project.

Notes

1. An earlier version of this paper has been recently published in Spanish in an issue devoted to Schiller and the French Revolution for the journal *Philosophical Readings* (cf. Acosta, María del Rosario, "La violencia de la razón: Schiller y Hegel sobre la Revolución Francesa," *Philosophical Readings*, 9:2 (2017: 141–50). The preparation of this chapter, both in this, its definitive version, and in the first version I presented for the conference on Schiller and the French Revolution at the Universidad Autónoma de Madrid in March of 2013, was made possible thanks to the postdoctoral fellowship granted to me by the Alexander von Humboldt Foundation (2013–2014). Additional thanks to the invitation of Prof. Christoph Menke, who helped me to enjoy a position as guest researcher at the Goethe Universität Frankfurt am Main. I especially wish to express my appreciation to Valerio Rocco and Laura Macor for having organized an event of such high academic quality. I hope to have included in this revised version of the text some of the suggestions resulting from our discussion during the conference. All errors and options remain my own.

2. Thus Jean-Luc Nancy, for example in *The Inoperative Community*, argues that certain categories proper to modern Western philosophy are directly connected to a way of conceiving community in terms of a subject, identical to and in absolute relationship with itself. (Nancy, Jean-Luc. "The Inoperative Community," in *The Inoperative Community*, trans. Peter Connor, Lisa Garbus, Michael Holland, and Simona Sawhney (Minneapolis: University of Minnesota Press, 1991): 1–42.) Such a reduction of being in common to a common being, according to Nancy, leads ultimately to a totalitarian conception of the political. The idea that there is only one step from here to the historical manifestation of said totalitarian, modern, political reason seems to be suggested occasionally by thinkers like Roberto Esposito and Nancy: whether in its most evident historical currents (National Socialism or "the Nazi myth," as Nancy calls it in his work with Philippe Lacoue-Labarthe, together with the totalitarian experiences of Soviet communism for example) or in that which in any case underlies the liberal notion of democracy. (Lacoue-Labarthe, Philippe and Nancy, Jean-Luc. "The Nazi Myth," trans. Brian Holmes, *Critical Inquiry* 16:2 (1990): 291–312.) In both cases, Nancy affirms, the political tends to be conceived of in terms of "Work" or project, that is as something to be realized, as a (common) goal of realization of what makes us qualify (or not) as "human." The political community in its modern Western configuration is thus characterized by a logic of inclusion by exclusion, a logic of "band" as Giorgio Agamben also states using this term coined by Nancy. (Giorgio Agamben, *Means Without End: Notes on Politics*, trans. Vincenzo Benetti and Cesare Casarino (Minneapolis: University of Minnesota Press, 2000, 9.) It is a logic that ends up, in Esposito's words, sacrificing individuals to their own survival. Thus, a sacrifice of the community marks the beginning of the path taken by modern Western reason and its political consequences; a path that, according to these thinkers, seems to lead almost inevitably towards a community of sacrifice. This is, in general terms, the same idea of the "camp" that also permeates Agamben's proposed diagnosis of the contemporary political situation. I have explored this contemporary tendency of philosophical criticism of the political in much greater detail elsewhere, cf. Acosta, María del Rosario, *Narrativas de la comunidad: de Hegel a los pensadores impolíticos* (Madrid: Abada, forthcoming).

3. By no means do I wish to suggest here that the abovementioned authors completely dismiss this possibility. It is rather a risk they run by insisting on the dangers entailed in the modern tradition: a risk both in terms of the reception of their own works, and in the paths that contemporary thought continues to take based on their statements. Nevertheless, a look at the work of Nancy, Esposito, and Agamben will suffice to show that, on the contrary, their philosophical projects are deeply indebted to a generous and careful reading of the modern Western tradition.

4. In this respect see Karl Mannheim's in-depth study, "Conservatism: its concept and its nature" in *Conservatism. A Contribution to the Sociology of Knowledge* (London: Routledge, 1997).

5. It is however interesting to recall the clarifications that Jacques D'Hondt has introduced in his biography of Hegel, and the historical, political, and cultural contexts that may possibly have led Hegel to hide, more than to deny, his critical political stance. Cf. Jacques D'Hondt, *Hegel: Biographie* (Paris: Calmann-Lévy, 1998).

6. The empty universality of the law, for instance, according to Hegel, must attempt therefore to "clothe itself with might" when it comes to its application. This is the expression he uses in one of his early writings, *The Spirit of Christianity and its Fate* (1798) where he first develops what would later evolve into his critiques of the violence of abstraction, closely related to the violence of the abstract universality of law and modern sovereignty. Cf. G. W. F. Hegel, *Early Theological Writings*, trans. T. M. Knox (New York: Harper, 1961), 226.

7. Cf. among other sources, Rebecca Comay's diagnosis of this idea of revolution in thought, and supposedly in thought alone, as the development of a "mourning process," in contrast to the "melancholical" attitude the Germans attributed to the French. Cf. Rebecca Comay, *Mourning Sickness* (Stanford, CA: Stanford University Press, 2010): 17–19; cf. a variation on the same topic in Rebecca Comay, "Dead Right: Hegel and the Terror," *The South Atlantic Quarterly* 103, no. 2/3 (2004): 375–95, particularly page 381.

8. Paul DeMan's article, "Kant and Schiller" in *The Aesthetic Ideology* ed. Andrzej Warminski (Minneapolis: University of Minnesota Press, 1996), 129–62 is a paradigmatic example of this. Another important influence has been Gadamer's reading of Schiller in Volume I of *Truth and Method* (London: Continuum, 1975), 70–76. I have discussed these interpretations of Schiller much more explicitly elsewhere. Cf. María del Rosario Acosta, "Making Other People's Feelings our Own: From the Aesthetic to the Political in Schiller's Aesthetic Letters," in *Who is This Schiller Now?* eds. Jeffrey High, Nicholas Martin, and Norbert Oellers (London: Camden House, 2011), 187–203.

9. A work that completely changes the panorama of reading Schiller in this sense, preoccupied with vindicating his importance as a philosophical thinker independently of Kant and Romanticism is Frederick Beiser's book, *Schiller as Philosopher* (New York: Oxford University Press, 2005). Beiser gives a better explanation of the "indigent" situation of reading Schiller as philosopher in the twentieth century in his article, "Un lamento: sobre la actualidad del pensamiento de Schiller," in *Friedrich Schiller: estética y libertad*, ed. María del Rosario Acosta (Bogotá: Universidad Nacional de Colombia, 2008), 131–51. Following in Beiser's footsteps, Laura Anna Macor has made an extraordinary effort to recover the originality of Schiller's thought prior to his reading and knowledge of Kantian philosophy. Cf. *Der morastige Zirkel der menschlichen Bestimmung. Friedrich Schillers Weg von der Aufklärung zu Kant* (Würzburg: Königshausen & Neumann, 2012).

10. For the latter, there is still a need for a detailed study of Schiller's generally tacit presence in the writings of Hegel. Some clues regarding this can be found in the works of Adrian Peperzak and of H. S. Harris. Cf. Peperzak, *Le Jeune Hegel et la vision morale du monde* (The Hague: Martinus Nijhoff, 1969), 72ff.; and Harris,

Hegel's Development: Toward the Sunlight 1770–1801 (New York: Oxford University Press, 1972), 194 and 253.

11. It is possible to find critical arguments regarding the French Revolution in many other places in the works of both Schiller and Hegel. Already in *The Legislation of Licurgus and Solon* (1790) and in the first drafts of the *Letters to Prince Friedrich von Schleswig* (1793), Schiller had begun to formulate his first reservations with respect to the political events in France. However, it is in *Letters on Aesthetic Education* that these arguments are exposed most systematically (if anything like this can be said in the case of Schiller), which is why I have decided to concentrate exclusively on said text. The choice is not so evident in the case of Hegel given that in the *Philosophy of Right* there is also an explicit critique of the violence of destruction, connected with the notion of negative freedom and with the concrete historical example of the French Revolution. However, as other authors have already argued, the figure of "absolute freedom" in the *Phenomenology* still presents a series of nuances and very concrete references to the specific case of the French Revolution that tend to disappear in Hegel's later analyses. Cf. for example in this respect Andrew Norris's "The Disappearance of the French Revolution in Hegel's *Phenomenology of Spirit*," *The Owl of Minerva* 44, no 1/2 (2012–2013): 37–66.

12. For a much more careful reading of Schiller's aesthetico-political proposal, as an outcome of his criticisms of the French Revolution, cf. chapters IV and V in my book, *La tragedia como conjuro: el problema de lo sublime en Friedrich Schiller* (Bogotá: Universidad de los Andes and Universidad Nacional de Colombia, 2008); and more recently, the already mentioned above "Making Other People's Feelings Our Own." For the case of Hegel, cf. for example the careful analysis by Angelica Nuzzo, "Arbitrariness and Freedom: Hegel on Rousseau and Revolution," in *Rousseau and Revolution*, eds. R. Lauristen and M. Thorup (London: Continuum, 2011), 64–82.

13. "On the Aesthetic Education of Man," trans. Elizabeth M. Wilkinson and L. A. Willoughby (1976), repr. in *Friedrich Schiller: Essays*, ed. Walter Hinderer and Daniel Dahlstrom (New York: Continuum, 2001), 86–178. Referred to throughout as "AL."

14. G. W. F. Hegel, *Phenomenology of Spirit*, tr. Terry Pinkard. This version of Hegel's *Phenomenology* used to be available online at http://terrypinkard.weebly.com/phenomenology-of-spirit-page.html. It is now announced as forthcoming, in a revised version, by Terry Pinkard and Michael Baur, in Cambridge University Press. For the purposes of this paper I will quote from the former available version and provide the number of the paragraph in addition to the page. PhS §51: 44.

15. Ibid., PhS §50: 43.

16. Ibid., PhS §51: 45.

17. This is a point that Schiller would insist on throughout his work, including his first writings on medicine. As he points out as early as 1780 in his essay "Connection between Animal and Spiritual Nature in Man," it is precisely the 'sensorial animal nature' that "initiates, if I may put it this way, the internal clockwork mechanism of spirit." (My translation. Cf. Friedrich Schiller, *Nationalausgabe*, eds. Helmut Koopman

and Benno von Wiese, vol. 20 (Weimar: Böhlaus, 1962, 37–75; 50). Also see my more detailed analysis of these early writings of Schiller in Acosta, *La tragedia como conjuro*, op. cit., chapter 1. Also cf. Laura Macor, *Der morastige Zirkel* (Würzburg: Königshause and Neuman) chapters 2 and 3.

18. Hegel, *Phenomenology of Spirit*, PhS §51: 45.
19. Hegel, *Phenomenology of Spirit*, PhS §51: 46.
20. Ibid., PhS §58: 53.
21. Ibid., PhS §58: 52.
22. Ibid., PhS §47: 40.
23. Cf. ibid. PhS §39: 33.
24. Cf. especially in this regard also the essay that Schiller wrote between 1796 and 1801, Friedrich Schiller, "Concerning the Sublime," trans. Daniel Dahlstrom, *Essays* (New York: Continuum, 2001), 70–85.
25. Cf. Hegel, Phenomenology of Spirit, PhS §64: 58.
26. Cf. F. Schiller, "Über die notwendigen Grenzen beim Gebrauch Schönen Formen," in Nationalausgabe, op. cit., vol. 21, 14. I have developed this conception of philosophical writing in Schiller's work, connected to a particular conception of the experience of philosophical thinking, in María del Rosario Acosta, "On the Poetical Nature of Philosophical Writing: A Controversy over Style between Schiller and Fichte," Charles Bambach and Theodore George (eds.), *Philosophy and its Poets* (Albany, NY: SUNY Press, forthcoming). For a very suggestive reflection on this point in the case of Hegel, cf. Jean-Luc Nancy, *La Remarque spéculative* (Un bon mot de Hegel) (Paris: Galilée, 1973).
27. Hegel, *Phenomenology of Spirit*, PhS §592: 527.
28. Ibid., PhS §584: 521.
29. Even in his early writings Hegel was already profoundly critical of the modern notion of sovereignty, which he linked to a kind of violence laying at the very heart of both the conception and the experience of law in Modern State. He points out that law, understood as the result of a merely "economic" contract between the individual and the State, establishes an "equal dependence of all on their invisible ruler" (cf. G. W. F. Hegel, *Early Theological Writings*, 198). This "invisible" sovereignty of the law, which in its formality presumes equality—and this is its apparent gain—ends up nevertheless establishing "equality among enemies" (Ibid., 216). Hegel points this out in clear reference to Hobbes. There is thus a very particular type of violence that establishes itself at the core of the modern State due to this contractual conception of the law—a conception that Hegel considers to have been surpassed, first by Rousseau and later by Kant, although this fact does not free their proposals from other types of violence related to their own conceptions of law and action.
30. Hegel, *Phenomenology of Spirit*, PhS §584: 521, emphasis mine.
31. Ibid., PhS §592: 527.
32. Ibid., PhS §580: 517.
33. Ibid., PhS §583: 520.

34. Ibid., PhS §584: 521.
35. Ibid., PhS §586: 522, emphasis mine.
36. Ibid., PhS §588: 523.
37. Ibid., PhS §585: 521.
38. Cf. Norris, "The Disappearance of the French Revolution," 37–66.
39. Comay speaks of this in a very suggestive way: "Terror is not just the result of philosophical abstraction: it is itself the abstraction that in leaping from "all to all" (Rousseau's perfect phrase) can in the end only elaborate itself as the repetitive production of nothing—the endless negativity of an unworked death" (Comay, "Dead Right," 388).
40. Hegel, *Phenomenology of Spirit*, PhS §587: 523, emphasis mine.
41. Ibid., PhS §588: 524.
42. Schiller has often been accused of being inconsequential with his idea of the moral state in the *Letters*. Although this is one of the targets of his criticism in the first *Letters*, he returns to it in the final ones as the end point of mediation through the aesthetic approach. Notwithstanding this fact, what one should keep in mind here, taking into account other texts such as *On Grace and Dignity*, is the type of moral ideal that Schiller has in mind for example in his criticism of Kant. Schiller does not intend to renounce morality, nor does he consider its demands to be too high. On the contrary, he wants to find a way to guarantee that the "moral state" will not be constantly threatened by a nature that has not been adequately prepared to put it into practice. Thus, the moral state (and the moral State as the political reflection of the former) are and continue to be the end point, but not in its immediate, empty, abstract form. This is what Schiller wants to bring into question in his earlier *Letters*, and what he expresses in his later *Letters* regarding the idea of an ideal aesthetic state. Aesthetics, Schiller clarifies, should not be understood simply as "arbitrariness," as is often the case; "our psyche in the aesthetic state does indeed act freely, is in the highest degree free from all compulsion, but it is in no way free from laws; . . . aesthetic freedom is distinguishable from . . . moral necessity, in willing, only by the fact that the laws according to which the psyche then behaves do not become apparent as such, and since they encounter no resistance, never appear as a constraint" (AL 146, emphasis mine).
43. Hegel, *Phenomenology of Spirit*, PhS §589: 524.
44. Ibid., PhS §589: 525.
45. Ibid., PhS §590: 526.
46. Cf. ibid., §5A.
47. Following the suggestions made by Norris (cf. "The Disappearance of the French Revolution," 37–66.), I have been careful here in presenting the "fury of disappearing" [*Furie des Verschwindes*] as a previous moment, different from—although necessarily connected to—the "fury of destruction" [*Furie des Zertörens*], i.e., the moment of death and terror exactly as Hegel has described them in the *Phenomenology*. The violence of disappearing refers, in general, to the way in which the general will, on the basis of its abstraction, establishes its relationship with individual consciousness. Destruction is the necessary consequence of this type of relationship: the death of the individual (a

dull, meaningless death) is the paradigmatic expression of said disappearance that has taken place as a result of the social contract. In *The Spirit of Christianity and its Fate*, Hegel very clearly connects both moments, following an argument very similar to that which he will present years later in the Phenomenology: "so long as laws are supreme, so long as there is no escape from them, so long must the individual be sacrificed to the universal, i.e., be put to death" (Hegel, *Early Theological Writings*, 226).

48. I recognize that these concepts require a much more detailed explanation. I have sought to show that this is the case for Hegel in other places (cf. Acosta, "Banquo's Ghost: Hegel on Law, Violence and Memory," *New Centennial Review* 14, no. 2 (2014): 29–48). In the case of Schiller, the statement refers to the effect he believes an aesthetic education would have on our character (and by extension also on our shared being), which would render the coercion of law superfluous and unnecessary. Underlying my suggestions is the assumption, which I will have to demonstrate elsewhere, that Schiller's proposal of aesthetic politics comes much closer than has previously been recognized to the way Hegel proposes to understand the destiny of Modern ethical life [*Sittlichkeit*].

5

Schiller and Pessimism

FREDERICK BEISER

Schiller a Pessimist?

On November 10, 1859, Julius Bahnsen, a school teacher in Anclam, a small town in the Prussian province of Pomerania, gave a speech to celebrate the centennial of Schiller's birth.[1] On the face of it Bahnsen's speech was like many of others given that year. However there was also something new and interesting about it, something that revealed the latest direction of Schiller interpretation. Bahnsen was a disciple of Arthur Schopenhauer, who was rapidly becoming the most famous philosopher in Germany. Thus Bahnsen began to interpret Schiller according to Schopenhauer's signature doctrine: pessimism. Schiller, in his view, was the poet of pessimism. "A deep pain with life goes through all of Schiller's poetry," he wrote.[2] "In all periods of the poet's life," he went on, "one could hear the old complaint . . . about the nothingness of human fate." Just like Sophocles, the choir from the *Braut von Messina* would intone: "never to be born is the highest human happiness"[3] Schiller was indeed "a thoroughly modern poet," Bahnsen averred, because "his heroes represent the turning away from the world and its pleasures."[4]

Bahnsen's interpretation raises an interesting question: was Schiller really a pessimist? Was Bahnsen right to claim him as the herald of Schopenhauer's bleak worldview?

Before we begin to answer this question, we need to be precise about the meaning of pessimism. In the writings of the pessimist thinkers who would dominate German philosophy from 1860 to 1900, the term had a definite meaning. The major pessimists—Arthur Schopenhauer (1788–1860), Eduard von Hartmann (1842–1906), Philipp Mainländer (1841–1876) and Julius Bahnsen (1830–1881)—agreed on the central thesis of pessimism. That thesis could not have been more depressing nor more shocking: that life is not worth living; that nothingness is better than being; that it would have been better were we not born at all. For this thesis, the pessimists gave two very different rationales: one was *eudemonic*, that life contains more suffering than happiness; the other was *idealistic*, that because of fate and circumstances, it is impossible to achieve our basic moral, political, and aesthetic ideals in this life.

The pessimist interpretation therefore maintains that Schiller held that life is not worth living. Allegedly, this is the message we receive from Schiller's poems and dramas. The aim of his dramas—so we are told—is to convey a tragic view of the world, according to which suffering is the normal lot of mankind and our basic ideals are unattainable. While he admitted that Schiller did not know the central thesis of pessimism since he died a half century too early for that, he still held that Schiller would have readily accepted it if he had lived into later in the nineteenth century. Schiller was therefore a pessimist *avant la lettre*.

Is this interpretation plausible? Was Schiller a pessimist in this precise sense? Did he really believe that life is not worth living? To answer these questions, we first need to have a better idea of the pessimistic interpretation of Schiller.[5]

Schopenhauer's Theory of Tragedy

Bahnsen's interpretation of Schiller was suggested to him by Schopenhauer's theory of tragedy, which he put forward in his masterwork, *Die Welt als Wille und Vorstellung*. Schopenhauer's theory, as he outlines it in §51 of volume I,[6] is short, simple, and straightforward. The purpose of tragedy, we are told in no uncertain terms, is "the presentation of the terrible side of life," the portrayal of "inexpressible pain, the misery of mankind, the triumph of evil, the mocking dominance of accident, and the irredeemable fall of the righteous and innocent."[7] All the great tragic heroes—Gretchen in Goethe's *Faust*, Hamlet, the maid of Orleans—abandon the goals they once sought and renounce the pleasures of the world. They all die "purified by suffering" after the will to live in them has been exhausted and extinguished.[8] What the spectator sees through tragedy, therefore, is the suffering and meaningless of life; through that insight he is able to turn away from "not merely life but the whole will to life itself." Schopenhauer made it plain that tragedy had nothing to do with "so-called poetic justice," according to which evil would be punished and virtue would be rewarded. That was the criterion by which "Dr. Samuel Johnson" had evaluated Shakespeare's plays and found them all wanting. But that judgment shows, Schopenhauer insists, a complete ignorance of the goals of tragedy. "The true meaning of tragedy is the deeper insight, that, what the hero suffers is not the result of his particular sins but of original sin, i.e., the guilt of existence itself."[9]

In volume II of *Die Welt als Wille und Vorstellung*, Schopenhauer went into a little more detail about his theory of tragedy. Here he made clear the effect that tragedy should have on the spectator. The tragic poet portrayed the bleakest aspect of life in the hope that the spectator would become disillusioned with life itself.[10] He showed the many ways in which the will is frustrated, so that the spectator would learn the value of resignation.[11] The terrible events played out on stage showed the spectator "the bitterness and worthlessness of life," and therefore "the futility of all his striving."[12] Schopenhauer then wrote: "The demand to turn against the will to life remains the true tendency of tragedy, the final purpose of the depiction of the suffering of humanity; and it is still the goal even when this resigned elevation of the mind is not shown in the hero himself but is aroused in the spectator through the sight of great, undeserved and even deserved suffering."[13] He went on to argue that the pleasure we derive from tragedy comes from "this elevation above all the goals and goods of life, this turning away from life and its enticements."[14] It did not derive from fear and pity, as Aristotle thought, because these are not really pleasant sensations; they could describe at best the means but not the end of tragedy.[15]

In short, this is Schopenhauer's theory of tragedy. But did Schopenhauer enlist Schiller into the ranks of his theory? Did he regard Schiller as one of his pessimist tragedians? It certainly seems so. In his original account of tragedy in *Die Welt as Wille und Vorstellung* Schopenhauer mentions no less than four of Schiller's plays: *Die Räuber, Braut von Messina, Don Carlos,* and *Wallenstein.* All of them are taken as evidence for his theory. Schopenhauer knew his Schiller well and would often cite him throughout his works.

These citations of Schiller appear, however, without any direct discussion of the playwright himself. It is as if Schopenhauer thought that Schiller gave evidence for his theory of tragedy only by default. There are, however, other references to Schiller in Schopenhauer's writings that show his explicit readiness to bring Schiller into his pessimistic view of the world. In his February 17, 1863, letter to Frauenstädt, for example, Schopenhauer remonstrated against his disciple's theory of tragedy on the grounds that it had revived the old "Protestant principle of poetic justice,"[16] according to which the just are rewarded and the unjust punished.[17] Frauenstädt had argued that tragedy must show a kind of justice where the hero suffers because of some misdeed of his own; "his suffering must be, directly or indirectly, the consequence of his deeds."[18] Tragedy, Schopenhauer insisted to the contrary, has nothing to do with justice because its aim is to show us the misery of life, pure and simple, and it does that best when we see how even the virtuous suffer and come to ruin. This is the case with all the great tragedians, Schopenhauer declares, having Sophocles, Calderon, Shakespeare, and Goethe in mind. However, he then adds, significantly, that the same generalization applies "even to Schiller." Schiller lets Don Carlos and Posa end miserably, and he even mocks the Protestant principle when he declares: "*Wenn sich das Laster erbricht, setzt sich die Tugend zu Tisch.*"[19]

It is even more striking that Schopenhauer cited Schiller's verse as evidence for his pessimistic view of the world. In his *Aphorismen zur Lebensweisheit*, for example, Schopenhauer twice referred to *Resignation* for his view that happiness and pleasure are only "*fata morgana*" and that only suffering and pain have reality in this life.[20] The sentiments behind the same poem also appear in a strategic place in §63 of *Die Welt als Wille und Vorstellung* where Schopenhauer develops his idea of "eternal justice."[21] According to that idea, everyone receives in life what they deserve. Everything that happens is the product of the will, so that whatever the will experiences in life it brings upon itself. If there is misery, torment, and death, that is only what the will deserves. It is in just this context that Schopenhauer announces, though without any direct citation of Schiller, that "*die Welt selbst ist das Weltgericht.*" That is, of course, a reference to the famous final lines of Schiller's poem.

Schopenhauer, then, certainly did see Schiller as a pessimistic philosopher. This was evident for him not only in Schiller's dramas, but also in his poems. When Bahnsen gave his lecture in 1859 he was simply making ideas of his master more explicit. Schiller was, as far as Schopenhauer and Bahnsen were concerned, a prime case in point of the poetic pessimist.

An Ex-Optimist

When Schiller was a young man at the *Karlschule* he expounded, in several school essays of 1779 and 1780, a very optimistic view of the world.[22] According to this worldview, God creates the world out of love for all its creatures. He makes everything according to a plan, which is for every human being to achieve perfection and happiness, first in this life and then in the hereafter. To know his duties, man needs to determine his place within the universe. A good action is one that perfects the system of the cosmos or promotes the end of God in creating us. An action therefore has moral worth insofar as it promotes the perfection and happiness of God's creatures. In this happy world, there is a perfect harmony between perfection and pleasure: what perfects myself is also what gives me pleasure and what destroys myself gives me pain. There is also a perfect concord between self-interest and social benefit: since I am a social being, I can be happy only by promoting the welfare of others. The egoist, who pursues his own good at the expense of others, isolates himself and eventually becomes miserable. The whole world system will operate smoothly—it will achieve its intended end—if people simply act in the same spirit as their creator: the spirit of love. It is love that makes the world go around, because through it I promote the happiness and perfection of myself as well as others, which is the whole purpose of creation.

There was, of course, not much new in Schiller's early philosophy. Such optimism was typical of the Enlightenment. Similar ideas could be found in the thinkers of the Scottish Enlightenment or in the Leibnizian-Wolffian school. Schopenhauer's pessimism was in fact a reaction against this optimism. From the very bottom of his heart, Schopenhauer hated the very sentiment behind optimism, which he regarded as "wicked" (*ruchlos*) because it made a mockery of the inexpressible suffering of mankind.[23] He denied categorically its every tenet of his universe: there is no God, there is no providence, there is no harmony between perfection and pleasure, and there is no concord between self-interest and the general happiness.

It did not take Schiller long to approach Schopenhauer's way of thinking. Already in the early 1780s he began to voice his doubts about his early optimism. In the short dialogue *Spaziergang unter den Linden*, which was published in 1782, Schiller has the character Wollmar express a view of nature diametrically opposed to his earlier view. Wollmar is a materialist who thinks "the fate of the soul is written in the body" (NA, XXII 76). In his concept of nature, there is no room for providence or immortality. Nature follows a cycle, reworking and feeding off her own creations, like "a dirty monster who feeds off her own excrement" (NA, XXII 76). The order of nature does not allow people to achieve perfection or happiness, because most of them most of the time, have to struggle merely to survive. While Schiller does not necessarily endorse the view of Wollmar, it is striking that he also does not refute it. The dialogue leaves us with an aporia between him and his idealistic interlocutor Edwin.

Some of the poems of the early 1780s also protest against the very idea of a providential order. In the poem *Freigeisterei der Leidenschaften*, which was written in 1782, the poet complains about the bonds of duty that demand repressing his passions for a married woman (NA, I 163–65). These bonds create enormous suffering, and there is no heavenly reward for following them. There is indeed, for all he knows, no higher good than satisfying these passions here on earth. The poem *Resignation*, which was published in 1786, voices a similar complaint: the poet now asks himself whether it was right for him to sacrifice his happiness on earth for moral redemption in the afterlife (NA, I 166–69). A spirit tells the poet that we have to choose between two principles: hope or enjoyment, the prospect for eternity or the pleasures of the earth. Schiller does not decide for one principle or the other; but it is striking that he thinks we must choose. In his early philosophy pleasure and eternity were not at odds but one reinforced the other.

Schiller's doubts about his early optimism reached their crescendo in his *Philosophische Briefe*,[24] which was first published in the *Thalia* in 1786. This work is both a confession and retraction, a statement and self-critique, of his earlier beliefs. In a section entitled *Theosophie des Julius*, Schiller gave a brief and passionate exposition of his earlier credo. It is striking, however, that he distances himself from this section, claiming that it came from an earlier essay he found among his papers. The beliefs expressed in it, he says, are the product of "a naïve and impetuous youth." While they express the needs of the heart, they cannot satisfy the demands of reason. Although Schiller does not abandon his early doctrine, he also does not know how to answer the doubts that can be charged against it. He refers to the general dangers of free-thinking and skepticism—"the paroxysms of the fever of the human spirit"—and he fears that the first shove of materialism will tumble his entire system. Schiller does not explain in detail how his new doubts affect his earlier beliefs. There is one place, however, where he expresses his doubts about one fundamental belief of his early philosophy: the belief in providence, the divine creation and government of the world. Schiller declares his puzzlement about the whole idea of creation; more specifically, he cannot understand why God has created man later than nature (PB 110). If God is perfect, and if the universe is better with man, then God should have created man at the very beginning. These doubts about the creation then lead to the point that

Schiller doubts the very existence of God. For he now asks if God is not a creator, is he really a God at all?

Where all these doubts were heading is not entirely clear. Schiller promised a sequel to the *Philosophische Briefe*, a much longer work where all the tensions would be resolved in "a general, purified and well-founded truth" (PB 108) but it was never written. Whether Schiller finally became an atheist has never been determined;[25] but it is clear enough that the idea of providence plays no role in his later thinking. After rejecting his early optimism, Schiller was free to write tragedies with no reflection on divine justice. These tragedies are based on the idea that either there is no providence—i.e., a divine order where virtue is rewarded and vice punished—or at least that we cannot know whether there is such. The heroes in Schiller's tragedies suffer or die with no prospect of reward for their virtues or punishment for their vices. Just as Schopenhauer would have it, then, Schiller had renounced "the Protestant principle of poetic justice" which would make tragedies into theodicies.

Freedom and Death

Although by the late 1780s Schiller was no longer an optimist, it hardly follows that he was a pessimist. After all, optimism and pessimism are not contradictory but contrary predicates, so that it is possible to deny one without affirming the other. Was then Schiller also a pessimist? The evidence stands heavily against this assumption. The more we examine Schiller's plays and the more we consider his philosophy itself, the more Schopenhauer's appropriation of Schiller proves to be not only highly tendentious but also wildly inaccurate.

Let us assume that Schopenhauer is entirely correct about Schiller's tragedies: that in each of his tragedies the hero or heroine suffers or dies through no fault of his or her own, and that there is no redemption for their suffering or death. It hardly follows from this that Schiller is a pessimist, i.e., someone who thinks that life is not worth living. For all that we know, Schiller thinks that tragedies are rare events in the history of mankind, that they happen to a few unfortunate individuals because of a peculiar concatenation of events. Even for those exceptional individuals who do suffer tragedy, it scarcely follows that their lives are worthless, or that they were better not born; their suffering and death still serve as instructive examples for others. This is indeed exactly how Schiller did view tragedy, because he tells us, in an early essay,[26] that the purpose of theater is to serve as a stage for moral instruction. From the theater we learn the attractions of virtue, the problems of vice, the depths of human passion, and how to bear misfortune. So Schiller does not think that tragedy should teach us to withdraw from life; on the contrary, it shows us how to better endure life.

Schopenhauer reasons that because tragedy shows us the inevitability of suffering and death, its ultimate intent is to disillusion us with life. He thinks that this general point applies to Schiller's tragedies as much as all others. But it is significant that Schopenhauer comes to this general conclusion irrespective of the *content* of any particular tragedies without considering their specific message, moral, or theme. The more we consider that content, however, the more we find that Schopenhauer's reasoning about tragedy is misleading. This is especially the case with Schiller's tragedies. Although Schiller does construct plots that result in the suffering and death of the hero or heroine, it is wrong to infer from this that he thinks that their lives are pointless or that their ideals are worthless. Let us briefly consider three of the tragedies that Schopenhauer refers to—*Die Räuber, Don Karlos,* and *Braut von Messina*—to see why his pessimistic analysis fails them.

Prima facie Schiller's *Die Räuber* complies with Schopenhauer's theory of tragedy. There is no cosmic justice, no rule of providence, to ensure that its virtuous characters are rewarded and that its vicious characters are punished. The hero and heroine suffer greatly, but they receive no redemption. The antihero, Karl Moor, deceived about his inheritance of the family estate, leads a life of the brigand as the head of a robber band. While he tries to behave like a Robin Hood, stealing from the rich to give to the poor, there are many innocent victims of his misdeeds. The character Amalia, Karl's fiancée, falls into the depths of despair because she is told that Karl is dead; although she remains completely devoted to him, he murders her in the end. The villain, Franz Moor, does pay for his crime—for deceiving Amalia and Karl Moor's father about his death—but this brings no justice or happiness for Amalia or Karl. Amalia never gets her man; Karl never gets his inheritance. The lack of cosmic justice is made apparent by Karl Moor in a revealing soliloquy where he asks why there is harmony for soulless nature but none for rational beings (NA, III 109). Life, Karl tells us, is the same for the wise man and the fool, for the coward and the brave, for the noble and the wretch. In true pessimist fashion, Karl finds it pointless to strive after ideals of happiness and perfection. "For what this hunger for happiness? Why this ideal of unattainable perfection?" he asks. The complete lack of cosmic justice is revealed at the close of the play when Karl declares "two men like me would destroy the whole moral order of creation" (NA, III 135). Yet the play remains, in the end, a remarkable affirmation of the human power of freedom and the need for the rule of justice. Rather than returning to his robber band, Karl resolves to turn himself in. There is the need for a sacrifice for all his injustice, and he makes himself that sacrifice. Precisely because there is no God to enforce the rules of justice, man himself has to perform that role; if he has committed crimes, he has to pay the price and sacrifice himself. What Karl will not surrender is his power of freedom, his pride in his autonomy. When pushed to the brink of suicide, he refuses to allow misery to take control over himself; he is too proud to surrender to misery (NA, III 109).

Schiller's *Don Karlos* lends itself less to a pessimistic interpretation than *Die Räuber*. Schopenhauer is right that *Don Karlos* ends with the death of its two heroes: Don Carlos and the Marquis de Posa. Both are conspirators for the rebellion in Holland, which is an act of high treason in the Spain of Phillip II. They are duly found guilty and have to suffer the consequences. However it hardly follows from this that Schiller regards their deaths as futile, as acts of hopeless and naïve idealism. The ideals for which they suffer are portrayed as noble and worthy of such sacrifice. These ideals are tolerance, basic human rights, and freedom of the individual. In his famous speech to the king where he sets forth these ideals, Posa admits that the time is not ripe for them, and that he comes centuries before his time (NA, VII/1 116). He knows that he will not be able to realize them in an age where absolutism is the prevailing political ethos. Still, he makes his stand and expresses his willingness to die for his ideals. That Schiller allows Posa and Karlos to die for these ideals is only his way of showing them as having the highest value and worth. In his *Briefe über Don Karlos* Schiller later explained that he wanted to show how republican ideals could be realized from above and that they did not require the clandestine activity of the Illuminati or Freemasons (NA, XXI 168–69). He said that it is perhaps worthwhile to see how the ideals of a Montesquieu could be applied and confirmed in a tragedy. While this was to push the political dimension of the play too far—nothing in the play shows us how these ideals could be applied—it still shows the great importance that Schiller gave to these ideals.

Of all Schiller's plays *Die Braut von Messina* seems to confirm best Schopenhauer's theory of tragedy. Two feuding brothers, Don Manuel and Don Cesar, are finally reconciled by their mother only to find that they love the same woman, Beatrice, who also happens to be their long lost sister. Don Cesar finds Beatrice in Don Manuel's arms, and feeling betrayed kills him in a jealous rage. After discovering that Beatrice is really his sister, Don Cesar resolves to kill himself to atone for his brother's death. "Death," Don Cesar tells us, "is a powerful mediator," having the power "to extinguish all flames of anger" and "to reconcile all hatred" (NA, X 120). Here is a fate so awful, and a life so dreadful, that the only rational decision seems to be to leave it. Don Cesar indeed regrets the day he was born, in true pessimist fashion. The choir too harbors Schopenhauerian sentiments, hoping that the reconciliation between the brothers will not last long because "man must have something to fear, to hope and be troubled about/so that he can bear the burden of existence" (NA, X 50). Yet, despite all this pessimism, one of the deep themes of the play is that life is not worth living under certain circumstances, and that one of these circumstances is a life sunken in guilt. The choir declares at the close of the play: "Life is not the highest good/the greatest evil of them is guilt" (NA, X 125). Don Cesar's suicide thus shows that there is something of higher value than life itself: freedom, the power to take responsibility for one's own actions and to be master over one's fate.

What we find in all three of Schiller's tragedies is the character's recognition of the value of freedom. This value is so great that it transcends that of life itself; it is something worth dying for. Thus Karl Moor decides to turn himself in; Don Carlos resolves to defend the political liberty even if it means betraying his father and death; and Don Cesar commits suicide rather than live with a guilty conscience. In each case the tragedy is the same. The character must die to demonstrate their freedom; to show their moral integrity, they must pay the ultimate price. Although all the characters must suffer and die, the point of Schiller's plays is not to demonstrate that life is not worth living but to show that people have a power of freedom whose value and power transcends life itself. This is anything but Schopenhauerian. Schiller is doing the very opposite of what Schopenhauer recommends: he is not denying the will but affirming it.

The paramount value that Schiller gives to freedom appears not simply in his tragedies themselves but in his theory of tragedy. In one of his first essays on tragedy, *Über die tragische Kunst*,[27] Schiller seemed at first to come close to Schopenhauer's definition of tragedy. He defines tragedy as "a poetic imitation of a connected series of events (a complete action) which shows that we human beings are in a state of suffering, and whose intention is to arouse our pity" (TK 164). Although the reference to pity is Aristotelian, the portrayal of human suffering fits Schopenhauer's requirements for tragedy. It is striking, however, that when Schiller goes on to explore the concept of tragic pleasure, he becomes decidedly anti-Schopenhauerian. Schiller explains that the pleasure we take in tragedy comes from perceiving our freedom, from sensing our power to act independent of the determination of the sensible world. We see in the tragic hero a struggle between reason and sensibility, a conflict between the demands of moral principle and those of personal happiness. The hero faces a predicament where he or she can fulfill moral obligations only by suffering, only by surrendering their hopes of personal happiness. On seeing the predicament of the tragic hero we have mixed feelings, feelings of both pain and pleasure. We feel pain because we empathize with the hero's suffering but we also feel pleasure because we sense his or her power to rise above all the forces of the physical world and to assert their moral power. We thus see the appearance of freedom in the hero's actions, which, according to the *Kallias Briefe*, is the basis of all beauty.

How is this *anti*-Schopenhauerian? Both Schiller and Schopenhauer think that the portrayal of human suffering in tragedy gives us a perception of our supersensible powers. In Schiller, it is our power of freedom to act contrary to sensibility, and in Schopenhauer, it is our power to turn against and renounce the sensible world. Nevertheless, Schiller and Schopenhauer still have very different conceptions of the purpose of tragedy. For Schiller, the aim of tragedy is not simply to arouse pity, as he at first suggests, but to give the spectator an awareness of his power to act upon and change the world. In other words, the purpose of tragedy is *to affirm* the power of the will. For Schopenhauer, however, the goal of tragedy is to give the spectator the awareness of his power to renounce the world. We have no real power to change the world, the eternal cycles of sorrow and suffering; but we can at least resolve not to enter that world and to stay outside it. Hence the purpose of tragedy is not to affirm but *to deny* the will. The difference is then between affirming and denying the will—a contrast that fits perfectly Schopenhauer's own account of the difference between optimism and pessimism.

Idealism versus Pessimism

There is a profoundly idealistic dimension to Schiller's thinking which makes it impossible to force him into a pessimistic mold. Schiller thinks that there is a highest good, unlike Schopenhauer,[28] and that human beings can, if they only strive with intelligence, make at least some progress toward achieving it. The highest good consists in the complete realization of all human powers, the harmony of reason and sensibility. The task of Schiller's *Anmut und Würde* is to explain this ideal, and the business of the *Ästhetische Briefe* is to lay down the political conditions for its realization.

This idealism is especially apparent in one of the guiding themes of Schiller's philosophy: that mankind should strive to achieve, through freedom, the unity and harmony with nature that had once been given to early man. It was the vocation of modern man to regain this lost unity and harmony, to achieve on a higher self-conscious and voluntary level what had been given to natural man on a lower subconscious and necessary level. Hence Schiller wrote in *Über naïve und sentimentalische Dichtung*:[29] "They [the objects of nature] are what we *were*; they are what we should *become*. We were nature, as they were, and our culture should take us, through the path of reason and freedom, back to nature" (NSD 414).

This utopian motive appears in various guises in Schiller's writings. It emerges in his ideal of grace, as he outlined it in his *Anmut und Würde*, according to which virtue means not acting contrary to inclination but incorporating it into one's character. It also appears in his account of the three stages of moral development: childhood, where we act according to our natural impulses and desires; youth, where we learn moral principles but feel constrained by them because they often command us to act contrary to our natural impulses; and maturity, where we act from moral principles from inclination and feel no constraint in acting on them. In the *Ästhetische Briefe* Schiller formulated a similar schema for history in general. There were the ancient Greeks, who lived in unity with nature; there were modern men, who lived by moral principles but who had lost that unity; and there would be the men of the future, who would recover the unity of the Greeks on a higher, self-conscious level.

While Schiller is under no illusion that humanity is far from realizing this ideal, he still thinks that it is possible to make some progress toward it, he still thinks that it is possible for it to make some progress, and it comes into existence, but only occasionally, in the lives of a few remarkable individuals. The aesthetic state outlined in the ultimate letter of the *Ästhetische Briefe* will exist "in the needs of every finely tuned soul" though "in fact only in a few select circles" (AB 412, AL 178). Still, this was a goal that mankind could, through constant striving, approach, even if they could never attain it. The mere fact that Schiller admits the possible existence of this ideal is significant because it shows that the world need not be as bad as Schopenhauer portrays. The amount of evil and suffering in the world can be diminished, and it can be made a better place by striving to realize the ideals of our human nature.

In his bleak portrait of the human condition in §§56–61 of *Die Welt as Wille und Vorstellung* Schopenhauer assumes that man will be a wolf to man, that he will act on his self-interest and compete with others. The world is such an unhappy place not least because human beings, whenever given the opportunity, harm one another to achieve their self-interests. Schopenhauer does think that there will be a few individuals who have the power to get beyond the competitive free-for-all. These are those lucky few who have the power to deny their natural desires and to renounce their will. They are the great exceptions, however, because they achieve their virtue by their innate inner character and not through education.

This is contrary to Schiller's famous theory of aesthetic education, as outlined in his *Ästhetische Briefe*. Through education everyone can learn to control their competitive instincts and to tame their self-seeking desires; they can learn to act on moral principles, and to do their duty from inclination. People have the power to create a world where they not only *respect* one another, because they obey moral principles, but also where they have the power to *play* with one another, because they develop their personalities in exchange with others.

There was always a *quietistic* element to Schopenhauer's pessimism, an element utterly alien to the spirit of Schiller's thinking. Schopenhauer explains in book IV of *Die Welt als Wille und Vorstellung* that the will can escape suffering only by denying itself, only by turning against the world, and by renouncing its own desires. We cannot change the world through our will, because it is precisely its activity, in whatever form it takes, that entraps us in the cycle of futile desire. Compared to Schopenhauer, Schiller's thinking is not quietist but activist. We can change the world for the better through our will; indeed it is through acting that we approach the highest good and begin to regain that unity with nature that we once lost.

The idealistic dimension of Schiller's thinking appears especially clearly in his philosophy of history. The civilized European of the eighteenth century, he wrote in his essay on world history,[30] should see himself as the benefactor of all the historical developments that lie before him. All the knowledge of the arts and sciences, which is the product of the centuries, has allowed mankind to control nature and to make life more comfortable. We can construct a narrative which shows how all the epochs of the past have been stages in the development of the culture of our own epoch. In this essay Schiller reveals himself to be a believer in progress, in the growing civilization of mankind through the ages. The contrast with Schopenhauer could not be more striking. Schopenhauer saw history not as a story of progress but as a cyclical tale, the repetition of the same events in slightly varied ways according to that old maxim "*idem sed aliter*" (the same but different).[31] We cannot ascribe a purpose or end to history, Schopenhauer argues, because it is only a collection of individual facts, one damn event after another. Since human beings are essentially the same, there is no sense in which we can talk about improvement through history.

Summa summarum, it is hard to imagine a greater contrast between two philosophers than that between Schiller and Schopenhauer. The idealism of the former clashes with the cynicism of the latter. But—*nota bene!*—the contrast is not that between optimism and pessimism, as if Schiller somehow believed that we can achieve happiness and perfection in life. In the great struggle between optimism and pessimism Schiller struggles for the *via media*; this is not the best of all possible worlds, but neither is it the worst. The world can be made a better place if human beings only learn to exercise wisely their greatest power: freedom. The aim of all Schiller's plays was to affirm this power, the very one which Schopenhauer would have us deny.

Notes

1. Julius Bahnsen, *Schiller. Eine Gedächtnissrede gehalten den 10ten November 1859 im Gymnasium zu Anclam.* (Anclam: Fr. Krüger, 1859). Bahnsen, it is worth noting, was the author of one of the best theories of tragedy of the nineteenth century: *Das Tragische als Weltgesetz und der Humor als ästhetische Gestalt des Metaphysischen.* (Lauenberg: F. Ferley, 1877).

2. Idem, 5.

3. Idem, 5.

4. Idem, 14.

5. We focus here on Schopenhauer's interpretation of Schiller. It was not the only pessimistic interpretation. See also Eduard von Hartmann, *Aphorismen über das Drama* (Berlin: W. Müller, 1870) reprinted in *Gesammelte Studien und Aufsätze Gemeinverständliche Inhalts* (Berlin: Duncker, 1876), 251–307. Although Hartmann does not explicitly discuss Schiller, he regards him as a pessimist. See *Studien und Aufsätze*, page 304, where he cites Schiller's *Braut von Messina* (though without mentioning the source).

6. Arthur Schopenhauer, *Sämtliche Werke*, ed. Wolfgang Freiherr von Löhneysen (Stuttgart: Cotta-Insel, 1968), I: 353–56.

7. Idem, 353.

8. Idem, 354.

9. Idem, 354.

10. Arthur Schopenhauer, 'Zur Ästhetik der Dichtkunst,' II: 555–62; 565.

11. Idem, 557.

12. Idem, 558.

13. Idem, 559.

14. Idem, 558.

15. Idem, 559.

16. Arthur Schopenhauer, *Gesammelte Briefe*, ed. Arthur Hübscher (Bonn: Bouvier, 1978), 303.

17. Schopenhauer discusses sections IX through XI of Frauenstädt's *Aesthetische Fragen* (Dessau: Gebrüder Katz, 1853), 95–124.

18. Frauenstädt, *Aesthetische Fragen*, 96.

19. The citation is not from *Don Carlos* but from the final verse of *Shakespeares Schatten* as in Schillers Werke: Nationalausgabe, i.A. des Goethe und Schiller-Archivs, des Schiller-Nationalmuseums und und der Deutschen Akademie, ed. Julius Petersen et al. vol. 2 (Weimar: Herrman Böhlaus Nachfolger, 1943, 2010), 307. All references will be this edition, and will be abbreviated as NA, followed by volume and page number.

20. Schopenhauer, *Werke*, IV: 487, 571.

21. Ibid., I: 480–81.

22. '*Rede über die Frage: Gehört allzuviel Güte, Leutseeligkeit und große Freygebigkeit im engsten Verstande zur Tugend?* NA XX: 3–9; and *Die Tugend in ihren Folgen betrachtet*, NA XX: 30–36.

23. Schopenhauer, *Die Welt als Wille und Vorstellung*, vol. I, §59, 447.

24. *Philosophische Briefe*, NA, XX: 107–29. From now on PB in in-text citations.

25. On the question of Schiller's religious beliefs, see M. Misch, "Schiller und die Religion" in *Schiller-Handbuch*, ed. Helmut Koopmann (Stuttgart: Kroner, 1998), 198–215.

26. "Was kann eine gute stehende Schaubühne eigentlich wirken?" NA, XX: 87–100.

27. *Über die tragische Kunst*, NA, XX, 148–70. From now on TK in in-text citations

28. Schopenhauer, *Die Welt als Wille und Vorstellung*, vol. I, §65, 492.

29. Cf. NA, XX: 413–503. From now on NSD, citations in text.

30. "Was heisst und zu welchem Ende studiert man Universalgeschichte?" NA, XVII: 359–76.

31. See Schopenhauer, *Die Welt als Wille und Vorstellung*, Band I, §35 & §53; and Band II, Kap. 38, *Über Geschichte*, 563–73.

Part II

Imagining Schiller Today

6

Naïve and Sentimental Character
Schiller's Poetic Phenomenology

Daniel Dahlstrom

Suchst du das Höchste, das Größte?
Die Pflanze kann es dich lehren.
Was sie Willenlos ist,
sey du es wollend—das ists![1]

Poets are, by definition, "the *preservers* of nature," but when they can no longer completely be so, they serve as its *witnesses*" and "*avengers*." In the former case, they are natural; in the latter, they seek the lost nature. In the former case, they imitate what is actual; in the latter, they portray something ideal. Every poet is accordingly "either naïve or sentimental." Even in the present day, Schiller insists, "nature is the only flame that nourishes the poetic spirit," a spirit that gathers all its power from nature and speaks to it alone even in the case of "artificial" human beings, caught in the grip of culture (NSD 196/432, 200f/436f).[2] In this way Schiller distinguishes between two basic kinds of poetry and poetic genius grounded in different relationships to nature.[3] Indeed, the development in Schiller's thinking from the *Letters on the Aesthetic Education of Man* to *On Naïve and Sentimental Poetry* is marked by the way that nature replaces reason as the center of gravity.[4] Each form of poetry possesses a distinctive and constitutive moral dimension that is sustained by their respective relationships to nature.

The distinction between naïve and sentimental poetry is easily misunderstood. Schiller is by no means claiming that a poet is always and necessarily only naïve or sentimental. The exclusive disjunction "either naïve or sentimental" stands, but only for a given poem or part of one. Thus, although he mainly treats the two forms as parallel with ancient and modern poetry respectively, Schiller reminds his readers that the distinction is not a matter of time, but "manner" (*Manier*).[5] Just as there is no lack of sentimental tropes in some ancient poetry, particularly in Latin, naïve poetry can be found in every class of modern poetry. Similarly, while both Homer and Shakespeare are naïve poets, the two forms of poetry are both on display in Goethe's *Werther's Suffering*.

Yet the two species fall under a common genus, namely a "poetic spirit" that, in drawing its nourishment solely from nature, is equivalent to being human (NSD 200/436). The concept of poetry itself is nothing but the concept of giving humanity its most complete possible expression, whether it be in a condition of natural simplicity where all human powers are acting harmoniously in nature or in a cultural condition where such a harmony is nothing more than an idea. The two forms of poetry correspond to these two conditions and so it is that the paths of poetry and the paths of humanity coincide, as do the two forms of poetry and the two sorts of human being (NSD 201f/437ff, 233/473f, 241/482). Schiller accordingly speaks of both a naïve "character" and a sentimental one (NSD 214/452, 221/459, 249f/491f). His reflections on naïve and sentimental poetry are thus at once poetic reflections on human character, on the dominant ways of being that constitute the human condition.

Yet while Schiller is intent on differentiating between the two characters of humanity and forms of poetry, according each its due and registering its respective advantages over the other, he does not simply present them as divergent characters, standing side-by-side one another. His reflections on naïve and sentimental characters is a reflection on what it means to be truly human, i.e., what it means to be human in the full sense of the term, which is not simply a matter of exhibiting a character that is sometimes naïve and other times sentimental. To the contrary, he outlines a fundamental and essential dynamic between the two characters. To the extent that the true nature of humanity can be realized, it requires moving beyond the naïve experience of nature and naturalness to the sentimental experience of nature. In other words, while Schiller attempts to establish the integrity of the two distinct species, he also privileges one over the other.

The pursuit of these two objectives gives rise to a deep tension in his reflections on poetry and humanity. A primary aim of the following paper is to examine this tension and its importance for his poetic reflections on human nature.[6] To that end this paper mainly reviews, in the first two sections, analyses of naïve and sentimental species of poetry as well as the dynamic between them. A secondary aim of the paper (pursued in a brief, concluding section) is to note how those analyses, anticipating central themes and moves of phenomenology, at once exemplify and supersede a poetic phenomenology of the human condition.

Nature over Art: The Moral Pleasure of Naïve Poetry

There are moments in life when we find ourselves cherishing the nature of a certain object, standing in awe of it, simply because it is natural, a part of nature. Two conditions are necessary for this feeling: first, the object must be part of nature or what we take to be nature, and, second, it must be naïve, "i.e., nature must contrast with art and put it to shame" (NSD 180/413). Schiller uses the term "art" in a broad but traditional sense, reminiscent of Aristotle's distinction between the natural and the artificial, the former having its principles of rest and motion internal to it, the latter external to it. Thus, "art" here designates the artificial in general, including every cultural phenomenon produced by human deliberation and execution. In Schiller's *Letters on the Aesthetic Education of Man*, art stands for the freedom of the aesthetic. By contrast, here it stands for the alienating culture, alienated from nature, dubiously set free from nature by reason and human device. The natural, when viewed in contrast to art so conceived, is naïve. The naïve is accordingly unaffected, devoid of any semblance of artificiality; it is unforced precisely because it involves no exertion, no design, and no work against what comes naturally.[7]

Nature is not automatically naïve; it becomes naïve when it is contrasted with the artificial surfaces. Nature, so considered, is the freedom that something enjoys when it obtains itself, existing according to its own laws, i.e., it is one with itself. Hence, Schiller adds, the pleasure that we take in the naïve is not aesthetic but moral; that is to say, it is not generated by observation alone but is mediated by an idea. What pleases us is not the beauty of a form but an idea exhibited by certain objects. "It is not these objects, it is an idea portrayed by them, that we cherish in them" (NSD 180/414). So, too, while the naïve poet imitates nature, it is not actual or ordinary nature but genuine nature instead (though no naïve poet, Schiller allows, has flawlessly pulled this off (NSD 236ff/476–79).

Given this analysis of what basically motivates our attraction to naïve phenomena, Schiller moves, without skipping a step, from objects in nature that are considered naïve to human behaviors displaying that same naïveté, and then to the poetic depictions and evocations of these naïve phenomena in general, i.e., to naïve poetry. Certain objects in nature and certain human behaviors are considered naïve on the basis of a particular way of experiencing them, namely, an experience of them mediated and motivated by the idea of a contrast with the artificial. The themes of naïve poetry are these naïve phenomena. In order to write such poetry, i.e., in order to be a naïve poet, one must obviously have the corresponding feelings and experiences. Something similar holds for the ability to appreciate such poems.

With this gloss of the general significance of the naïve in hand, Schiller introduces his basic distinction regarding poetry and poets. There are, at the base, two kinds of poets: those who are natural and those who seek to be. As noted at the outset of this paper, the former, "the *guardians* of nature," are naïve poets; the latter, "nature's *witnesses* and *avengers*," are sentimental poets (NSD 196/432, 200/436).[8] The sort of poet one is depends upon the character of the age in which one lives or on the impact of contingent circumstances upon the poet. Thus, Greek poetry is paradigmatically but by no means unfailingly naïve, while modern poetry is typically, but not invariably sentimental (NSD 197/433, 203n/437n). Yet whether it is history or circumstances that determines the kind of poet, what they determine in either case is the poet's relationship to nature. If the poet is one with nature, simply safeguarding it, her poetry is naïve; if the poet feels the loss of nature and, thus, the need to bear witness to it, even to avenge it, her poetry is sentimental. Where the poet's expression of her own sentiments, self-expression, is missing in naïve poetry, it is the hallmark of sentimental poetry.

While Schiller applies the adjective "naïve" to a broad palette of phenomena (objects, behaviors, experiences, poems, poets), what they have in common is their naturalness and the moral pleasure produced by that naturalness. Yet the experience of this pleasure is complex because its emergence depends upon awareness of its opposite, i.e., the contrast with art and artificiality. The tenuousness of this dependence is patent since it means that we have to go beyond mere observation of something in order to consider and enjoy its naïve character. In other words, we have to reflect on the phenomenon, comparing it to its mirror image, in order to appreciate its unreflective character.

The basic significance of the naïve for Schiller is, as noted, the experience of nature in contrast with the artificial. The experience is itself pleasurable but it is a "moral pleasure." There are two sorts of naïveté and, accordingly, two forms of poetry that produce this moral pleasure. Behavior that is unexpected and thus, as a rule, laughable is deemed "naïve" ("the naïveté of surprise"), but so is behavior that simply displays a wholesome disregard of convention and culture ("the naïveté of character").⁹ An example of the former has already been given, i.e., the actions and expressions of children. However, as noted earlier, the example holds only to the extent that we indulge the illusion that they could be artificial and act otherwise. Strictly speaking, only those who are capable of acting otherwise (acting artificially) can display the childlike, unintended behavior that takes the form of being surprising. Thus, for example, public displays of such behavior in situations that are embarrassing (if not for the person responsible for the behavior then for others) typically produce a combination of mirth, respect, and melancholy.¹⁰ While we laugh at the surprising (i.e., unmannerly, unconventional, improper, indecorous, etc.) behavior, we also admire it for its naturalness and freedom from conceit, even as we also poignantly note our own lack of that freedom (NSD 185/420).¹¹

While nature commands our attention in this case, the person behaving so is in the other species of naïve subject matter, the naïve temperament. We not only experience a moral pleasure, but we experience it regarding a moral object, and while nature is in the right in both cases, it is nature in the form of a person's honorableness in the latter case. The expression of nature here is not simply a spontaneity that amuses because it ridicules social convention; it is instead the sort of deliberate action that wins our respect for the agent. So while the common theme remains the same, i.e., the contrast of nature with art that puts the latter to shame, the notion of nature is not the same in each sort of naïveté.

Schiller gives three examples of the naïveté of character: the action of a child who, upon hearing that someone is perishing from poverty, immediately gives her father's wallet to the poor man; an honest, trusting person's act of sharing a confidence with another who is bent on betraying that trust; and Pope Adrian VI's frank and public admission to the Church's adversaries of its misdeeds (though the respect for the admission diminishes—think of a politician's tears—to the extent that it appears to be more a matter of prudence than candor). In all three cases, the action puts the state of the actual world to shame, the world of human creation, as the nature of the individuals in each case follows "*its moral constitution*" (NSD 185/420).¹² As evidenced by this last remark, the conception of nature at work in Schiller's account is the source of a moral character that overrides anything artificial or cultural, at least aesthetically, and any human institution not in keeping with it.

In the immediate wake of presenting these examples of a naïve temperament and thinking (*Denkart*), Schiller makes the claim that every true genius is naïve. The claim is unsurprising in certain respects, given the tradition of thinking about genius that traces back to Kant. Genius is nature's way of providing rules for art, almost behind the backs of the geniuses themselves. A genius has no clue to how she comes upon the ideas of what to produce; she has no control over them and no capacity to convey them in the form of directions (from which Kant infers that genius is to be found only in fine arts and not in science).[13]

Schiller expands on this Kantian account by addressing the "naïve grace" with which a genius expresses her thoughts. This genius for naïve expression supposedly flows at once freely and by inner necessity from the naïve type of thinking. The "ingenuity" and "esprit" of the poetic genius's writing style consists in making its subject matter fully alive and transparent, presumably rendering all commentary superfluous, as "the sign completely disappears in what is signified." Thus, in the naïve expression, words, thoughts, and reality are in perfect alignment; the words of poetic genius ("divine decrees from the mouth of a child") render what is thought fully present, even if for the first and only time. This naïveté of expression stands in stark contrast to affected, inauthentic ways of speaking in everyday social life, where "people often say something other than [what] they are thinking" (NSD 190f/425f). If the words inspired by poetic genius disappear in what is said naïvely, so, too, does the naïve poet: "The *naïve poet* is the work and the work is the *naïve poet*" (NSD 197/433).

Schiller augments Kant's gloss on genius by extending it to the genius's intellectual and moral character and even to the genius's gender.[14] Significantly, if also somewhat ambiguously, he contends that genius, acting not on principles but on "insights and feelings," expands nature itself. At a first reading, this contention may seem at odds with Kant's view that genius is nature's way of giving rules to art. How can it make sense on this view that genius "expands" nature? However, it bears recalling that even in Kant's view, genius consists in each case in an originality, i.e., in the supposition of nature's fecundity for art. Second, it must be remembered that genius, precisely in its naïveté not only portrays what is natural, but is itself natural. Thus, the naïve genius is part of or even better an active participant in nature's fecundity.

From these observations, it follows that the naïveté of genius requires an understanding of nature as superseding itself, that is to say, superseding what it, at any point, affords or presents itself as. So, too, the experience of the naïve is never an experience of nature simply or as something simply given. In other words, the naïveté of nature is not natural, at least not in the sense of an unmediated nature, a point to which I return below.[15]

Schiller reinforces this general point by adding a developmental aspect to the naïve experience, an aspect that is nostalgic in one direction and obligatory in another. Referring to naïve objects, he writes: "They are what we were; they are what we *should become* again." Thus, small children provide us with a pure impression of the naïve, as long as we ignore the fact that they are incapable of being artificial and contrast them with ourselves. So construed, they are "holy objects," exhibiting an "integrity" of which we can only dream. Identifying the naïve with "a childlikeness where it is not expected," Schiller notes how naïve phenomena remind us of "our lost childhood" and thereby introduce a certain melancholy. At the same time, they exhibit "our highest perfection in the ideal" and, hence, stir sublime feelings in us. Culture's task, he adds, is to lead us back, "along the path of reason and freedom," to nature (NSD 180f/414f).[16]

Nature Superseding Itself through Art: The Moral Longing of Sentimental Poetry

The foregoing accounts of the species of naïveté, together with the naïveté characteristic of genius, fill out the picture of the distinctive conception of nature supposed and portrayed by naïve poetry. The nature that we find in naïve phenomena is morally pleasing because it represents possibilities of honest self-expression not beholden to convention, making our nature clear to ourselves and others. Yet it does so paradoxically, as noted above, given its dependence upon a conception of a dissembling, cultural conventionality.

As Schiller segues into his discussion of sentimental poetry, he makes this conception of naïve nature explicit by elaborating two sorts of longing for nature. He challenges his readers to consider what they long for when, fed up with social affectedness and cultural conventions, they pine for nature. The nostalgia that we feel when, for example, we experience a child's naïveté can make us long for the happiness or perfection of nature. The former sort of longing is motivated by sensory desires, the latter only by moral aspirations. While it is clear that Schiller associates nature in naïve poetry with the longing motivated by moral aspirations, he also makes clear the necessity of refusing to identify with it. Indeed, it is necessary to forgo the happiness that comes from nature alone in order to pursue its perfection or the lost completeness of it. As Schiller puts it, while only a sensual individual complains about the loss of purely natural happiness, "only a moral individual can mourn the loss of nature's completeness." Indeed, together with that loss, submitting to all the evils of culture is, he states "the natural condition of all that is good."[17] Hence, he concludes with the conditional admonition, "if you can take consolation in the loss of natural happiness, then let its completeness serve as the model of your heart" (NSD 192f/428).

When Schiller turns to sentimental poetry, the two different sorts of longing for nature, i.e., for natural happiness and for natural completeness, give rise to different senses of "nature," i.e., a crude, unrefined nature and a refined, but pure nature. While the latter alone is the theme of both naïve and sentimental poetry, it can only be expressed sentimentally, that is ideally once culture and art have laid their hands on the human being (NSD 200f/436f). Since Schiller countenances naïve poetry in modernity, he presumably means that it can be expressed only in times when we are in the grip of culture and art. In such circumstances, our unnaturalness is the catalyst for our urge for simplicity, *for finding outside us in nature what is no longer in us*. Hence the moral nostalgia we feel for our lost childhood. Sometimes Schiller speaks of culture, the culprit in this regard, without qualification; other times he is referring to modern culture, such as when he contrasts his contemporaries with the Greeks. What comes naturally for the Greeks, we have to objectify and transform into an idea. Thus, Schiller observes, "they felt naturally, while we feel the natural." The edifice of their social life was erected on "feelings," not "on some clumsy work of art," and "culture had not degenerated to such a degree that nature was left behind in the process" (NSD 195f/430f).

Schiller makes clear, as already noted, that the gloss of the difference between ancient and modern poetry merely registers tendencies (a respective "spirit") since forms of naïve and sentimental poetry can be found in every era and even in a single poet. Nevertheless, registering these tendencies in such historical terms is not insignificant since we can no more return to the ancient world than deny its legacy. Naïve poetry and sentimental poetry represent the beginning and the end of this transition, respectively, the passage from an actual oneness with nature to a moral, ideal unity with it. Moreover, as also noted above, he regards this poetic transition as indispensable to human development and maturation. Thus, in a key passage, after remarking that ancient poets touch us through their sensuous truth and modern poets through ideas, he observes: "This road taken by the modern poets is . . . the same road humans in general must travel, both as individuals and as a whole. Nature makes a human being one with himself, art separates and divides him; by means of the ideal he returns to the unity" (NSD 202/438).

On the basis of this observation, Schiller claims a certain priority for sentimental poetry, precisely because its self-conscious character, i.e., the consciousness of its lack of naturalness entails infinite horizons. The claim is somewhat paradoxical for two reasons: first, the model of the nature sought is the nature portrayed by naïve poetry, i.e., the nature that puts art to shame; and, second, the sentimental consciousness of being unnatural is itself natural, inherent to human nature, albeit dominant in a certain stripe of human personality. Moreover, the sentimental poet's material must be naïve in certain respects. Thus, in the course of defending a poet's liberties, Schiller argues that their naïveté justifies them. As long as the material is "naïve and combines the mind and the heart, it is . . . worthy of acclaim, regardless of all the objections of a frigid sense of decency" (NSD 224f/463f).

It would be wrong to infer that the superior poetry here seeks to be what the other species of poetry is already. After all, the very consciousness that constitutes naïve poetry presupposes the consciousness of the contrast between nature and art; hence, there is a sentimentality at the heart of any experience of the naïve. Thus to access to the pre-reflective character of experience, the naïve, there is no other recourse than reflection, i.e., sentimental poetry.[18]

Schiller allows that in a certain, undeniable way, a cultured human being can never be as complete as someone who is so naturally. Nevertheless, "the goal for which the human being *strives* through culture is infinitely superior to the goal that he *attains* through nature." Hence, if, as noted above, culture is the culprit when it comes to the loss of a simple, unaffected naturalness, it is also the means to something more, the endless progression toward "an infinite greatness" (NSD 202/438). Since culture and art are as natural to human nature as human reason is (indeed, they are expressions of it), sentimental poetry is, in effect, nature's way of exceeding itself (or "superseding itself," as we put it in the case of genius).

This cultural detour to the natural ideal reveals itself in the sentimental poet's need to move beyond merely depicting nature outside her to expressing her nature, her own feelings and reflections or, even better, her reflected feelings. Thus, while the naïve poet simply follows her natural feelings in imitating reality, the sentimental poet "*reflects* on the impression the objects make on her and only on the basis of the reflection is the emotion founded, into which she is transported and into which she transports us." The sentimental poet is thus forced to negotiate mixed feelings that spring from two conflicting sources, "the actual world as a limit and her idea as something infinite" (NSD 204/441). The themes of sentimental poetry are always mediated by the poet's need to reflect on and express her feelings. "This mentality can endure no impression without at the same time looking to the play of its own mind and, by reflection, setting up outside itself and opposite itself what it has in itself." This happens, Schiller adds, even when the sentimental poet wants to show us his own feelings (NSD 214f/452f).[19]

Based upon this confrontation of the limited actual world and the infinite idea in the mind of the sentimental poet, Schiller identifies three manners of feeling that are operative: the *satire*, the *idyll*, and the *elegy*, respectively.[20] A feeling of the contradictory relation between actuality and the idea informs satire, a sense of their agreement dominates in the idyll, and the alternation between the pain of contradiction and the joy of agreement animates the elegy. Since all sentimental feelings fall under this threefold disjunction, these three types completely delineate the field of sentimental poetry.[21]

Satire belabors the actual world's deficiencies in comparison with the ideal ("the supreme reality"). "Censuring" (also dubbed "pathetic") and "mocking" (also dubbed "amusing") satires express an aversion to the actual world in serious and humorous manners, respectively. Works of Juvenal and Swift epitomize pathetic satire, while Horace, Cervantes, and Fielding are masters of amusing satire.[22] The indignation expressed by pathetic satire and the sarcasm expressed by amusing satires must both arise from an ideal. That is to say, whatever form the satire takes, it must take its bearings from the ideal or "it will have no poetic effect at all." What Schiller understands by the poetic effect is precisely the awakening of the ideal in the mind of the reader.[23]

The communication of the ideal is also the defining feature of the *elegy*. An elegy is a lamentation, but it is poetry only if the sadness expressed springs from a conception of the ideal. Sadness over losses can serve as material for elegy only if what is lamented can also be represented as an "object of moral harmony" (NSD 212/450).[24] Schiller lauds "our Klopstock"—"the musical poet"—as the indisputable master of the elegiac genre, though his praise also includes choice remarks about the poet's and genre's limitations (NSD 217–20/455-58).

The idyll portrays human beings in a state of innocence, "in harmony and at peace with himself and his surroundings." Both peoples and individuals have their paradises; they recall their respective state of innocence, their respective golden age, and this recollection informs the pastoral idyll. Indeed, Schiller considers Milton's *Paradise Lost* as "the most beautiful idyll in the sentimental genre." Though the usual setting for the idyll is pastoral, a place before the onset of culture, the harmonious existence portrayed by the idyll is in fact culture's final goal. The idyll provides tangible confirmation of the plausibility of the idea of this harmony. Nevertheless, Schiller makes a point of its limitations, given its focus on a place before the onset of culture.

> Unfortunately, they [idylls] place behind us the goal toward which they are supposed to lead us. Thus they can inspire in us only the sad feeling of a loss, not the joyous feeling of hope. . . . They can only heal the sick mind, they cannot nourish the healthy one. They cannot motivate, they can only soothe. (NSD 227-31/466-71)

None of the arts of poetry, Schiller adds, have been able to make up for this defect rooted in the essence of the pastoral idyll.

Schiller concludes his treatment of the two forms of poetry with a comparison of their respective perils and limitations. Just as the naïve poet always runs the risk of imitating vulgar reality or actual nature instead of genuine nature, so the sentimental poet runs the risk of over-idealizing her subject matter. The naïve poet's sensibility, her naïve feelings, can fail to remain "sufficiently exalted," while sentimental poet's spontaneity can fail to remain "sufficiently restrained." As a result, while triviality (triteness) and vulgarity are constant temptations for the naïve poet, the sentimental poet must contend with the temptations of exaggeration and fantasy (NSD 236-44/474-86). Analogously, just as the recreation (alternatively, the recovery or convalescence: *Erholung*) provided by naïve poetry is too often related one-sidedly to the real needs of sensuous life, so, too, the ennoblement prompted by sentimental poetry is frequently defined one-sidedly in terms of ideas alone.[25] As this last comparison suggests, neither the naïve nor the sentimental character can completely capture "the ideal of beautiful humanity, an ideal that can only emerge from the union of both" (NSD 249/491).

Schiller's Poetic Phenomenology

The task of poetry in Schiller's eyes is, as iterated and illustrated on the preceding pages, to give full expression to human nature. With this thought in mind, he analyzes naïve and sentimental species of poetry in terms of two fundamental, but mutually exclusive types of human feelings. For purely logical reasons, i.e., based upon some straightforward, exclusive disjunctions, he considers his analysis, both of the basic structures of these two species and their subdivisions, to be complete. Naïve poetry moves us by capturing feelings of "nature, individuality, and a vivid sensuality," while sentimental poetry does so through the medium of "ideas and a lofty spirituality" (NSD 220/459). Whereas naïve poetry produces a feeling of restful motion, sentimental poetry creates one of restless motion (NSD 233/474). Yet only the union of these two feelings yields, as noted, "the ideal of beautiful humanity," but the yield—always a matter of approximation—is found only in a poetic mood (*Stimmung*).[26]

The aim of the first two sections of this paper has been to provide brief clarification of these analyses and their conclusions. The aim of the following concluding section is to flag how these analyses anticipate problems and moves of twentieth-century phenomenology. To put the matter anachronistically but aptly, this final section demonstrates key ways in which Schiller's essay on naïve and sentimental poetry provides a paradigm for a poetic phenomenology.[27]

The status of nature within naïve and sentimental feelings is a bit of a paradox. The naturalness of these feelings is negatively determined; that is to say, what makes them natural is what they are not, i.e., not artificial, not contrived, not affected, non-conformist, etc. In the case of naïve feelings, the naturalness is simply registered (imitated); in the case of sentimental feelings, it is felt as something both lost and longed for. Hence, in an important sense, both naïve and sentimental phenomena derive their meanings from the modes of experience that they supposedly exclude. Yet it is sentimental poetry that inherently aspires to a nature that is more than what is presently given to us; it is culture's (art's) means of signaling nature as something lying beyond it. Culture exploits naïve phenomena for moral purposes or, better, as a way of articulating those purposes. To the extent that sentimental poetry longs for and sets up a certain naturalness as an ideal, it also must contend with this reliance upon a conception that is principally, if not wholly, determined negatively.[28]

The paradox of naturalness supposed by naïve and sentimental poetry is related to the ironic difference between the ancient and the modern experience of nature. As Schiller points out, one finds little sentimentality in ancient poetry, least of all for nature as the modern world conceives of it. Thus, ancient poetry focuses preeminently on objects, treating them all without distinction, whether natural or artificial. While we moderns are enthralled by nature's "serene necessity," the Greeks are innocently personifying it at every turn, "ascribing to the will influence where a blind necessity reigns." In this way, they overcome the very aspect of nature that is its singular attraction for us. What is ironic, in other words, is the fact that, while the Greeks surpass us in everything that is natural, we alone revere nature as such, i.e., the naïveté of nature, nature in contrast to art (NSD 193ff/429ff).

The reason for this reverence, Schiller submits, lies in our unnaturalness when contrasted with the Greeks. Since the Greeks had not lost nature in their humanity, they had no need to rediscover it outside them nor were they surprised to find nature outside them. "They felt naturally, while we feel the natural" (NSD 195/431). This irony (the fact that the Greeks did not experience the naïve because their experiences were naïve) points to the paradoxical character of the two species of poetry and the experiences underlying them. Both naïve poetry and sentimental poetry derive from and are motivated by a sense of nature heightened by the experience of unnaturalness.[29]

One might argue, however, that there is not so much paradox and irony as there is a poetic sleight of hand (an allusion) or even an illusion at work in Schiller's account. How can nature—or, alternatively, being natural or authentic—be the aim of human striving if the naïve experience of nature or, even better, the experience of nature as something naïve, is not the way that we experience nature? How can we strive for what we do not know, or know at best through the nostalgia for a bygone time, i.e., our childhood? Or if we do know it, how can we establish that it is given to us and thus avoid the inference that it is our product? How can we avoid concluding that the naïve is artificial, an artifice, a sentimental invention?

The constellation of issues underlying such questions corresponds to some basic issues for phenomenology. One such issue is that of the objective or given status of any phenomenon or experience, i.e., the pretension of specifying it without the artful and historical trappings of a subjectivity that would distort it. To be sure, there is no phenomenon at all that does not have some subject to which it appears the way that it does. Providing an objective account of phenomena requires negotiating the perspective, designs, and concepts that the subject brings with it to the experience. Husserl's phenomenology attempts to return to the matters themselves by bracketing presuppositions in an effort to describe the givenness of things. But such negotiating and bracketing, difficult in any case, is acute when it comes to the sort of phenomena that Schiller deems naïve. Given that the hallmark of the naïve is the contrast with the artificial, one might well ask whether the naïve can be given at all.[30]

Since "naïve" designates what is natural precisely in contrast to what is mediated by reflection, it may be said to designate immediate experience. "Reflection" is a word that Schiller uses to gloss the sentimental; particularly given some common uses of "sentimental," some critics prefer to employ "reflective" over "sentimental" to characterize this species of poetry and experience.[31] "Reflection" is also the term that Husserl uses to designate the phenomenologist's only recourse to recovering immediate, "naïve" experiences.[32] The issue for the phenomenologist, then, is how reflecting on experience can yield the essence of the unreflected experience. In this respect, Schiller's reflections on naïve and sentimental poetry are analogous, on one level, to phenomenological reflections on pre-reflective experience.[33] On another level, given the issues that have been raised in the last few paragraphs, they exemplify a sort of irreducible differentiation, the determination of which, exceeding both sides of their difference, must be constantly deferred.[34] Moreover, on both these levels, Schiller's poetic phenomenology enjoys the considerable advantage of availing itself of the phenomenological work already done by the poets.

Yet the experience of the naïve is not simply theoretical. It is, above all, pleasurable and, indeed, a "moral pleasure," as Schiller characterizes it. This characterization brings it closer to existential questions of being authentic (Heidegger) and acting in good faith (Sartre). The pleasure in question is, as already noted, precisely the sort that we take in displays of naturalness and, not least, in ways of acting that contrast with the artificial, purely conventional, or calculating sorts of behavior. The supposition here is that there is a kind of integrity to nature and that culture, including art, represents a rupture, a break with naturalness. The unity with itself that Schiller attributes to nature as the subject of naïve poetry and the aspiration of sentimental poetry represents nothing less than the existential ideal of authenticity.

Flagging these phenomenological cognates to Schiller's interpretation provides some contemporary context for evaluating his interpretation and its potential significance. His endeavor to give a viable interpretation of these phenomena coincides with basic philosophical questions about achieving objectivity, accessing our experiences, and being authentic, not least in deferring the differentiation of objectivity or authenticity and their opposites. However, there is more to Schiller's endeavor—more promise—than a mere historical coincidence. Without by any means resolving these questions, Schiller's reflections suggest a neglected and fertile way of addressing them, namely through poetry. Taking poetry as a means of disclosing what is essential in human experience, Schiller's poetic phenomenology, i.e., his reflections on the basic species of poetry, succeeds in articulating something essential to being human.

In *Ideas I* Husserl makes the striking claim "that 'fiction' makes up the vital element of phenomenology," a claim that corresponds to his conception of phantasy as a form of "neutrality modification," i.e., the sort of "neutralization" (bracketing and suspending) necessary to attend to consciousness itself.[35] In the neutralization of the natural attitude, the contents of what is given in that attitude, far from being lost or forfeited, take center stage as the phenomenologist retains and reflects upon them, in an attempt to discern their essential nature. In a similar way, the neutralization is the work of both naïve and sentimental poetry, and it remains for the poetic phenomenologist to reflect on their contents, attempting to discern the essential character and structure of human feelings. Despite his ardent defense of the process of reflection, Husserl was deeply aware that the process is fraught,[36] just as Derrida was aware that we have to make do merely with traces (and simultaneously erased traces at that) of the difference between the unreflected (the naïve) and the reflected (the sentimental).[37]

Schiller's poetic phenomenology underscores that this difference is—for most of us at least—the permanent tension at the core of being human, a tension that must be constantly revisited since the reconciliation of naïveté and sentimentality can only be an ideal.[38] Yet, in a way that is perhaps true to his account if at odds with its phenomenological character, Schiller cannot leave us with this reference to the ideal alone. To be sure, he refuses to say whether a class of people exists in a setting that allows them to combine the naïve and the sentimental characters in such a way that avoids the excesses of both, thereby realizing the ideal. He iterates his contention that it is futile to try to resolve the conflict between the realistic and idealistic feelings that underlie naïve and sentimental poetry respectively. Yet, in the course of the argument, he observes that the conflict will hardly be resolved "other than in a few, rare individuals, who hopefully there always have been and always will be" (NSD 248-50/490-92). While reaffirming the results of his poetic phenomenology in one sense (after all, the tension still characterizes the human condition), the observation also moves squarely beyond a strictly phenomenological investigation. Yet perhaps this move demonstrates that phenomenology, even a poetic phenomenology, for all its resources, also has its naïve and sentimental limitations, limitations that only reality—and no ideal—can overcome.

Notes

1. Friedrich Schiller, *Werke* (Nationalausgabe), Band I, trans. Julius Petersen und Hermann Schneider (Weimar: Böhlaus, 1943), 259.

2. All parenthetical references in this paper refer to the pages of the English translation of *Über naïve und sentimentalische Dichtung* in *Friedrich Schiller: Essays*, ed. Walter Hinderer and Daniel O. Dahlstrom (New York: Continuum, 1993), followed by the original in German in *Schillers Werke* (Nationalausgabe), Band 20, trans. Benno von Wiese (Weimar: Böhlau, 1962). Hereafter referred to as NSD.

3. Although every true genius must be naïve, there are both naïve and sentimental geniuses (NSD 189/424, 240f/482).

4. See Benno von Wiese *Schiller* (Stuttgart: Metzler, 1963), 531. The development between the two works is not a leap, however, since Schiller already speaks of "noble

nature" in the 6th and 9th Letters. The distinction between naïve and sentimental is sometimes traced to Schiller's defensive sense of how his poetry differs from that of Goethe, as suggested by Goethe himself in a March 21, 1830 letter to Eckermann: "The concept of classical and romantic poetry that is now spreading over the entire world and causes so much debate and ruptures . . . originally sprung from Schiller and me. In poetry I had the maxim of objectively proceeding and wanted this alone to count. But Schiller who created [*wirkte*] entirely subjectively, considered his kind [of poetry] the right kind and, in order to defend himself against me, he wrote the essay on naïve and sentimental poetry. He proved to me that I myself, against my will, was romantic and my *Iphigenie*, thanks to the dominance of feeling, is in no way as classical and in the ancient sense, as one would like to have believed." See Johann Wolfgang Goethe, *Gedenkausgabe der Werke, Briefe und Gespräche*, Band 24, trans. Ernst Beutler (Zürich: Artemis, 1948), 405f. Schiller depicts the author of *Werther*, *Tasso*, and *Faust* as a naïve poet working with sentimental material (220f/459f).

5. Presumably this conception of *Manier* differs from that indicated by Schiller in a letter to Körner a few years earlier. There he contrasts the manner, expressing the taste or mentality peculiar to the poet or artist, with style, "the highest independence of the presentation from all subjective and all objectively contingent determinations. . . . Pure objectivity is the essence of good style, the supreme principle of the arts." See *Schillers Werke*, Nationalausgabe, Band 26, trans. Edith Nahler und Horst Nahler (Weimar: Böhlaus, 1992), 225f. Also see Goethe, Johann Wolfgang "Einfache Nachahmung der Natur, Manier, Stil" (1789) in Gedenkausgabe, Band 13, trans. Christian Beutler (Zürich: Artemis, 1954), 66–71.

6. In a certain sense, this paper pursues what Schiller himself deliberately left unsaid. Thus, he alludes to "the idea of humanity" that coincides with the concept that encompasses both naïve and sentimental poetry, but he adds that "this is not the place to pursue this thought further" (NSD 201/437). This paper is an attempt to pursue this thought, given the many clues to it provided by Schiller's essay. Also see his remark that naïve and sentimental poetry are incomparable without recourse to a higher concept of poetry—and that "there actually is such a concept" (NSD 202/439).

7. In several respects, Mendelssohn's discussion of the naïve anticipates Schiller's account, even down to the examples used; see Moses Mendelssohn, "On the sublime and naive in fine sciences" in *Philosophical Writings*, trans. and ed. D. O. Dahlstrom (Cambridge: Cambridge University Press, 1997), 222-32. It may be the case, as Sharpe observes, that Schiller's conception of the naïve is idiosyncratic, but if so, it is due in part to Schiller's extension of the term's traditional meaning from the subject matter and the expressions of it to the poets responsible for those expressions; see Lesley Sharpe, *Schiller: Drama, Thought and Politics* (Cambridge: Cambridge University Press, 1991), 176.

8. An analogous distinction can be found in Mendelssohn, *On the Sublime*, 226.

9. Mendelssohn makes a similar distinction between comic and noble forms of naïveté; ibid., 222.

10. As Schiller notes, Kant gives this analysis of the naive, but in Schiller's view the analysis falls short on two counts: first, because it applies at best only to one of the species of naïve phenomena and second, because it fails to recognize the moral dimension that underlies our experience of the like. See Immanuel Kant, *Kritik der Urteilskraft* (Hamburg: Meiner, 1974), §54, S. 193.

11. In *Pygmalion* George Bernard Shaw repeatedly exploits the contrast between the naïveté of the "guttersnipe" of a flower girl, Eliza, and the urbane sophistication of Henry Higgins, the scholar of phonetics who is trying to win a bet that he can transform Eliza into a "fair lady" by changing, above all, how she speaks. There is one scene in *My Fair Lady* (based upon *Pygmalion*) that exemplifies Schiller's first species of naïveté. Higgins has brought Eliza to a high-society event, the Ascot Races, to measure her progress. Watching the race with a crowd of "Ladies and Gentlemen" who observe a reserved decorum indistinguishable from boredom, Eliza cannot restrain her excitement. The Ladies and Gentlemen begin to stare at her, as she encourages her favorite "Come on, come on, Dover!" and they moan—the Ladies feint fainting—when she finally shouts "Move your bloomin' arse!!!" (*My Fair Lady*, directed by George Cukor (1964; Burbank, CA: Warner Home Video).

12. Frank Capra's *Mr. Smith Goes to Washington* is built around this sort of naïvete.

13. Kant, *Kritik der Urteilskraft*, §46-47, 160-64.

14. Schiller's gloss of the genius' naïveté in these respects leaves much to be desired. His depiction of the genius's "childlike" character may be an encomium to Goethe, but in any case the claim that the same or at least some of the same qualities of a genius's work surface in her "private life and morals" is undoubtedly true, but it is also misleading if it supposed to suggest something stronger, for example, that the same virtues *must* be found or even that they are *usually* found in the genius's personal life. Moreover, Schiller's gloss on those qualities strongly suggests that he intends one of these stronger claims. At the same time, while admitting that little is known about the private lives of the greatest geniuses, he contends that his gloss is "confirmed even by the little that has been preserved for us" (NSD 190/425). In addition to omitting further analysis of this aspect of Schiller's account, I also set aside further consideration of his passing contrast of the sexes in terms of naïveté, since this topic also warrants a separate treatment.

15. The way that nature supersedes itself in the naïve genius is, to be sure, different from the way that the moral pleasure we take in naïve phenomena or poetry trades on something more than and typically contrasting with the natural. In the former case, the superseding is unthinking; in the latter case, the thought of what is—relatively speaking—unnatural is essential. Yet in both cases the contrast between a given state of nature and its transcending is central.

16. Our feeling for nature is intimately related to our protests against the passing of childhood and its innocence, since "our childhood is the only un-mutilated nature that we still encounter in cultivated humanity. Thus, it is no wonder if each footstep of nature outside us leads us back to our childhood" (NSD 195/430). In this

connection, see the image of the playing child in Schiller's *Der spielende Knabe, Natur und Schule*, and *Der philosophische Egoist*. In all these poems the image of the child playing displays the natural as the self-evident agreement of individual act and general law, being and consciousness, necessity and freedom.

17. This observation reinforces the way that sentimental poetry, the pursuit of the ideal, is itself natural; that is to say, it is nature's way—as in the case of genius—of superseding itself, i.e., what it is at any given moment.

18. Not only are reflection and, with it, sentimental poetry no less natural than naïve poetry, they are essential to a human being's "true" or "real" nature. So construed, sentimental poetry is anything but an expression of sentimentalism (*Empfindeley*) where "tender feelings," devoid of ideas and the reflection that they demand dominate (NSD 222/460). For similar reasons, Schiller distinguishes what makes up "a beautiful work" from one that we "read with great pleasure" (NSD 222f/461).

19. In other words, what makes a poem sentimental is, oddly enough, a certain lack of sentiment, i.e., the fact it communicates not a poet's immediate feelings but her reflection on them. Sentimental feelings are, to put it another way, always mixed feelings, i.e., a mix of immediate feelings and mediated feelings, the feelings resulting from reflection on what is immediately felt (NSD 198/434, 204/441, 214f/452). Schiller mixes three things together here: (1) the mere intrusion of the first person, the poet's own feelings, into the poem; (2) the poet's expression of her reflection on what she feels and/or portrays; and (3) the mixed feeling of the sentimental, alternating between imagination and ideas, finite and infinite, actual and ideal.

20. Schiller's discussion of these three species of sentimental poetry is not uniform. He introduces this threefold distinction later in his essay, after initially (1) distinguishing just two basic types of feeling, satirical and elegiac, where the emphasis is on presenting the actual world or the ideal respectively; and then (b) distinguishing under the latter (the elegiac feeling), elegy in a narrow sense whose themes are objects of mourning, from idyll in a broad sense whose themes are objects of joy. He defends his inclusion of idyll under the elegiac by contending that, even should a poet present us with "a portrait of nature unspoiled or the ideal fulfilled perfectly," the contrast with the actual world will betray itself; see NSD 211f/448ff, especially the footnote on these pages.

21. Schiller stresses that his concern is with the manners of feeling common to these three species of poetry, respectively, and not with a taxonomy of poem types. Thus, it may not be possible to specify certain genres (e.g., the epic, the novel, or the tragedy) in terms of the manner of feeling, though a novel or a tragedy may well be satirical or elegiac. Since the paradigm for some of these genres is provided by ancient, naïve poetry, there is every reason to expect the paradigm to be broken by modern, sentimental poets, as experience has shown frequently to be the case. See the lengthy footnote on NSD 226ff/466f.

22. Schiller notes that both the tone of censuring and that of mocking are alien to the poet's purpose, since the former alone is too serious and the latter too frivolous

for the "play" that poetry should always be. The only solution is for the pathetic satire to achieve poetic freedom by becoming something sublime, and for the amusing satire to become something beautiful (NSD 205/442).

23. It is certainly possible for a "vulgar satirist" to makes us feel an aversion to the actual world, based upon its failure to satisfy certain inclinations. Yet the feelings awakened do not constitute "genuinely poetic pathos . . . recognizable by a preponderance of spontaneity and by a freedom of mind persisting in the midst of passion." According to Schiller, communication of the ideal must motivate the poet and this communication only succeeds by producing a "free play" of reason and sentiment in readers.

24. Schiller notably finds that both Ovid and Rousseau fall short as elegists, the former because need, not inspiration, motivates his mourning for Rome, the latter because "a need for physical *peace* is more visible than a need for moral *harmony*" in the ideal he sets up (NSD 212ff/450ff). In order to get rid of the conflict in humanity as quickly as possible, Rousseau "would rather see it led back to the spiritually empty uniformity of its original condition rather than see the battle ended in the spiritually rich harmony of a thoroughly developed culture" (NSD 214/452).

25. Schiller addresses the two traditional principles that poetry should please and that it should educate, i.e., that it should be a means of both recreation and ennoblement (NSD 244-49/486-91). The pursuit of pleasure and recreation can degenerate into "a kind of indulgence that works like a sedative," while the pursuit of the ideal of ennoblement can lead to fanaticism and exaggeration, something "far too removed from experience." In this connection, naïve and sentimental poetry each counteracts a potential misstep by the other. "While the naïve would protect the mind from exaggeration, the sentimental would ensure it against listlessness" (NSD 240/491).

26. The approximation to the ideal must remain incomplete given the "psychological antagonism" addressed by Schiller on the final pages of his essay, an antagonism that serves as a fundamental breach in humanity. He elaborates this antagonism in the form of contrast between realists and idealists that emerges when the poetic nature is removed from the naïve and the sentimental character, respectively. Far from favoring one over the other, his purpose is to underscore the need to include both in order to do justice to "the rational concept of humanity" (NSD 249f/491f).

27. A further anticipation, not addressed in the following remarks, also deserves flagging. Much like Husserl's analysis of the transcendental ego or Heidegger's analysis of Dasein, Schiller's reflections are removed from any empirical or biographical level of consideration. In a manner analogous to the strictures of the phenomenological method (aimed at isolating and analyzing the transcendentally purified contents of consciousness), Schiller's reflections remain at the level of the impersonal or pre-personal. Thus, the naïve character and the sentimental one apply to the human condition, prior to differentiation into individual or collective egos, but clearly applying to both (NSD 228/468, 232/472).

28. By way of explaining the moral, not aesthetic interest that we take in nature via naïve phenomena, Schiller gives an Aristotelian characterization of nature as something that acts on its own (in contrast to the artificial) (NSD 180/413). As also noted above, he differentiates nature that is "genuine" (NSD 236/476f), "pure" (NSD 185/420, 191/427, 200/436), "wholesome" (NSD 186/421, 180/424), "real" and "beautiful" (NSD 224/463) from nature that is "unrefined" (NSD 200/436), "ordinary" (NSD 237-40/477-81), and "actual" (NSD 236/476). Given that general Aristotelian characterization as well as these differently qualified meanings of "nature," it is perhaps incorrect to conclude that he determines nature only negatively. Still, the negative determinations seem to do the heavy lifting in his reflections. The issue is a fundamental one: if x can only be defined in terms of its difference from y, i.e., if no property (no essential, necessary feature) other than that of being different from y can be assigned to x, then x is essentially dependent upon y.

29. In short, just as the concept of the sentimental derives from the aspiration to be naïve, so the concept of the naïve or, alternatively, the experience of things as naïve is deeply, irretrievably sentimental.

30. A closely related issue concerns the artificiality of what is deemed "natural." Their distinction of appearing with a certain naturalness, devoid of anything that resembles or betrays human artifice or design, depends upon both an historical concept of what counts as natural and a subject who brings that concept to bear on those appearances. The concept is an historical artifact. What counts as naïve phenomena is dependent upon ideas of nature that are artificial and historical, i.e., ideas that are the historical product of human interaction with their environment. In other words, how are we to make sense of Schiller's talk of our accessibility to the natural, given the fact that its significance appears so clearly to be an historical construct?

31. See "The Reflective Poet" in William Witte, *Schiller* (Oxford: Clarendon Press, 1949), 53-68; also Mainland's introductory remarks to Schiller, *Über naïve und sentimentalische Dichtung*, edited with Introduction and annotation by William F. Mainland (Oxford: Blackwell, 1957), xxvii-xxviii.

32. Edmund Husserl, *Ideas I*, trans. Daniel O. Dahlstrom (Indianapolis, IN: Hackett, 2014), 67f, 91, 139f.

33. Ibid., 226f, 241, 291f; Jean-Paul Sartre, *L'être et le néant: Essai d'ontologie phénoménologique* (Paris: Gallimard, 1943), 16-22.

34. The reference here is obviously to the notion of *différance*; see Jacques Derrida, *Marges de la philosophie* (Paris: Les editions de minuit, 1972), 1-29.

35. Husserl, *Ideas I*, 127, 147, 213-16.

36. Ibid., 146-52, 173.

37. Derrida, *Marges*, 25f: "La <<trace matinale>> de la différence s'est perdue dans une invisibilité sans retour et pourtant sa perte même est abritée, gardée, regardée, retardée. Dans une texte. Sous la forme de la présence. De la propriété. Qui n'est elle-même qu'un effet d'écriture."

38. The inherent need to revisit this tension is reminiscent of Heidegger's talk of being free for the possibility of taking back previous decisions, and his identification of this freedom with the authentic resoluteness to repeat itself; see Martin Heidegger, *Sein und Zeit* (Tübingen: Niemeyer, 1972), 308.

7

Schiller and the Aesthetic Promise

Jacques Rancière

Translated by Owen Glyn-Williams

At the end of the fifteenth of his *Letters on the Aesthetic Education of Man*, Schiller states a paradox and makes a promise. He asserts that man "is only fully a human being when he plays."[1] To those who might think he is joking, he announces that this paradox is capable of "bearing the whole edifice of the art of the beautiful, and the still more difficult art of living" (AL 131). He asserts that there exists a specific form of sensory experience, the experience of aesthetic play (*jeu aesthetique*), and that this experience, properly understood, carries the promise of a new world of art as well as a new lived world.

The entire singularity of the pronouncement of course lies in the conjunction that it produces. To those who see the new world of art as opposing mimetic servitude to an autonomous, or even auto-referential art, the statement proposes a union of apparent opposites. This "play" establishes what is proper to art *and* a new form of life. In order to comprehend the paradox and the promise, we must first understand what play means. Play is the activity *par excellence* that has no other end than itself, which attempts no actual seizure of power over objects or people. Within the context in which Schiller is invoking it, the general meaning of the term is of course specified by the Kantian analysis of aesthetic experience. Indeed, Kant characterizes this experience as a "free play of the faculties," which is to say as a double suspension: the suspension of the cognitive powers of the understanding that determine sensible givens in accordance with its categories, and the power of sensibility which imposes its objects of desire. This double interruption, this *neither* . . . *nor* at once suspends an activity and passivity in favor of a neutral state: the free play wherein the normally "active" faculty, the understanding, and the normally "passive" faculty of sensibility relate to one another without concept.

It is in this power of suspension that Schiller situates, under the specific title of an *aesthetic state*, the potential for a new world of art and a new form of life. He does this by means of a series of transformations, the first of which appears paradoxically to make neutrality lean on the side of inactivity, to make of the free player a spectator—the powerless spectator of an inactivity. Indeed, at the end of the very same letter, he places us, in an imaginary manner, before a Greek statue known as the *Juno Ludovisi*. The statue, he tells us, is self-contained. It expresses the fundamental character of divinity: idleness, the absence of not only all care but also of all will. The spectator is therefore there to do nothing before this deity whose sovereignty consists in doing nothing. Meanwhile the work of the sculptor itself appears to be absorbed in this circle of inactivity that promises to man a full humanity *in the image of the divine*.

This is the first side of the paradox: the whole edifice of beautiful art henceforth rests on the suspension of activity, the suspension of will proper to aesthetic play. Yet this exceptional situation is presented by Schiller as characteristic of the founding of a new art of living. And by this must be understood not only the art of living as individuals, but the art of life in common, or what we generally call politics. This text, written in 1795, is thoroughly marked by the French Revolution, and it tells us that aesthetic free play is the principle that must allow us to do what the Revolution was not able to: to engender a community of free men. Beyond the immediate political exigency it invokes, it decisively links what some persistently want to separate: the autonomy of aesthetic experience *and* the transformation of this experience into the principle of a new community.

Traditional debates surrounding art and politics effectively pose the problem in terms of the relation between two separate domains. They ask us whether art should engage in politics (*faire de la politique*), and if it does not thereby risk betraying its proper essence. On the other hand, they tell us that the so-called autonomy of art is the veil under which it submits to the institutions of the state, to the law of the market, and to activities of cultural distinction. Both positions presuppose that the existence of the two is related in this way. It goes without saying that there is politics because there is power and that there is art because there are painters, musicians, or poets. The Schillerian conception, however, reminds us that these two presuppositions are equally questionable.

There can be—as has most often been the case—musicians, painters, and poets without their work being identified as art. In order for it to be "art," their know-how or their acts must be understood as having a common mode of being, a distinct mode of visibility and a specific form of intelligibility. Similarly, the fact that humans everywhere obey leaders in no way implies the existence of a political sphere; the identification of specific common objects relies on a shared capacity to identify them and put them into speech and practices. For there to be art and for there to be politics, there must be a certain partitioning of spheres of experience, a certain relationship between practices and the forms of visibility, and intelligibility of these practices. There must be a distribution of the sensible (*partage du sensible*): a distribution of spaces and times, of functions and capacities, of the visible—and the invisible—and of the sayable. An identification of art presupposes a certain distribution of the sensible, a certain distribution of what can be done, sensed, and thought. This also implies an idea of politics as a distribution of the common.

The "art of the beautiful" thus names a certain mode of being for art objects and the subjects who appreciate them. The *Juno Ludovisi* is—that is to say the text makes of her—a "free appearance," an appearance that is not governed by any "reality": neither the reality of an object of faith nor that of a model to be imitated. The statue is not experienced as an image of a deity, which would entail knowing whether or not it really is divine, if it is legitimate in representing divinity, and if it ought to be represented in this way. Nor is it perceived as the result of the sculptor's ability to put life into the stone, and to reconcile the monumentality that befits the image of the divine with the character traits that individualize it by lending it the human sentiments. The *Juno Ludovisi* is not the imperious goddess or the jealous wife described by the poets. She is an *idle* figure, defined by a pure quality of separation. The sculpture is thus removed from the order of representation that judged it as an either failed or successful encounter between a manual capacity and the representation of an idea. "Aesthetics" means such: the object of art is defined henceforth by its belonging to a specific mode of being (a mode of being "idle," that is to say separated from the *concerns* of knowledge and the will) and no longer as the successful result of a kind of making. The free play of the faculties that appreciate this free appearance marks, in turn, the annulment of a hierarchy. The sovereign goddess, *precisely because* she is without will and commandment, nullifies the representational hierarchy of form imposed on matter, the opposition between an intelligence that commands and a materiality that obeys or resists.

The mode of being of the deity-without-will is thus emblematic of a new identification of art; the first that identifies it in *the singular*, which creates a generic concept of a specific domain of experience. In effect, the "fine arts" only signified, from within the multiplicity of technical capacities, a specific class of "art" whose hierarchical position, conditions of inclusion, and declared or undeclared rules are analogous to the hierarchies of an ordered society. The new mode of existence of the object of art, however, defies any analogy between the order of the arts and the order of domination. Of course, it does not do so at any random time. The force of Schiller's text is to highlight the political implications, at once general and immediate, of the new status that the *Critique of the Power of Judgment* gives to the beautiful, as the correlate of free play, of the play of the faculties "without concept." Certainly, the revolution involved in this free play is much more than the annulment of the established norms of the beautiful proper to the order of representation. It is the revocation of the essential principle of this order: the power of active form over passive matter.

That this revocation has decisive implications not only for "the art of the beautiful" but for the "still more difficult" art of living is already revealed, a few months after the taking of the Bastille, in paragraph 60 of the *Critique of the Power of Judgment*. The aesthetic *sensus communis* promised an answer to the problem of a time when "the vigorous drive towards the lawful sociability"[2] was confronted with the problem of "uniting freedom (and thus also equality) with coercion (more from respect and subjection to duty than from fear)."[3] The solution to the political question posited as a prerequisite a form of aesthetic universality, the constitution of a common sensorium, allowing for "reciprocal communication of the ideas of the most educated part with the cruder,"[4] offering the middle term between the *refinement* of the first and the *originality* of the second, between *superior culture* and *simple nature*.

Schiller radicalizes this prerequisite, carrying out a double transposition of the Kantian transcendental scene. The relation between understanding and sensibility becomes first and foremost an anthropological opposition, an opposition between two fundamental *drives*: the *form* drive, the active will of spirit to everywhere leave its mark, i.e., the mark of autonomy; and the *sense* drive, the force of material sensibility that, in wanting to impose the anarchy of its desires, tends more fundamentally to the triumph of passivity, to the law of heteronomy that governs them. The free play of the faculties thus becomes a theatre of the drives that reveals aesthetic autonomy as the solution to the impasses of another autonomy, that of the understanding that imposes its concepts or its "forms" on the given, the rational will that wants to impose itself directly on material sensibility.

But this anthropological transposition is itself ruled by a thoroughly political exigency. The power of form over matter that is suspended by the third drive—the *play drive*—is directly translatable into political terms. It is the power of statist universality over the anarchy of individuals and the masses. This power itself realizes another: the power of "culture" over "nature," which is to say of the leisure class over the classes—natural or savage—of work and simple reproduction. The failure of the French Revolution, its becoming-terror, for Schiller, stems from its will to directly achieve the reign of liberty and equality as the reign of the law, or the statist universal. The revolutionary reign of law reproduces the traditional domination of a class of universality imposing itself on the anarchy of particularities. It once again reproduces that which must be abolished: the separation of two humanities. The true revolution would be a revolution in the very distribution of the sensible that separates two humanities into one destined to the autonomy of acting and the other to the heteronomy of passive materiality.

It is this separation of two humanities that constitutes the essential challenge, at once designated and masked by the ruin of the criteria of fine art and by the decapitation of the monarch. In order for the political overthrowing of the ordered society and of sovereignty to avoid being a simple reversal of hierarchy, it must come to grips with that which is most profoundly implicated in the revocation of power and of "form." Not simply the collapse of the hierarchy of the arts, of subjects, and genres, a hierarchy analogous to the social and sovereign order, but a putting into question of the distribution of "sensibilities" according to places occupied in the order of "occupations," i.e., the ways that individuals and groups use their time to occupy the place to which they are assigned.

If that which revokes the order of *mimesis* is called *play*, and if this play appears far from any futility, as proper to the divine, therefore as proper to a new humanity, it is because play traditionally plays the role of the exception to the order of places and occupations—an exception that, as expected, confirms the rule of order. This play of rule and exception is summed up in the Platonic pair seriousness (*spoude*) and amusement (*paidia*). The Platonic republic seriously strives to reproduce divine play in the human order. But reproducing this play in no way means having fun. It means constituting an order that prohibits play to those who could only be poor players, who would disfigure the resemblance of divine play. They cannot play, they do not *know how* to play, these artisans who *do not have the time* to do anything other than their *proper task*—the fabrication of use objects and the reproduction of reproductive life. They are bad players, cheaters even, these mimetic poets who want to play with appearances while they do not even know how to discern what is an appearance and what is reality. Only those who know what is play and what is serious are permitted to play. Only those who know what reality and its imitation are can imitate. The same principle that permits the exclusion of the professional mimetic artist (*mimeticien*) keeps the artisan in his place. This principle is that one cannot do two things at once: working and ruling, being oneself and a fictional character. The exclusion of free appearance is consubstantial to a distribution of the sensible in which the difference of functions is presented as identical with a difference in natures, and in which the forms of sensible experience, time and space, itself attest to this identity. It is consubstantial with this distribution that reserves the caring for common affairs for those who know how to play and who *have the time* for play because they can afford leisure.

It is this distribution of play and seriousness that is essential to the undoing of Aristotelian form. Free play and aesthetic free appearance subvert the order of *places* that ensured the exclusion of both play and knowledge of appearances. They challenge the distribution of the sensible that grounded domination in the separation of two humanities. They manifest a feeling of freedom and equality that is uniquely able to transform into reality what the French Revolution had enclosed in the abstract ideality of the law. The rule of the law is still the rule of free form over servile material, of the universal state over the anarchy of individuals and the masses. On the other hand, the idleness of the goddess manifests a freedom that no longer suppresses any resistant materiality, a non-oppressive freedom without power. It thereby carries the principle of another revolution, aesthetic revolution, one in the form of sensible experience that precedes and predetermines the instituted forms of the state and of social hierarchy. "Common sense" no longer simply carries the promise of communication between refined culture and savage nature. It is no longer simply the site of mediation between the high and the low. It carries the essential principle of a new humanity characterized by a new sensorium, but in the very exceptionality that defines it. Common sense is a common sense of exception—or, if you will—a dissensual common sense.

This dissensuality is sensible in the relation between the two powers brought into play. The Kantian "free play" of the faculties, the resolution of the opposition between formal instinct and the sensible instinct in the play instinct is, in Schiller, no longer a peaceful agreement. It manifests a tension in which passive power and active power are together suspended at the extreme of their opposition and transformed into their contrary. The active power becomes receptive, and the receptive power becomes active (AL 123). This tension that characterizes free appearance does not resolve itself in the calm assurance of the judgment of the beautiful. It is translated into a sensible state of exception. The subject does not peacefully enjoy form. He or she is taken up in an internal conflict in which one autonomy wins at the expense of another one: the formal autonomy of the understanding and the will. By the encounter with free appearance, the subject finds itself in a contradictory state of supreme repose and supreme agitation, of attraction and repulsion. The goddess who attracts her spectator with her charm at the same time pushes the latter back with her self-sufficiency.

Our contemporaries, particularly following Lyotard's analyses, are accustomed to splitting Kantian aesthetics in two, relegating the analytic of the Beautiful to a classical thinking of harmony in order to privilege the analytic of the Sublime, conceived as an irreconcilable tension between the imagination and reason, between the idea and all forms of sensible presentation. It is in this way that the aesthetic of the sublime is for Lyotard the very working principle of the artistic avant-gardes.[5] But this opposition, which paradoxically centers the Kantian "aesthetic" around the point that marks for Kant the departure from the aesthetic and the entry into the universe of moral freedom, is only possible by means of an inversion of the primary operation carried out by Schiller. In the Schillerian scene, the reconciliation of the beautiful is not opposed to sublime irreconcilability. The experience of the beautiful, that of the *neither . . . nor . . .* , is already the experience of a tension of opposites. It is already an experience of *dissensus*, the effective rupture of a given constitution of the sensible and its "law." The aesthetic free play is, in the strongest sense of the term, a suspensive state, a state that suspends the logic of domination by actualizing a freedom that is the seed of a new humanity, because it is a freedom without opposite, or rather one that has *partialness* as its only opposite, the separation of functions and of humanities.

It is because it is intrinsically dissensual that aesthetic autonomy is immediately tied to its apparent opposite, the promise of a new community. There is no opposition between an autonomous art and an art submitted to political heteronomy. There is a specific nexus of autonomy and heteronomy, a "politics" included in the very definition of the new "edifice" of art. This inclusion is in no way the simple personal affirmation of a thinker of two centuries ago. It has not ceased to govern—beyond the false quarrels between pure and engaged art—two centuries of relations between that which is proper to art and the principle of community. Schiller says that the play drive will at once reconstruct the edifice of art and communal life. The militant workers of the 1840s break the cycle of domination by reading not popular nor militant but "great" literature. The bourgeois critics of 1860 denounce Flaubert's posture of "art for art's sake" as the embodiment of democratic equality. Mallarmé wants to separate poetic language from common speech so poetry can "prepare the celebrations of the future" and to give the community the "seal" it is missing. Adorno wants art to be entirely separated from life, but only in order for it to better attest to society's contradictions. We could extend the list indefinitely. One will always see the same paradox at work, initially stated by Schiller. It is the "purity" of aesthetic experience that ensures its political promise.

Thus the autonomy demonstrated by the aesthetic regime of art is not the autonomy of work, of a product of making. It is the autonomy of a mode of experience in which this product is felt. The self-sufficiency of the *Juno Ludovisi* has nothing to do with an "autotelism" of art and a consecration in the name of genius, of demiurgic artistry that takes itself as its sole norm. This self-sufficiency is, rather, "idleness," absence of will, of an end pursued. Paradoxically, the statue embodies the properties of something that has not been made, of something that has not been the recipient of a purpose, of thought imposed on resistant material. In short, she embodies the properties of that which is not a work of art (this, by the way, is the core of the tiresome claims "this is" and "this is not" art). The property of being an art object is henceforth defined by the identity of the properties of this object with the properties of its opposite, the properties of that which *is not art*. There is one important consequence for the autonomy of the aesthetic subject to be drawn from this. Faced with the free appearance, the subject senses an autonomy that is every bit as much a dispossession, a withdrawal of power. The "free appearance" persists in front of the subject, unapproachable, unavailable for its knowledge, desires, and ends. But it is precisely in this way that it delivers a promise. By way of aesthetic experience, the subject is promised the possession of a new world of sensible liberty and equality by this figure that cannot be possessed. The subject as spectator and the goddess are brought together in this sensorium that annuls the oppositions of activity and passivity, will and resistance, appropriation and disappropriation.

The autonomy of art does not oppose political heteronomy. What does oppose it are two different ways of connecting autonomy and heteronomy, of positing the relation of "that which is proper to art" to the sensible configuration of the community, of thinking about the identity of art and non-art. These two ways, the conflict between which has yet to be settled, are already in tension in Schiller's own text.

In effect, there are two ways to think of the same self-sufficiency. First of all, self-sufficiency means *heterogeneity*. Aesthetic experience is one of a sphere of the sensible in which relations that normally govern sensible experience are suspended. The statue carries its promise for as long as it is radically foreign to the subject who comes across it for as long as it cannot be an object of attained knowledge or fulfilled desire. However this self-sufficiency very soon takes on another meaning. Free appearance is actually the appearance of a certain freedom. The goddess is free because of a certain freedom, a certain self-sufficiency or autonomy is expressed in her. This freedom, according to Schiller and those following him, is that of a people, the ancient Greeks. The credibility accorded to this representation of ancient Greece matters little. The important thing is to identify what is contained in this autonomy. Greek life is thus understood as a free life, autonomous in the sense that it is a life that does not submit to forms of authority governing separate spheres of experience. It is the life of a people whose activities are not severed into distinct spheres governed by exclusive laws, where the same mode of being is expressed in both private life and in public life, in religious beliefs and in celebrations and monuments in civic life. The free people is the one that knows no division of functions and domains, no severing of morality and politics, of politics and religion, of religion and art, etc.

The freedom of the Greek statue, that seemed henceforth to embody the existence of an unfamiliar, heterogeneous sphere of experience, comes to embody the exact opposite: a life that knows no separation of heterogeneous spheres of experience, that knows no aesthetic experience because the aesthetic is equally ethical, political, or religious. The autonomy that the statue embodies in front of us is the representation of an autonomy, of a non-separation (*inseparation*) that took place in the past. She carries the promise of a newly non-separated world, one where art will no longer exist as a separate sphere, but where the practices of artists will be identical to the active forms of elaboration of a common world.

This also assumes that free appearance is no longer the simple suspension of oppositions between form and matter, between activity and passivity. The whole problem is concentrated in the characterization of this neutral state as neither active nor passive. How does one think about that which is neither active nor passive? Or rather how does one avoid always thinking of it as an absorption of one opposite by the other: *either* a becoming-passive of activity *or* a becoming-active of passivity? Here again the *Aesthetic Letters* attest to a significant tension between two manners of presenting the same neutralization. The two first parts strive to separate aesthetic autonomy from the activism of the "form drive"—of its will to impose the autonomy that characterizes its self-relation on all matter. We must, without doubt, protect each drive against the encroachment of the other. But in this double prevention, the dominant emphasis is put on the need to protect sensible materiality, to protect passivity.

The acknowledged target of every will is to transform the world into a resemblance of reason.⁶ However the third part, in an apparent continuity of reasoning, presents a shift in the relation that tends toward a reversal of this priority. Free appearance is less and less presented as a heterogeneous, suspensive state. It is increasingly identified with the product of a human spirit that wants to transform the entire order of sensible appearances into a new sensorium in which it could contemplate its own activity in a mirror.⁷ For the contemplation of the inapproachable divinity of the stone is substituted with the description of the passage from the state of nature to that of civilization, the manner in which the savage learns to take a fresh look at his weapons, his implements or his adornments, to separate the enjoyment of the appearance from the functionality of the objects or bodily marks. Aesthetic free play, suspending the power of active form over passive matter and promising a still unheard of equality, gives way to a new scenario in which matter submits to the law of spirit, a scenario of self-education in which humanity emancipates itself from materiality and transforms the world into its own image.

The aesthetic education that must fulfill the promise of "free play" finds itself henceforth drawn into a fundamental polarity defined by two antagonistic scenarios. The first scenario is that of aesthetic revolution: the revolution of sensible existence that must accomplish the task necessarily uncompleted by a political revolution that was partial in nature. It is this scenario that inspired the famous *Oldest Systematic Program of German Idealism*, co-authored by Hegel, Schelling, and Hölderlin. This scenario makes political dissensus vanish in the sheer opposition between the dead mechanism of the State and the living power of the community framed by the power of incarnated thought. The task of poetry, of aesthetic education, is to render ideas sensible, to transform them into beliefs and living images, offering the modern equivalent of ancient mythology: a fabric of common sense experience, shared by the elite and by the people.⁸ This draft is not just a forgotten dream of the 1800s. It imparts a new idea of revolution: a revolution of the sensible—the *human* revolution as the young Marx would say—in which philosophy must complete itself by annulling its status as separated thought. It is on this basis that, in the 1920s, the artistic avant-garde was briefly able to link up with the Marxist avant-garde, agreeing on the same program: the construction of new forms of life that at once suppressed both the specificity of politics and of art. This entailed, moreover, the suppression of the logic of aesthetic free appearance, which is appearance released from reference to any truth. In becoming the expression of a form of life, it finds itself once more with a truth as its guarantor. One step further, and this incarnated truth is once again opposed to the lie of appearances. The fulfillment of the aesthetic promise thus becomes the act of a subject who liquidates all those appearances that are nothing other than the "the dream of something he must possess in reality."

It took no more than three years for the Schillerien *mise en scène* of the aesthetic state to be transformed, in the *Oldest Program*, into a scenario of aesthetic revolution. Three years were also enough for two of its authors to announce its end, elaborating a counter-scenario of "aesthetic education," a scenario that is nothing other than the constitution of aesthetics as we know it: aesthetics as a regime of thinking about art, as the narrative of its life, of the manner in which its spirit is embodied. It is this counter-movement that Schelling inaugurates in the last chapter of the *System of Transcendental Idealism* and for which Hegel provides in completed form in his *Lectures on Aesthetics* of the 1820s.

That which stands opposed to aesthetic revolution as the transformation of aesthetic foreignness into the principle of an autonomous life in formation, is precisely the life of forms. We could look at the museum not as the locale and institution where dead masterpieces of culture are placed, but as the idea and sensorium of their proper life. This counter-scenario of the life of forms transfers the properties of the aesthetic state to the works, which means that it invalidates the transfer of these properties to a new form of collective life. The equality of activity and passivity, of form and matter, of art and non-art, thus takes on a new sense. Henceforth, it characterizes the very terms of the works. The "aesthetic" work is defined as the identity of a having-been-willed and a not-having-been-willed, of being-made and a having-not-been-made, of consciousness and an absence of consciousness. The success of the work thus becomes identical to the revealed contradiction of a form and a content, whether the perfection of a statue without concern expressing the spiritual void of Greek religion, or the intensifying of the forms of Gothic statuary expressing the impossibility of translating Christian interiority into the coarseness of the stone. The work, then, promises no new life of the community. The life of a collectivity has already taken place in it. It is conserved as a gap between that which the artist meant to do and what he did. This is the new sense of aesthetic heterogeneity that the Hegelian scenario establishes. The work constitutes art for us to the extent that for he who has created it, it was not art but the manifestation of a belief or a mode of being. It is art because it *was* life and will not return to it. The only future of art, the only suppression of the approaching divide, is therefore the pure and simple suppression of art conceived of as a specific form of thought: not its transformation into rule over bodies animated by common thought, but its banalization, decorative or doxic, correlative to the modern separation of spheres of rationality.

It is not simply the barren idea of the end of art that derives from this counter-scenario. If we return to the Hegelian exposition, from it stems an idea of its survival, an idea of its new life, which is also another idea of its politicity. The work is alive for as long as it reproduces the tension of the original scene, the tension embodied by the captivating and yet inaccessible goddess. It holds the promise of a collective life to come for as long as it is the manifest contradiction of a form and a content, as it presents the face of a contradiction and makes the sound of a dissonance heard. There is no need for the musician's chords to be actually dissonant. Adorno provides the exemplary proof of this: the sweetest of post-romantic melodies can be conceived as dissonant if the musician—Mahler in this case—substitutes, in order to introduce it, his brother's crude post horn for the noble horn of the symphony orchestra. The veiled sound of the plebeian instrument, playing the simple little melody, is enough to corrupt harmonious perfection. It is enough to highlight once again that which underlies this "modern" rationality of the separation of functions that strips—or claims to strip—art of its content, that claims to know the original sin of Western reason, namely the separation of work and enjoyment, of Ulysses's calculations and the singing of the sirens. It recalls, along with the singularity of the aesthetic state, "the promise without which breath could not for a second be drawn," the promise of a free, or undivided life.[9] Symmetrically, the inhuman perfection of the dodecaphonic system, in being more mechanical, is even more inhuman than Taylorist rationality, and has the virtue of letting the mark of the repressed appear on the surface, thus denouncing this aestheticized art that serves as an approval of commercial life and as a complement to exploitation.

The only thing the proof requires is the purity of its theater, the radical separation of the work and of life that leaves the latter no other place to appear but as the contradiction of the work, that never lets it express itself in any other way than as forbidden life, as a return of the repressed. The banality of modernist and formalist argumentation, which wants to make the advances of art correspond with those of the century, intentionally forgets the constitutive paradox whose precise logic is only made visible by the light of the primitive Schillerian scene. The work must be sharply separated from life for it to hold the promise of a new life. This is necessary because it is in its foreignness, in its heterogeneity that the entire promise of the future lies. This potential can only be preserved at the price of forever remaining potential, of being radically excluded from any compromise with the actual, from the risk of losing itself in realizing itself. It is, at the limit, the impossibility of the promise ever being fulfilled that alone ensures its validity.

Saving the heterogeneous sensible to save the aesthetic promise of autonomy: this mantra, consubstantial with the scenario of the life of forms, perhaps only escapes banality at the price of finally reversing the meaning of this heterogeneity. In a second step, it indeed consists of nothing more than saving the heterogeneous sensible in order to save heterogeneity. And, in the final stage, saving the heterogeneous means saving heteronomy as such. It is this limit that is exemplarily reached by the Lyotardian aesthetics of the sublime. The Adornian fixation on safeguarding heterogeneity, the prohibition of any flattering mélange in the name of the contradiction that attests to alienation, becomes a complete inversion of the aesthetic logic. The dissonant purity of the work thus becomes the pure trait of heteronomy, the pure inscription of a condition of irremediable dependence in the face of the Other and irredeemable guilt before the forgetting of this dependence. The properly aesthetic dissensus that Schiller stages is thus returned to the pure and simple gap of the Kantian Sublime: the gap between the idea of reason and the powerless effort of the imagination to elevate the most grandiose sensible spectacle to its height. This "return to Kant" is a pure and simple transformation of aesthetic singularity into ethical "respect." However, this transformation is itself a total inversion of the Kantian logic. What the powerlessness of the imagination showed reason, in Kant, is its properly unconditioned power. What it introduced to it is the world of freedom, of the autonomy of legislating reason. In Lyotard, however, the power of art demonstrates the complete opposite: by means of the discord between idea and materiality, it demonstrates the pure and simple law of heteronomy, the dependence of reason vis-à-vis an Other to whom it will never finish paying its debt.[10] In its very radicality, this transformation of the Kantian law into Mosaic law might already very well be the form, purely inverted but equally intense, of the promise attached to aesthetic heterogeneity: as if the power that Schiller tied to the declaration of aesthetic freedom lead once again to this declaration of servitude.

Notes

1. Friedrich Schiller. "On the Aesthetic Education of Man," trans. Elizabeth M. Wilkinson and L. A. Willoughby (1976), repr. in *Friedrich Schiller: Essays*, eds. Walter Hinderer and Daniel Dahlstrom (New York: Continuum, 2001), 131. From here, referred to in text as AL.

2. Immanuel Kant. *Critique of the Power of Judgment*, trans. Paul Guyer and Eric Matthews (Cambridge: Cambridge University Press, 2001), 229.

3. Ibid.

4. Ibid.

5. Jean-François Lyotard. "After the Sublime, the State of Aesthetics" in *The Inhuman*, trans. Geoffery Bennington and Rachel Bowlby (Stanford, CA: Stanford University Press, 1991), 135–43.

6. On the need to "protect" passivity from the encroachment of active power, see the 13th letter in particular. On the political consequences of this "encroachment," the terror of law with respect to life, see the 3rd letter.

7. Cf. in particular the 27th and final letter: "The things he possesses, the things he produces, may no longer bear upon them the marks of their use, their form no longer be merely a timid expression of their function; in addition to the service they exist to render, they must at the same time reflect the genial mind that conceived them, the loving hand that wrought them, the serene and liberal spirit that chose ad displayed them." (AL 174.)

8. See J-L. Nancy and Phillipe Lacoue-Labarthe. *The Literary Absolute*, trans. Philip Barnard and Cheryl Lester (Albany, NY: SUNY Press, 1998), 27–28.

9. Theodor Adorno. *Mahler: A Musical Physiognomy*, trans. Edmund Jephcott (Chicago: University of Chicago Press, 1992), 37. The melody referred to is found in the third movement. *Scherzando*. of Mahler's Third Symphony.

10. Cf. in particular Jean-François Lyotard, "Anima Minima" in *Moralité Postmodernes* (Paris: Galilée, 1993), 199–210.

8

On the Fate of Aesthetic Education
Rancière, Posa, and *The Police*

CHRISTOPH MENKE

TRANSLATED BY ELIZA LITTLE

In the middle of the most tense dramatic action, immediately before the Marquis Posa meets King Philipp's summons, and immediately after Posa has spoken the decisive word, "act" ("Whether it is or not, the same! With this belief I will act") Schiller's *Don Carlos* ascribes the following actions to Posa: "He paces through the room a few times, finally coming to stand in quiet contemplation before a painting." The text goes on: "the King appears in the adjoining room, where he gives some orders. He then enters, pausing in the door frame to observe the Marquis for some time, without the latter noticing."[1] This is the first time in Schiller's piece, so full of courtly intrigues, political declamations, and ethical reflections, that an aesthetic attitude, an attitude of "quiet contemplation," is depicted. What this means, or rather, that this is what is meant, is immediately clear because the King is also brought to a standstill as he stops to observe the Marquis's contemplation of the painting. This is the moment in which the King, "the experienced expert / proficient in the matters of human souls,"[2] understands Posa and comes to recognize the quality of Posa's virtue.

In a later conversation with the Queen in which Posa outlines the program of aesthetic education that he had devised for her former fiancé and current stepson Don Carlos, Posa himself describes his aims thus: "I want to direct him to excellence / I want to lift him up to the highest beauty."[3] Posa later describes his understanding of the aesthetic contemplation that he himself practices in the following way:

> What is it to King Philipp, if
> The Transfiguration in the Escorial
> Ignites the painter who stands before it with eternity?
> Do the sweet harmonies that
> Lie dormant in the lute belong to the buyer
> Who guards it with a deaf ear?
> He has bought the right to beat it into pieces
> But not the art to call the silver tones
> And to melt in the song's delight.
> Truth is present for the wise man
> Beauty for the feeling heart.[4]

The depiction of a heart, and thus of a virtue, that is "feeling," stands in contrast with the morality of the Spanish court. This virtue is not a "principle . . . wrung from hot blood / by means of cunning and hard battle,"[5] but rather an "ideal" that "from the soul's maternal soil, / conceived in proud, beautiful grace, / sprouts voluntarily."[6] Scarcely a decade later, Schiller himself would present a conception of aesthetic education identical to the one his Marquis Posa puts forward here. One of the central theses that Jacques Rancière has brought forth in recent years against postmodern aesthetic theory and its distorted image of modernity is that this concept of aesthetic education, which has been ridiculed as a misjudgment of the seriousness of the political and dismissed for overestimating the value of aesthetic play is the theoretical heart of the modern—or, as Rancière puts it, "aesthetic"—regime of art. Furthermore, according to Rancière, the basic elements of the theory of aesthetic education can (and should) be defended against postmodernity's critique.

As can already be seen in *Don Carlos*, there are two such basic elements. Rancière has worked these out from the concept of play described in Schiller's *Letters on the Aesthetic Education of Man*.[7] The first element of the concept of play inheres in a redefinition of what art itself is. The old Aristotelian model of art, valid for over two thousand years, determined the exemplary modes of artistic presentation, the various necessary arts, as well as the appropriate "poetic" techniques (taking that term in its broadest sense). In the same way, the central placement of the concept of play in the new model demonstrates that what "beautiful" art is and can do must be determined through the practices that are bound up with it. One of the foundational tenets of the specifically modern "aesthetic" regime of art, the program of which is formulated in Schiller's concept of play, is the idea that art is defined by its presence to its surrounding subjects:

> In this regime, the statue of Juno [which Schiller mentions in his 15th Aesthetic Letter] does not draw its property of being an artwork from the conformity of the sculptor's work to an adequate idea of divinity or to the canons of representation. It draws it from its belonging to a specific sensorium.[8]

Furthermore, the statue of Juno belongs to the category of art because of its existence as "free appearance [*freier Erscheinung*]" for a "specific form of sensory apprehension" or a "specific experience which suspends the ordinary connections not only between appearance and reality, but also between form and matter, activity and passivity, understanding and sensibility."[9] The concept of play conceives of art as practice [*Praxis*] rather than as representation. This aesthetic practice is, in Rancière's words, defined as a "specific" one because play transforms the "ordinary" hierarchical ordering of understanding and sensibility, activity and passivity, and brings about a new or, even better, a "playful or "free" relationship between them.

The second basic element of Schiller's concept of play that Rancière brings to the fore is the relationship between beautiful art and the "art of life" (or *Lebenskunst* as it is termed by Schiller,[10] and later by Friedrich Schlegel and Bertolt Brecht). Schiller uses the concept of play to define not only a new kind of art, but also a "new form of life-in-common," or even a new form of "humanity."[11] Rancière reformulates the political implications that Schiller attributes to aesthetic play as follows: aesthetic practice can be called "playful" because it dissolves the relationship of "domination" that fixes it between the designated poles—appearance and reality, form and matter, activity and passivity, understanding and sensibility—in everyday social practices. Aesthetic play belongs to a "sensorium different to that of domination."[12] More precisely, in the same way that Rancière grounds relations of political domination in a specific "distribution of the sensible," the practice of aesthetic play creates a different "distribution of the sensible" that is opposed to the paradigm of domination: namely, a distribution based on "equality." Thus, the actual enactment of the concept of play consists in carrying out a determination of the aesthetic in its specificity or autonomy. The autonomy of the aesthetic is, however, not to be understood here as "the autonomy of 'artistic' making [*faire* artistique] celebrated by modernism. It is the autonomy of a form of sensory experience; and it is precisely this experience which appears as the germ of a new humanity, of a new form of individual and collective life."[13] Rancière's (thrice repeated) conclusion from this account reads: "thus, there is no conflict between the purity of art and its politicization."[14]

Rancière also points out the strategic import of this conclusion, namely, that if there is no conflict between aesthetic autonomy and the political significance of art in the modern regime, then there can be no "postmodern rupture."[15] The postmodern has traditionally been understood as beginning with a claim about the breaking apart of the modern unity of art and politics. Rancière wants to repudiate this claim and, along with it, the right of postmodern critique in general. This is also why he does not claim a tensionless success for the modern "project." On the contrary, according to Rancière it is precisely through this tension, which can be more strongly characterized as a "paradox" or a "contradiction," that the "dialectic" of the modern concept of art is constituted.[16] However, the contradiction he describes doesn't pertain to the systematic coherence of art and politics but rather to the place—more correctly, to the *time*—of its realization. If the medium of art comes to be thought of as a communal practice that fulfills the political promise of the aesthetic here and now, in the (temporal and spatial) presence of the artwork, then art loses the power of negation that it holds against the prevailing politics of domination—this is Adorno's objection to the classic *avant-garde*. Conversely, if art comes to be thought of as an instance of negation that promises different politics that never come into being, then this political promise is empty; this is Brecht's objection to purely formal art.

Rancière rightly sees this conflict as the central dialectical tension of modern aesthetics.[17] However both parties to this argument share with each other and with Rancière (or Rancière shares with them) the conviction that the autonomous character of aesthetic practice can bring forth a politics of non-domination (whenever, wherever, and to whatever extent this other politics is actually possible) because the aesthetic practice of play provides the model for such a different politics. More precisely, play provides the model for a different "distribution of the sensible," which in turn grounds a different politics. A position could thus be called "postmodern" if it were to contest this idea (admittedly, this definition would make Hegel and Nietzsche postmodern). Such a position would claim that the Schillerian concept of aesthetic education that Rancière takes up as the archetype of aesthetic modernity necessarily fails on conceptual grounds. Indeed, there are two such grounds: the aesthetic education of man can be stymied either by the autonomy of the aesthetic or by the power of the political.

∽

The first objection to the concept of an aesthetic education runs thus: if such an education is supposed to be able to succeed—that is, if it is supposed to be able to change something politically—then it negates the autonomy of the very aesthetic medium through which (or in which) aesthetic education is supposed to take place. In order to see how this objection applies to Schiller, it is necessary to revisit our previous sketch of his position. Our specific concern is how Schiller understands the opposition between the two contrasting paradigms of the "distribution of the sensible" to which Rancière refers respectively as domination and aesthetic regimes.[18] Schiller's analysis states that the logical structure of sociopolitical domination is that of a scission. More precisely, it is a scission between the elements that must be taken together and be bound up with one another in order to constitute the capacity that Kant and Schiller call "humanity," i.e., the capacity for free subjectivity. When these elements are mediated by and reconciled with one another they comprise the capacity for subjectivity. However, in Schiller's account, these elements are socially torn apart and separated from one another.

The structure of domination of the present society offers an image of subjectivity as a death's head. The unity of the subject has disintegrated; its dismembered, estranged parts are divided socially amongst different socioeconomic classes. The scission of the subject mirrors the matrix of class domination. This is Schiller's reformulation of the old Platonic thesis of the reflexive reciprocity between disorder in the soul and disorder in society (a theory that would turn out to be foundational for the tradition of critical theory of bourgeois society from the young Hegel to Marx up to Lukàcs and Adorno). The capacity for free subjectivity is inherent in the ability to freely bring together activity and passivity, spontaneity and receptivity, understanding (or reason) and sense perception. Following Schiller, it can thus be seen that sociopolitical domination is first inherent in the bringing forth of individuals who each *in themselves* organize these elements in relationships of domination of one side over another, be it the dominion of the understanding over sense perception or, conversely, the dominion of sense perception over the understanding. Schiller writes:

> But man can be at odds with himself in two ways: either as a savage, when feeling predominates over principles, or as a barbarian,

when principles destroy feeling. The savage despises civilization and acknowledges nature as his sovereign ruler. The barbarian derides and dishonors nature, but, more contemptible than the savage, as often as not continues to be the slave of his slave [i.e., nature]. (AL 95)

Thus, individuals form two classes that are defined respectively by two opposing relations of domination between the understanding and sensibility. Sociopolitical domination consists of the production of a relationship of domination that places one of these two classes of self-ruling individuals in power over the other. The class of individuals for whom understanding rules over sensibility thereby also rules over the class of individuals whose understanding is dominated by sensibility. Both classes of individuals are equally depraved, insofar as both have equally lost the capacity for subjectivity or humanity.

The first question posed by the critique we are currently considering concerns the general suitability of such a theoretical matrix of subjectivity for critical social analysis. Schiller's class theory may indeed be crude. It is, however, convincing to describe also contemporary figures of class domination by the forms of subjectification on which class domination is based or which it enforces. Schiller's further assumption that these modes of subjectification are not merely equivalent but rather are deficient in complimentary ways is more problematic. On this view, these two forms are understood as parts of a shattered unity that can once again be assembled into a whole. This view is bound up with the normative relationship between Schiller's critical analysis of domination and his concept of subjectivity or "humanity." Furthermore, this normative relationship is definitive not only for Schiller's social critique, but also for his idea of aesthetic education, insofar as aesthetic education is nothing other than the process of transformation that makes free subjects out of self-suppressing individuals. It therefore includes, to use Posa's previously quoted words, the process by means of which a virtue that must be wrung out of "hot blood," i.e., that represses sensibility for the sake of its principles, is transformed into a virtue that sprouts "from the soul's maternal soil . . . voluntarily."[19] Such an education to free subjectivity is meant to result from taking part in an aesthetic praxis with beautiful objects. According to Schiller, this education occurs by means of the activity of play. This is so because, in play, the determinations of the subject that are sundered from and opposed to one another in relations of domination undergo a "reciprocal action [*Wechselwirkung*]" or a "reciprocal proportion [*Wechselverhältnis*]" because *each* determination is differently enacted. Specifically, each is made manifest in a limited, rather than in an absolutely fixed manner, in a free, rather than in a compulsory manner (cf. AL 126).

Schiller formulates what Rancière describes as the tensionless relationship between aesthetic autonomy and political subjectification thus: the political—and, simultaneously, the rational or rationally grounded—imperative "humanity should exist" is identical to the aesthetic imperative (one could even say the aesthetic "law") "beauty should exist" (AL 129). This is so because the aesthetic law states that the human being plays. Play, in turn, allows both the two drives and the relationship of domination between them that is the ground of sociopolitical domination to come into being in a different way, such that this relationship can also be instantiated differently. In this way, human beings (re)claim their capacity for subjectivity by means of aesthetic play.

The aesthetic price that Schiller's theory has to pay for the overlapping of free play and free subjectivity is readily apparent in his text: aesthetic play must enter into the teleology of subject-constitution. Thus, it must also be the case that in the aesthetic mode, which leads to a full accomplishment of sensibility and understanding, activity and passivity, spontaneity and receptivity—i.e., the aesthetic mode that displaces these elements from their usual relations of domination—nothing different and nothing else comes to pass than precisely *this* transformation of the two elements: their transformation into elements which stand in the relation of "reciprocal proportion" which defines the unity of subjectivity. That this is the case is, however, merely a claim. Prior to Schiller, Kant had already put forth the corresponding claim that the aesthetic state is a "quickening of both faculties (imagination and understanding) to an activity that is indeterminate but yet, as a result of the prompting of the given representation, nonetheless unified,"[20] in order to give a coherent explanation for why we experience pleasure in this state. In Kant's view, pleasure must be grounded in a positive judgment stating the suitability of the aesthetically experienced condition of a force or a drive for the faculty of subjectivity in general.

Schiller abandons this (not very convincing) premise about the concept of aesthetic pleasure by driving his aesthetic phenomenology to an understanding of the pleasure of the subject in the aesthetic state as a pleasure in being merely "null": "In the aesthetic state, then, man is *naught*" (AL 147). This aesthetic state of nullity is that of the freedom of "indetermination," a condition of unboundedness and endlessness that is only "the ground of possibility of everything" because it is the grounds of nothing (AL 148–49). Put differently, this state can only function as grounds because it is not such at all. In this state, the 'subject' is not in any way an incipient or responsible actor. The elementary sense of aesthetic freedom according to which Schiller understands this connection is thus not politically (or "meta-politically") suitable. Such aesthetic freedom does not contribute to the previously described interaction of faculties, which, when it succeeds, constitutes (free) subjectivity and dissolves the domination of one class over another by dissolving self-domination within individuals.

∾

The second objection to the concept of aesthetic education is thus: the success of aesthetic education would seem to demonstrate that the possibility for changing something politically entails taking for granted and making use of the very same structures of domination that such an education is directed against. This is less apparent in Schiller's theoretical writings on aesthetic education than it is in his dramatic texts, which themselves perform his program of aesthetic education.

Understanding Schiller's dramatic works in this way requires a preliminary methodological remark. How is it that the role of artistic presentation [*Zeigen*] or exhibition [*Darstellen*] in the modern—or, following Rancière, "aesthetic"—regime of art breaks with the traditional "representative" regime? This contrast should obviously not be taken to mean that, in Rancière's view, art in the aesthetic regime does not present anything. Beautiful art can only bring about the aesthetic practice of play by means of presenting something, particularly by *the way in which* it presents it. In the aesthetic regime of art, what an artwork presents is not supplanted by the artwork's effect on the spectator; rather, the thing presented is defined in terms of this effect. The art under discussion here, however, as exemplified by Schiller's dramatic art, presents yet something else, and in another way it presents the effect that its own presentation has on the spectator. *This* presentation can no longer be determined by its aesthetic effect, because it consists in the presentation *of* aesthetic effect. Beautiful art is not only a part of or a medium for the aesthetic practice of play. Rather, it exhibits this practice for which it is a part or a medium in itself.[21] In this way, the presentation that characterizes this art is (self-)reflexive. It is a reflection of art itself on the very aesthetic regime to which it belongs. Art is not simply situated in an aesthetic regime; it is never totally dominated by any regime. The aesthetic regime does not define and control art. Art is rather the medium of the reflexive exhibition and the critical cross-examination of the aesthetic regime itself.

Schiller's dramatic art (which, like all contemporary dramatic art is metadramatic or meta-theatrical) exemplifies how the political-aesthetic education that Schiller postulates as the effect of art (and hence also the effect of his plays) presents and reflects on itself. His plays make visible the preconditions for—and also the limitations of—his program of political-aesthetic education. In order to see what these preconditions and limitations are, it is necessary to recall that Schiller's initial question is a political one: namely, the question of the Revolution. More accurately, it is the question of how a political subject can arise, one whose capacity for self-government is as removed from the savagery of a sensibility deprived of reason as it is from the barbarism of a reason that represses sensibility. According to the Fichtean thesis that serves as Schiller's point of departure, subjectivity in this political sense cannot be produced by means of politics. Rather it "can be acquired and increased only through culture."[22] As Schiller sees it, this is the German answer to the French failure: revolutionary politics must become cultural politics. In contrast to Fichte, who places the emphasis on the education of the scholar, Schiller conceives of aesthetic education as providing such a revolutionary cultural politics. Pursuantly, Schiller's plays demonstrate why the anticipated revolutionary effects fail to come about. On this topic, two brief remarks follow.

First, *Don Carlos, Infante of Spain* centers on a struggle between two forms of virtue: a repressive, dominating virtue, and a beautiful or free virtue. Representing the first form are King Philipp and the Princess of Eboli, the latter of whom goes from being the unrequited lover of Don Carlos to being the King's mistress, scheming against the Queen. Representing the second form are, of course, the Marquis Posa and the Queen herself. Carlos is the object and prize of their struggle. It is a struggle over his soul, a struggle over who and what he will become through his education. The aim of Posa's educational efforts makes his accusation against Carlos clear; Carlos's obsessive love for the Queen, who is now his stepmother, has lost him his aesthetic freedom:

> Yes, once / Once it was very different. Then you were so rich, / so warm, so rich! The whole world's circle found / ample space within your breast. All that / is now a bygone, is swallowed up/ in this one passion, paltry selfishness. / Your heart is dead. No tears, not one tear more / for Flanders and her monstrous destiny.[23]

The accusation Posa makes against Carlos here describes the one-sided limitation of the "drives" that Schiller's *Letters on the Aesthetic Education of Man* will later diagnose as the grounds of domination. This is the very same limitation that the *Letters* hope to be able to break out of and overcome through the aesthetic practice of play. Posa wants Carlos to become a *whole* human being and thus also a whole *human being*. Any of the ways in which this can take place must be political insofar as Carlos is the Infante of Spain. The play is about the education of a prince, about the subjectification of a sovereign, that is, about him becoming a whole human being.[24] This is the reason why Posa cannot seize upon the obvious political option of placing himself at the head of the rebellion that breaks out in Madrid when Carlos's incarceration becomes public knowledge. To do so would threaten the very structure of political domination that must remain intact, that must be *taken over* intact from the enemy, in order to demonstrate the political impact of Posa's educational program. "One stroke of the pen by your hand and the world / will be created anew. Give men / the right to think!"[25]—this demand that Posa addresses to King Philipp while "throwing himself at his feet," and which borders on parody in its connection of chancellory and eschatology, describes precisely the concept of sovereignty that the aesthetic educator wants to confirm rather than struggle against. Only a political sovereign, one who has the power to remake the world with a stroke of a pen, can make his own aesthetic freedom everyone's freedom. The revolution that takes place by means of aesthetic education and that, according to Rancière, aims at a new "distribution of the sensible" (i.e., a distribution made in terms of equality), must issue from the very same sovereign domination that it is directed against.

In the broader scope of the modern history of aesthetic education, this fact is demonstrated by the double-meaning of the concept of the *avant-garde* pointed out by Rancière, which he attributes to the opposition between two different conceptions of political subjectivity: "the archi-political idea of a party, that is to say the idea of a political intelligence that sums up the essential conditions for change, and the meta-political idea of a global political subjectivity, the idea of the potentiality inherent in the innovative sensible modes that anticipate a community to come."[26] It is critical for the concept of the *avant-garde* that these two conceptions of political subjectivity not be detached from one another. If the subjectivity of play that is possible in aesthetic practice is to become operative, it must either take over the instruments of political domination (from the State) or create them (in the party). Lukàcs's problem regarding the indissoluble connection and the irreconcilable tension between tactics and ethics is repeated here, however this time between tactics and aesthetics.

A brief glance at the play fragment that Schiller composed shortly after completing *Don Carlos* reveals that the political question of aesthetic education is therein further complicated. The fragment is titled *The Police* or alternately *The Children of the House*. *The Police* is complementary to *Don Carlos* in many respects, not least that the draft addresses the other half of the Oedipal material dealt with in *Don Carlos*. While *Don Carlos* foregrounds the incestuous motivation of the Oedipus complex, *The Police* centers on the similarly Oedipal connection between destiny and the search for truth. Destiny comes on the scene in Schiller's fragment in a twofold manner, both as tragic and as comic. In both cases, however, it appears as *just* (in the Platonic sense of the word). As a tragedy, *The Police* recounts the uncovering of the crimes of hypocritical virtue; as a comedy, it tells of the uncovering of the innocence of true virtue. This double uncovering occurs by means of the police force, insofar as it is permitted its "free course." Schiller describes the police force as a machine that is set "in motion like a series of interlocking gears."[27]

That this leads to "poetic justice," the rewarding of virtue and the punishment of vice, is not, however, because the police force would be committed to these objectives. The views that Schiller ascribes to Police Chief d'Argenson certainly do not speak to an interest in such justice: "[t]he Police Chief looked upon humanity as a species of wild animal and treated it accordingly."[28] Additionally, in response to the "famous plea" with which the criminal attempts to justify himself ("But I have to make a living somehow"), d'Argenson replies, "I don't see it that way."[29] However, another fact is decisive. It is not so much the case that the police force pursues an end other than justice, rather, in some sense, it does not pursue an end at all. Indeed, in the notes to Mercier's *Tableau de Paris*, whose reading had inspired Schiller's project, Schiller writes: "Paris is a jail, it is in the power of the monarch, who has here a million under lock and key."[30] Yet, in spite of all of the traditional attributes of sovereignty that Schiller ascribes to the Police Chief, such as mildness and "saving caution,"[31] the "police regime"[32] is not an order of political sovereignty. Thus, the police force in Schiller's piece, in contrast to the way it is presented at the beginning of the play, is not in actuality "all-knowing" or equipped with an "all-seeing eye."[33]

In both the tragic and the comic readings of the play, the resolution comes about not through police mediation, but rather by chance. Thus, the Police Chief is not a sovereign in the traditional sense; the police-machinery has neither a center that integrates everything nor an all-controlling focal point. This means, however, that the potential addressee of aesthetic education is also lacking. If there is no sovereign, there is no longer any issue about what kind of human being he or she is or whether the virtue he or she displays is forced or voluntary. Schiller describes the Police Chief thus:

> D'Argenson has seen people too frequently in their shameful aspect to have a noble concept of human nature. Yet, although he has become skeptic of the good and more tolerant of the bad, he has

not lost his feeling for the beautiful and, when he encounters it unequivocally, he is stirred all the more strongly. In this latter case, he comes and pays homage to proven virtue . . . In the course of the piece, he appears in his private life, where he demonstrates a very different character, one that is jovial and pleasing. He also acquires benevolence and respect as an upstanding member of society and a man of the heart and spirit. In spite of his stern exterior, he can be kind; he really finds a heart that loves him and his beautiful conduct earns him a kindly wife.[34]

D'Argenson is an archetypical student of aesthetic education; equipped with a feeling for beauty, he is stirred by it, and, as a result, becomes capable of being virtuous, pleasant, and kind. This earns him an even kinder wife. D'Argenson is the incarnation of that "aesthetic culture" from which Schiller expects nothing less than another Revolution. But d'Argenson is the Police Chief, a high-ranking civil servant who does his duty. He is not aesthetic in the "house of the police" but rather in his own home as a private person.[35] This fact is not inconsequential, rather it reflects the place of subjectivity in a post-sovereign political order. In the regime of the police, this place is the private sphere. Here, therefore, aesthetic education cannot go any further.

∾

I have indicated here two senses in which the relationship between art and politics must fail if Schiller's idea of aesthetic education is understood as exemplifying the modern aesthetic regime. First, this relationship fails on account of the recalcitrance of the aesthetic and, second, it fails on account of the constitution of the political. Thus, there is an indissoluble tension in the very concept of aesthetic education. Does this mean that the idea of a link between art and politics that is both systematic and has normative consequences ought to be entirely abandoned? That only the celebration of pure aesthetic experiences and resignation before the unchangeable character of political circumstance (one could also call this "postmodern") is left to us? By no means.

Admittedly, it does mean that the analogical matrix by means of which modern thought defines the relationship between art and politics must be abandoned. It was Kant who first described the relationship between the beautiful and the ethical as "analogous."[36] He did so in order to make two claims: first, that this relationship is not one of hierarchical domination of either one over the other and, second, that this relationship is regulated by the fact that both the ethical and the beautiful, in spite of their differences, operate in reference to a single ideal. (For Kant, this is the autonomy of both aesthetic and ethical reflection). Kant's claims about the analogous operation of aesthetics and ethics serve as the impetus for the subsequent attempt to define the relationship between art and politics by relying on the assumption that, at least on some abstract level, they must operate according to the same model or in service of the same idea. Such a way of looking at the problem guarantees that the two will be perceived as being interchangeable.

The alternative lies in (to speak with Bataille) replacing the "limited" economy of the exchange of equivalents with a "general economy" in which non-equivalents are exchanged. Less metaphorically, the relationship between art and politics must come to be thought in such a way that it does not rely on the idea that the two terms symbolize or stand in for one another because of their supposed analogy or "similarity" (Kant). Rather, they should be thought of as different, heterogeneous, conflicting moments of a combined unity. Moreover, this combined unity must be understood as capable of altering both art and politics once they enter into its realm, while not being itself either artistic or political.

In this way, not only the structure of the relationship between art and politics, but also the status of this relationship is altered with respect to the modern concept. The relationship itself changes from an analogical to an agonal structure. The analogical model assumes that the connection between the two terms is already given. This connection is supposed to consist in the fact of their analogy, in which all cases must be recognized and brought to consciousness. If, on the other hand, it is the playing out of the conflict between the two terms that constitutes their relationship, then this relationship exists only when and insofar as this conflict actually occurs. In this latter case, art is neither made analogous to politics nor permanently cordoned off from the political. Rather, art is brought into conflict with politics and, in this way, comes to stand in relation to it.

Notes

1. Friedrich Schiller, "Don Carlos, Infant von Spanien," in *Sämtliche Werke*, eds. Gerhard Fricke, Herbert G. Göpfert (München: Hanser, 1981), Bd. 2, Act III, Scene 9.
2. Ibid., Act II, Scene 10, verses 2996-97.
3. Ibid., Act IV, Scene 21, verses 4334-35.
4. Ibid., Act IV, Scene 21, verses 4352-63.

5. Ibid., Act II, Scene 15, verses 2336-38.
6. Ibid., Act II, Scene 15, verses 2329-32.
7. Compare to Jacques Rancière, "L'esthétique comme politique," in *Malaise dans l'esthétique* (Paris: Galilée, 2004), 31-64. Cf. in English: "Aesthetics as Politics," in *Aesthetics and its Discontents* (Malden, MA: Polity, 2009), 19-44.
8. Ibid., 44 (cf. English trans., 29).
9. Ibid., 45 (cf. English trans., 30).
10. Friedrich Schiller, "Letters on the Aesthetic Education of Man" trans. Elizabeth M. Wilkinson and L. A. Willoughby in *Essays*, eds. Walter Hinderer and Daniel Dahlstrom (New York: Continuum, 2001), 86-178. From now on AL followed by the page number.
11. Rancière, "L'esthétique comme politique," 46 and 47 (cf. English trans., 30 and 31).
12. Ibid., 46 cf. English trans., 30).
13. Ibid., 48 (cf. English trans., 32)
14. Ibid., 48, 49, 50 (cf. English trans., 32, 33, and 34).
15. Ibid., 53 (cf. English trans., 36)
16. Compare to ibid., 50 and 60.
17. Compare to ibid., 52-63.
18. Compare also with Jacques Rancière, "Les antinomies du modernisme," in *Malaise dans l'esthétique* (Paris: Galilée, 2004), 130 ff. (cf. "The antinomies of Modernism," in *Aesthetics and its Discontents*, 61ff).
19. Schiller, "Don Carlos," Act I1, Scene 15, verses v. 2330 ff.
20. Immanuel Kant, "Kritik der Urteilskraft," in *Werke*, ed. Wilhelm Weischedel, Darmstadt 1983, Bd. V, §9, B31. English translation: Werner S. Pluhar *Critique of Judgment* (Indianapolis, IN: Hackett Publishing Company, 1987) with some emendations.
21. Compare to Christoph Menke, *Tragic Play. Irony and Theater from Sophocles to Beckett*, New York: Columbia University Press 2009, 108-27.
22. Fichte, Johann Gottlieb, "Einige Vorlesungen über die Bestimmung des Gelehrten," in *Werke*, ed. Immanuel Hermann Fichte (Berlin: Theater der Zeit, 1971), Bd. VI, 311. (Cf. English Translation D. Braezaele in *Early Philosophical Writings* (Ithaca, NY: Cornell University Press, 1988), 160.
23. Schiller, "Don Carlos," Act II, Scene 15, verses 2409-19.
24. Schiller's political problem is this: the Sovereign is not a subject, not a person. This is not necessarily because he is inhuman, wicked, or without virtue (like Monteverdi's Nero, who is not a subject because he is missing the subject constituting capacity of practical self-relation), but rather because he is virtuous in the wrong way: his virtue is to oppress others. Compare with Christoph Menke, "Die Depotenzierung des Souveräns im Gesang. Claudio Monteverdis *Die Krönung der Poppea* und die Demokratie," in *Literatur als Philosophie—Philosophie als Literatur*, eds. Eva Horn, Bettine Menke, and Christoph Menke (München: Fink, 2005), 281-96.

25. Schiller, "Don Carlos," Act III, Scene 10, verses 3212–14.
26. Jacques Rancière, J, *Le partage du sensible. Esthétique et politique* (Paris: Wilhelm Fink, 2000), 45. (Cf. English translation: Jacques Rancière, trans. Gabriel Rockhill, *The Politics of Aesthetics: The Distribution of the Sensible* (New York: Continuum International Publishing Group, 2004), 30.
27. Schiller, Friedrich, "*Die Polizei*," in *Sämtliche Werke*, eds. Gerhard Fricke, Herbert G. Göpfert (München: Hanser, 1981), Bd. 3, p. 207 and 209.
28. Ibid., 192.
29. Ibid., 192.
30. Ibid., 194.
31. Ibid., 193.
32. Ibid., 193.
33. Ibid., 193.
34. Ibid., 190–91.
35. Ibid., 191 and 197.
36. Kant: *Kritik der Urteilskraft*, §59, B 255. (Cf. English trans., 227)

9

Kant, Schiller, and Aesthetic Transformation

JEFFREY L. POWELL

In his seminal essay from 1936, "The Work of Art in the Age of Mechanical Reproduction," Walter Benjamin proposes a difficulty for those working in the continental tradition who are interested in attempting to marry politics and aesthetics. This is not a new marriage as even the most rudimentary reflection on Greek tragedy will reveal, but it has not been an easy one. Perhaps, though, Greek tragedy supplied humanity with the portents of such a marriage, portents that were little seen until Benjamin's arrival. For Benjamin, the difficulties experienced by these two reached their nadir through a certain realization only accomplished through technological development made possible through the material conditions of the industrial revolution. Once a work of art was definitively abstracted from the authentic materiality of its productive place and time—an abstraction that technology really only just makes apparent—it was then ripe for being put to use for whatever means possible, especially political purposes. When this occurs, this putting to use for any political purpose whatsoever can only result in the attempted realization of a vision that results from an arbitrary decision. It is this arbitrary decision that is most often at issue in appeals to the well-known formulation with which Benjamin closes his essay: "'Fiat ars—pereat mundus', says fascism, expecting from war, as Marinetti admits, the artistic gratification of a sense perception altered by technology . . . *Such is the aestheticizing of politics, as practiced by fascism. Communism replies by politicizing art.*"[1] If we are at all confused about what Benjamin means by the fascistic rendering of the aesthetic, we need only read the preceding page of his essay, for while the essay as a whole offers enough to challenge our comprehension, in this case we would be the source of any confusion: "*All efforts to aestheticize politics culminate in one point. That one point is war.*"[2] Benjamin's essay has been frequently enough the object of critical reflection, and the distinction between an aesthetic politics and a political aesthetics has been equally cited enough. However, the critical work is hardly homogeneous in its treatment, and the citing of this passage has never, to my knowledge, been unpacked in any significant way despite the many visions it has spawned. That the latter has not occurred has been partly accounted for by Benjamin's claim that he is "completely unusable" for fascism (which, as we will shortly see, means being unusable for what he means by "political art") and the treatment Benjamin gets by at least Alex Düttmann and Peter Fenves.[3] To quickly gloss over this claim, one can say that the "usable," which requires a kind of reproducibility and repeatability, is essentially synonymous with fascism insofar as its usability is inseparable from the political regardless of whether one identifies with the left or the right.

So, aside from the judgment that an aesthetic politics necessarily results in war and fascism, what might Benjamin more concretely mean by this aesthetic rendering for political means? In order to find our way to Benjamin's meaning, let us first begin with a common understanding of what might be meant by an aesthetic politics. By aesthetic politics, it seems safe to presume an understanding of the political through aesthetic means. That is, that some political end be realized through aesthetic means. In this case, a representative of the political, or the representative of some political view, would appeal to aesthetic sensibility, some specific αἴσθησις, not for the purpose of delineating the content or form of that phenomenon. Rather, the appeal would be made on behalf of some further end or purpose designated under the guise of political interest. This would seem to capture the appeal made by all politicians to what is called the base, an appeal that is through and through aesthetic. This appeal seems to be so thorough that it is difficult to imagine anyone voting on what are called "the issues" over what is aesthetically appealing about either the politician or what he aesthetically represents. Even if this were the case, even if "the issues" were to at least limit the possible candidates to a relatively small list—perhaps even only one—how is one to decide between what is an issue and what is an aesthetic object? If "the issues" to which one is drawn in a candidate are indeed moral rather than merely procedural or founded on a kind of technē, then we can easily draw from Kant's *Critique of Judgment* and aesthetic beauty as the symbol of morality.

Before we return to Benjamin, we would do well to briefly recall Kant's analysis of the beautiful as a symbol of morality. This analysis occurs in the final section of part I of the *Critique of Judgment* in §59. Kant begins this section by first appealing to an issue of crucial importance for the *Critique of Pure Reason*, that concerning the schematism. Assuming the section under consideration was among the last of those written by Kant, they could not have been completed after 1792. In 1797, well after the completion of the manuscript now known as the *Critique of Judgment*, although before the publication in 1799 of the third edition, Kant had written in a letter, which is cited by Heidegger in his reading of the schematism in *Kant and the Problem of Metaphysics*: "In general, the Schematism is one of the most difficult points. Even Herr Beck cannot find his way therein.—I hold this chapter to be one of the most important."[4] One might well ask why there is mention here of the schematism. Kant's framing of beauty as the symbol of morality immediately tells us why, for he begins the section as follows: "To demonstrate the reality of our concepts, intuitions are always required. If they are empirical concepts, then the latter are called **examples**. If they are pure concepts of the understanding, then the latter are called **schemata**."[5] Thus the demonstration of empirical concepts is achieved through the presentation of the concept in an empirical intuition. The empirical concept of a chair is provided by the empirical presentation of a particular chair, an empirical experience of the thing as example designated by the concept. Likewise, the demonstration of a pure concept of the understanding would be achieved through the empirical presentation of such a concept in empirical experience. Guyer explains the schemata as follows: "For pure concepts of the understanding, *schemata* may be furnished—for the pure concepts of causation, we may supply the appropriately defined schema of temporal succession."[6]

These are explanations of two of the three types of *hypotyposis* treated by Kant. The third is the one that concerns us most, which is the symbolic rendering of an intuition as opposed to the direct empirical rendering of either pure or empirical concepts. For the symbolic rendering of an intuition, the operation occurs, not as a direct presentation of the pure or empirical concept, but rather as an indirect rendering of a concept or idea of reason, which is a rendering of the supersensible (freedom or morality). Such concepts or ideas of reason may be only indirectly presented because they extend beyond any possible intuition: "since no intuition adequate to them can be given at all,"[7] says Kant. Any direct or immediate presentation is impossible. This indirect representation of an idea of reason operates by means of analogy, an analogy whereby empirical intuitions are employed in the rendering of what can only be thought but not empirically perceived. Interestingly for our purposes, when Kant goes on to explain the more specific operation of analogy in the forming of an empirically represented symbol, he does so by appealing to political representations. However, the very manner in which the political representation he offers operates is anything but clearly presented. Here is his description of the process of analogy:

> All **hypotyposis** . . . is one of two kinds: either **schematic** . . . or **symbolic**, where to a concept which only reason can think, and to which no sensible intuition can be adequate, an intuition is attributed with which the power of judgment proceeds in a way merely analogous to that which it observes in schematization, i.e., it is merely the rule of this procedure, not of the intuition itself, and thus merely the form of the reflection, not the content, which corresponds to the concept.[8]

The type of *hypotyposis* that concerns us cannot be of the schematic form, for in the earlier language of the third *Critique* it would then concern theoretical cognition. Since this symbolic representation concerns morality, it must have to do with freedom, not theoretical cognition. Furthermore, since the symbolic representation also concerns beauty, it cannot concern the object of the intuition but rather the judgment concerned with the representation. In other words, as already stated, it concerns not the content but the form of intuition. In this case, a concern with the form of intuition is a concern with merely the form of schematization, as explained by Kant in the previous citation. So, what is important in beauty as the symbol of morality is the form the analogy takes regarding the content of what is related by analogy. The terms through which this analogy of form would operate are supplied by Kant as follows: "Thus a monarchical state is represented by a body with a soul if it is ruled in accordance with laws internal to the people, but by a mere machine (like a hand mill) if it is ruled by a single absolute will, but in both cases it is represented only **symbolically**."[9] Against any temptation to view the analogy as one concerning content, Kant quickly observes that there is not any similarity between a despotic state and a hand mill, just as there is not any similarity between a monarchical state and the body and soul of a human being. This also means, according to Guyer, that "there is no intrinsic connection between a symbol and what it stands for."[10] However, there is a similarity between how what is presented can be indirectly presented by means of symbols, such as in the symbolic representation of morality, or the structure of reflection that is analogous between the terms of symbolization.

The rule for analogy giving rise to the two respective symbols (body/soul, hand mill) that indirectly represent the state would presumably work as follows. A monarchical state is analogous to the body and soul of a human being in that just as the soul provides the rules internal to the operations of the body, the monarchical state provides the rules inherent to the people ruled. A despotic state, on the other hand, subdues and subjugates those ruled by means of rules external to those who are ruled. In the latter, the hand mill grinds the grain just as the despotic ruler "grinds" or subjugates the people, and where the hand mill produces flour, the despotic ruler produces slaves. So, the general form of reflection provided in the analogous symbolization is the subjugation of the second term by the first, or, better, the rule of the first by a law or series of laws instituted by the second but external to the first. Within the monarchical state, the rule of reflection is different. Just as the soul is thought to rule over the body in such a manner that it designates the rule inherent and determined by the whole (body and soul), the monarchical state is believed to rule over the whole (the δῆμος) in accord with a rule or rules inherent to the whole, i.e., inherent to the people in its universality. Thus the monarchy would rule over its subjects in accord with a rule, "of, for, and by the people." The rule of law in a monarchical state, or monarchical democracy, would then be a kind of self-rule like that expressed by Locke somewhere between 1679 and 1681, depending on whom one believes.

Now, the question still remains: what does this have to do with beauty as the symbol of morality? It would seem to be the following. Beauty as the symbol of morality would itself operate as a symbol, a symbol that would operate in accord with a rule of analogy attributed to reflection. As we know, from the entirety of the first part of Kant's *Critique of Judgment*, an aesthetic judgment of beauty gives rise to a pleasure that is devoid of interest, is subjectively universal, is purposive without a purpose, and gives rise to a necessity founded on *sensus communis*. While these four moments that Kant identifies with judgments of taste are not all analogous to the reflective structure associated with moral judgments, it is nevertheless the case that both judgments of beauty and judgments of freedom give rise to a kind of feeling. Whether that feeling can in both cases be called pleasure is subject to debate, but both do indeed give rise to a feeling that cannot be simply attributed to what Kant calls subjective contingent interest. Unlike judgments of taste, there is indeed an interest associated with moral judgments, but it is certainly not to be characterized as a subjectively contingent one; rather it is a universal interest attributed to reason. The analogous structure of reflection, then, between aesthetic judgments and moral judgments, the structure that makes possible the symbolization of morality by beauty, is precisely this feeling just described. That is, just as the reflective judgment in judgments of taste gives rise to the feeling of pleasure, moral judgments give rise to the feeling of respect or reverence, *Achtung*. It is this particular view of the human being that at once offers, not only the content of one pole of the analogy that serves to connect art to morality, but it is also what serves as what Kant in §17 calls the ideal of beauty, an ideal that for us will further serve in thinking about the relationship between art and politics.

When Kant speaks of the ideal of beauty, he argues that it is the human being and the human being alone that meets the requirements for such an ideal. "It is *man* alone among all objects in the world, who admits of an ideal of *beauty*."[11] Within the order of purposiveness, it is only the human being who, because of reason, can supply himself with his own purposes. No other being is capable of such an act.[12] Furthermore, the human being is also capable of comparing his purposes or intentions "with essential and universal purposes" of nature and can judge the rational 'purposes' harmony with the latter ones aesthetically."[13] Now, the ability to make such a judgment for political purposes would require an analogy whereby a harmony would be established between an aesthetic ideal and what one perceives as "the issues" noted above. Thus, one's politics, and by this I mean the determination of how one votes, would be an aesthetic determination that attempts to bring the ideal of beauty into harmony, which is the rational moral form constitutive of the Kantian ideal of beauty, and the perceived political issues just noted. Two things are of note here: first, the political issues must meet the requirements of the form of ideal beauty, which is to say they must be in accord with the moral form of the human being. Second, with regard to beauty as the symbol of morality, the validity of this analogy is dependent upon the belief that the relationship between body and soul is actually reducible to the soul or reason as the universal nature or essence (*Wesen*) of the ideal form of beauty. This is certainly Kant's position in the *Critique of Judgment*. To put this in a slightly different form, we might say that what we take to be the political issues are a more primary judgment concerning the nature of the human being, and the nature of that being is provided, not so much through an appeal to an intelligible concept of the human being, but through an appeal to an aesthetic judgment concerning the ideal form of beauty. The latter, at least in Kant's view, is the form we have just treated. We will return to this later through an examination of the first appendix to Kant's *Perpetual Peace*, an examination that will focus on a similarity between Benjamin's formulation with which we began (aesthetic politics/political aesthetics) and Kant's formulation of the political moralist and the moral politician.

Let us now return to Benjamin's analysis of the work of art, reproducibility, and the political. It would seem appropriate to ask: what are the means through which these ends, war and fascism, are achieved? While Benjamin does not provide a microscopic view of the manner in which this occurs, he does provide both the general historical conditions for such a movement as well as an example of its results.[14] Benjamin's example of the results of such a rendering, drawn from the Futurist and Italian fascist sympathizer, Filippo Tommaso Emilio Marinetti, was a sign of the times. The example was in support of yet another formulation of an aesthetic politics, a formulation we should keep in the forefront of our minds as we consider the example. The formulation that Benjamin identified as the political one was as follows: "War, and war only, makes it possible to set a goal for mass movements on the grandest scale while preserving traditional property relations."[15] For Benjamin, the property system that is preserved is ownership of only a few for whom the proletarian masses work. What is preserved for the proletarian masses is the chance to express themselves, a chance that should not be confused with right. This chance for expression reaches its acme in the consolidation of the masses as warriors under a nationalist sign. "I am fighting for my country and its beliefs, which are the same beliefs as mine," says the proletariat just before being shipped off to the front. Benjamin next offers what he calls the "technological formula" for this formulation: "only war makes it possible to mobilize all of today's technological resources while maintaining property relations."[16] It is easy enough to provide examples of not only the application of advances in technology for purposes of war or what we today like to call self-defense, but even more greatly the development of technological advances under the sign of some future war. However, what is important here is that technology is itself the dialectical result of the self-sublation of myth in the expression of art. It is here, then, that Benjamin's claim concerning the aestheticization of politics gains traction.

Now the example drawn from Marinetti as he addressed the Ethiopian colonial war. It is a long citation, but its entirety is required for the full effect:

> For twenty-seven years, we Futurists have rebelled against the idea that war is anti-aesthetic [an error for which Marinetti will provide the antidote] . . . We therefore state: . . . War is beautiful because—thanks to its gas masks, its terrifying megaphones, its flame throwers, and light tanks—it establishes man's dominion over the subjugated machine. War is beautiful because it inaugurates

the dreamed-of metallization of the human body. War is beautiful because it enriches a flowering meadow with the fiery orchids of machine-guns. War is beautiful because it combines gunfire, barrages, cease-fires, scents, and the fragrance of putrefaction into a symphony. War is beautiful because it creates new architectures, like those of armored tanks, geometric squadrons of aircraft, spirals of smoke from burning villages, and much more. . . . Poets and artists of Futurism, . . . remember these principles of an aesthetic of war, that they may illuminate . . . your struggle for a new poetry and a new sculpture![17]

This entire process resulting in the aestheticization of politics or fascism is not absolutely necessary, although most of the forces of history and contemporary life would seem to be aligned with its success, if it can be called that. The appearance of a necessity annexed to this aestheticization is due, according to Benjamin, to the "decay of aura" in the work of art.[18] Aura is thought by Benjamin as "A strange tissue of space and time: the unique apparition of a distance."[19] It does not matter if the distance is near or far, for what the distance impresses upon us is the uniqueness of what is distant. Perhaps nearness better indicates the absolute distance of what distinguishes us from the work of art than does what is understood to be far. That is, regardless of how close we might come to the work of art, there is never an identification, or, in the later language of German Idealism, the distance will never be fully appropriated through the investment of spirit by means of the negation of its own externalization and subsequent interiorization (*Erinnerung*). The distance is never overcome. In remaining distant, then, the work of art has the status of uniqueness, a uniqueness that is not reproducible. Speaking in only a slightly different idiom, Adorno says of Benjamin's thoughts on the aura of the work of art that "To perceive the aura in nature in the way Benjamin demands in his illustration of the concept requires recognizing in nature what it is that essentially makes an artwork an artwork. This, however, is that objective meaning that surpasses subjective intentions."[20] Nevertheless, for all of that, the aura of an art work was inseparable from the historical conditions in which it existed, it was "identical to its imbeddedness in the context of tradition,"[21] says Benjamin.[22] This is most obvious when one appeals to those earlier historical traditions in which art was situated within ritual and cult. Echoing Nietzsche before him, Benjamin notes that "the earliest artworks originated in the service of rituals,"[23] such as that of Greek tragedy.[24] This simple observation of the historical conditions of the work of art is a lynchpin for the later proposition concerning aesthetics and politics, for the historical conditions determining the very sensible qualities that permit the recognition of an object as a work of art are also what determine the decay of aura that is fully realized in the invention of the photograph. There is neither time nor space to pursue it here, but this is an analogue for what Jacques Rancière will come to think of, in our own time, as *Le partage du sensible*, the partition or distribution of the sensible. Those historical conditions enabling the decay of aura and the invention of the photograph are the same material conditions of the industrial revolution that equally enabled the increasing technological sophistication, and this latter increase has done nothing to abate the preservation of the principle of private property. Although perhaps not intended in exactly the same manner (Adorno would most likely contest this), Benjamin inadvertently makes the point even more strongly in some reflections following a meeting with Bertolt Brecht in 1934.[25] Benjamin recounts the meeting and conversation with Brecht concerning his "The Author as Producer" as follows:

> Brecht thought the theory I develop in the essay—that the attainment of technical progress in literature eventually changes the function of art forms (hence also of the intellectual means of production) and is therefore a criterion for judging the revolutionary function of literary works—applies to artists of only one type, the writers of the upper bourgeoisie, among whom he counts himself.[26]

What is so obvious here, when viewed from contemporary life, is precisely the extent to which technological progress as the teleological negation of aura in the formation of art has further embedded the work of art within technology, to such an extent that one must have the technological means to both create and communicate art work in the current day.[27] This elaborate technological requirement is simply the outcome of the preservation of private property from which we drew just a few moments ago in our beginning analysis of the aestheticization of politics resulting in fascism or war. In fact, the increasing importance of private property along with all the contradictions it carries along with it, contradictions addressed by both Marx and Hegel before him are, not surprisingly, cut from the same cloth as the decay of aura. Once again, Benjamin: *"the desire of the present-day masses to 'get closer' to things" is equally joined by a "passionate concern for overcoming each thing's uniqueness [Überwindung des Einmaligen jeder Gegebenheit] by assimilating it as a reproduction."*[28]

Despite all this, according to Benjamin, it is only through the decay of aura that art becomes liberated from its dependence on ritual and cult. Rather than art being bound to the expression of ritual and cult, one discovers an emphasis on art for art's sake, the battle-cry of *l'art pour l'art*. The more art is loosened from its bonds to ritual, the greater the decay of aura; and the greater the decay of aura, the more art is realized through the technological means that are the material conditions of the then (and now) current culture. The more art is able to be produced through technological means, the less its value is founded on its unique character, a character that was only achieved through the aura that had decayed. The less art is founded on uniqueness and authenticity, the more value it consequently potentially acquires in its reproducibility. The more it is possible, through technological means, to produce art through reproducibility, the more valid it becomes as an object ready for reproducibility. Stated differently, the very reproducibility of the object now qualifies it for becoming art. This all leads Benjamin to say that "*But as soon as the criterion of authenticity ceases to be applied to artistic production, the whole social function of art is revolutionized. Instead of being founded on ritual, it is based on a different practice: politics.*"[29]

Regardless of what Benjamin says, the decay of aura, or the negation of aura due to the material conditions that give rise to technology, does not liberate art from its dependence on ritual and cult.[30] This is not to say that the decay of aura has no effect on this relationship, but rather the ritual and cult upon which art was dependent becomes transformed. The material conditions that give rise to the object of art through technological reproduction do serve to remove the distance of the object of art under the sign of aura, but the cult value of the art is transformed into the cult value of science. The work of art then becomes more and more transformed by the degree to which it can be produced through scientific means. Art is no longer limited to the creative activities of writing, painting, sculpting, music, and the like, but it now also includes photography and film. Art becomes less and less the product of some unaccountable creative force for which reason is at a loss, and more and more the expression of a rational order hidden from view but made available through scientific-technological means. The more the aura of authenticity decays, the greater the distance required for that authenticity to collapse and be transformed into an identification with the products of technological reproducibility, for example, the character on the screen or the gaze of the face in the photograph. This character and this gaze would seem to be what captured the imagination of Benjamin in "The Little History of Photography" from 1931. There Benjamin writes the following:

> No matter how artful the photographer, no matter how carefully posed his subject, the beholder feels an irresistible urge to search

a picture for the tiny spark of contingency, of the here and now, with which reality has (so to speak) seared the subject, to find the inconspicuous spot where in the immediacy of that long-forgotten moment the future nests so eloquently that we, looking back, may rediscover it. For it is another nature which speaks to the camera rather than to the eye: "other" above all in the sense that a space informed by human consciousness gives way to a space informed by the unconscious.[31]

The technology through which the work of art is now produced performs its task so well because art and what it represents, which is preserved through the aura, has been transformed into some new third thing, which is the identification of what lies behind the image with the technology that reveals it. What might be a disorganized mess lying behind the image of the human being has now been transformed by technology in such way that the distance of aura, formerly preserved through the distance maintained by the particularity of the object, has now been internalized as a distance within the formerly Kantian subject, a self-differing through which the innermost recesses of the subjective are, in a language foreign to Benjamin, both deferred and differed. This is the interpenetration of which Benjamin speaks when he writes: *"Hence, the presentation of reality in film is incomparably the more significant for people of today, since it provides the equipment-free aspect of reality they are entitled to demand from a work of art, and does so precisely on the basis of the most intensive interpenetration of reality with equipment."*[32]

But this interpenetration and internalization of aura is anything but innocent, for it carries along with it the possibility of both the democratization of art, as well as the fulfillment of art through politics; in other words, the possibility of either political art or the aestheticization of politics. As to the latter, the closure or formalization of the internalized gap of the self-differing of the internalized aura is attempted; the former resists a kind of subjective definition, whether that definition be one pertaining to a kind of particularity without resolve, or the defining or designating of a group identity for the purposes of politics.[33] This is why we find the double-edged sword with the change of the material conditions of art from the authenticity of the aura to technological reproduction. Once again Benjamin: *"But as soon as the criterion of authenticity ceases to be applied to artistic production, the whole social function of art is revolutionized. Instead of being founded on ritual, it is based on a different practice: politics."*[34] Political art hacks at the hegemony of what sustains the difference between what enables political power and those subjugated to its exercise. With the aestheticization of politics, we discover the edge that cuts into and fractures the identity required for traditional property relations, the wound required for the identification of him to whom property "rightfully" belongs. This wound must be healed, the subject to whom property belongs must be restored, restored into the beauty of some ideal form of the human being. Let me tell you the truth of who you are says the director in service to the politician. You are the beauty lying within, the beauty that makes the difficult, arduous work of the moral politician worthwhile.

This turn of phrase, the moral politician, is set in contrast to the political moralist in Appendix I of Kant's *Perpetual Peace*. Entitled "On the Opposition Between Morality and Politics with Respect to Perpetual Peace," here Kant attempts to provide a kind of roadmap for the transition from morality to politics, a roadmap in which would be achieved in an empirical form of life corresponding to the universal will of the moral law. This transition could only ever occur through a treatment of the sensible natural body along with all its desires with the beautiful medicine of morality. This would be the resolution of an antinomy between the political moralist and the moral politician. Early in the appendix, Kant writes that "I can easily conceive of a moral politician, i.e., one who so chooses political principles that they are consistent with those of morality; but I cannot conceive of a political moralist, one who forges a morality in such a way that it conforms to the statesman's advantage."[35] This resolution is nothing short of what would be the attempt to bridge the gap between a human being of the natural order (the *Critique of Pure Reason*) and the moral order of freedom (the *Critique of Practical Reason*). Thus, this resolution would be achieved by a reflective judgment such as the aesthetic one of the *Critique of Judgment*. Kant will even refer to this activity, the activity of political rule, as "the *art* of using this mechanism [nature] for governing men."[36]

Ultimately, for Kant, political rule and political resolution is to be achieved through the appeal to morality for Kant. When difficulties of the political order cannot be achieved merely through technical procedural changes—or, really, even when they would be achieved in that manner—the guide will always be the moral guide one, to bring all law under the form of universal law. The achievement of this guide and goal, whether realizable or not, is what Kant calls the Kingdom of Ends, or with regard to the discussion concerning politics, perpetual peace. "Then it may be said," says Kant, "Seek ye first the kingdom of pure practical reason and its righteousness, and your end (the blessing of perpetual peace) will necessarily follow" (appendix I). However, there is a problem here, a problem that surfaces through the analyses of Benjamin, as well as in Schiller's letters compiled in *On the Aesthetic Education of Man*.

The problem posed by Benjamin, assuming Benjamin is correct, and the moral solution posed by Kant is the aestheticizing of the political, first through "beauty as the symbol of morality" wherein the ideal beauty for symbolization is the form of the human being as moral being, the human being as a free being of reason. What Benjamin shows is that even beyond Kant and the context in which he was writing, this view of art and morality, at one time bound to the authenticity and singularity to which the aura gave rise, dialectically resolves itself into a new set of material conditions resulting in the reproducibility of art for the sake of politics, a politics that preserves all the privileges of private property and fascism. Schiller, on the other hand, often presented as a ventriloquizer of Kant, can actually be used as a model for the theoretical representation of what Benjamin calls political aesthetics. In the first half of his text, a text that is squarely immersed in and respondent to the French Revolution, Schiller first addresses, in Kantian terms, the situation of the Revolution. The monarchy has functioned very much like what Kant called the political moralist, or again, "one who forges a morality in such a way that it conforms to the statesman's advantage."[37] It is this very situation that has given rise to the Revolution and that Schiller addresses throughout his essay. This is a difficulty that is seemingly an intransigent part of the Western political order first clarified through the character of Thrasymachus in Plato's *Republic*. The more modern expression, still relevant for today, perhaps even more so in recent times, is provided by Marx in what Balibar analyzes as "intellectual difference." Says Marx,

> Division of labour only becomes truly such from the moment when a division of material and mental labour appears. From this moment onwards consciousness *can* really flatter itself that it is something other than consciousness of existing practice, that it *really* represents something without representing something real; from now on consciousness is in a position to emancipate itself from the world. . . .[38]

Schiller's version of this problem is clearly stated in Letter VII of his essay:

> The present age, far from exhibiting that form of humanity which we have recognized as the necessary condition of any moral reform of the State, shows us rather the exact opposite. If, therefore, the principles I have laid down are correct, and if experience confirms my portrayal of the present age, we must continue to regard every

attempt at political reform as untimely, and every hope based upon it as chimerical, as long as the split within man is not healed, and his nature so restored to wholeness that it can itself become the artificer of the State, and guarantee the reality of this political creation of Reason.[39]

The monarchy functions in this case in the service of his subjectively contingent desires, which is to say that he acts animal-like. The proletariat, on the other hand, functions much the same way, although in its case subjectively contingent desire is limited to seeking of the means of subjective subsistence. Both, then, the monarch and proletariat alike, are seemingly concerned with what is restricted to each their own subjectivity. Now, according to Schiller, at the beginning of the Revolution the proletariat was morally justified in its actions. The Revolution was a moral one in the attempt to attain what was rightfully its own, which was nothing short of its own moral freedom guaranteed by a representative government. Thus, for the purpose of moral-political action the Revolution was justified by the very form of the human being who is simply his moral form.

With the success of the Revolution, a new set of problems arose. Included in the denial of a Kantian essential freedom was the denial of a total lack of education, including moral education. It seems safe to say that both Kant and Schiller would agree on such a need. Schiller is explicit about it; Kant is not. Nevertheless, on behalf of Kant, it would seem safe to say that such an education would be required if the new form of government were to be so structured that its principal players could act as moral politicians and not political moralists. Only moral politicians would be capable of negotiating the complex conflicts of the state with other states on the way to perpetual peace. Now, for Kant, the struggle is ultimately a moral struggle and a moral struggle alone. If aesthetic reflective judgment is difficult to make or even to recognize, and it is certainly that as anyone will know who has read the *Critique of Judgment*, it might well be that its difficulty is due to the moral impingement it imposes on us.

Or it might be that its difficulty is due to other reasons of which the Kantian system is seemingly unaware, reasons that Schiller sometimes gives the impression of having stumbled upon, but that Benjamin seems to confront head on. For Schiller the political conflict of the French Revolution will never be resolved through an appeal solely to morality. Why? Because the turn to morality exchanges one kind of subjugation for another. That is, the subjugation that gives rise to the Revolution is the subjugation of one subjectively contingent will by another, the subjugation of the subjective will of the proletariat by that of the monarch. The Revolution requires the recognition of the universality of reason and morality, the domain of freedom, which can only be achieved through the negation of the subjective will of both the proletariat and the monarch. But for this negation of subjective contingency by the universality of reason and morality to be maintained and put to work requires, not perpetual peace, but rather the perpetual subjugation of the subjective contingency of the will, the particularity of the human being. For that reason, Schiller views the success of morality as the potential destruction of what we are as temporal beings within the order of becoming. At one point, Schiller calls the two drives, impulses, or forces—one having to do with sensuous, temporal existence, the second having to do with universal, moral being, the giver of laws—the seeming exhaustion of our concept of humanity:

> The first of these, which I will call the *sensuous* drive, proceeds from the physical existence of man, or his sensuous nature . . . The second of the two drives, which we may call the *formal drive*, proceeds from the absolute existence of man, or from his rational nature, and is intent on giving him the freedom to bring harmony into the diversity of his manifestations. (AL 118)

As long as these two remain at odds, or as long as one remains in subjugation to the other, or as long as they are taken to be in opposition, the only outcome is war or, according to Benjamin, fascism. Schiller is very clear about this: "The two are, therefore, not by nature opposed," he writes in the Thirteenth Letter (AL 121). Thus the problems of politics are not to be resolved through an appeal to morality nor will its resolution be effectively surmounted if morality is viewed in opposition to the sensuous existence of singularity. Much of the Thirteenth Letter addresses the formal problems associated with viewing the two forces as oppositional and their inadequate resolution through the subordination of one to the other.

For Schiller, then, the resolution, if one could rightly call it that, is the absolute unity of the two drives, a coming together of the two drives not only as a creative act, but a creative act that infinitely resists this coming together in accord with a rule, for any and all rules would only once again be the subjugation of the particular by the universal. Nor can the equation simply be reversed, not even in the form of a kind of historical materialism, the resolution of which would appear to be the kind of dialectical materialism proposed by Lefebvre.[40] Further, although this is an exercise that is only initially proposed by reason, "This reciprocal relation between the two drives is, admittedly, a task of reason,"[41] writes Schiller, the fulfillment of this task cannot be accomplished by reason. Rather, this task gleaned by reason will discover its resolution in a turn toward what will become the crucial sticking point for German Romanticism, for this is "an exercise that man is only capable of resolving completely in the consummation of his existence" (AL 125).[42] That is to say, in the full realization of the human being's sensuous and rational existence or, alternatively, in the realization of the two drives, a realization achieved only as the enactment of freedom. However, Schiller's notion of freedom is a far cry from that of Kant, as one might easily already surmise. Whereas Kant sees freedom solely within the domain of the human being's moral domain, for Schiller that kind of freedom could only be a freedom from the subjugation of one's natural constitution. Thus Schiller writes at the beginning of his Twentieth Letter that freedom "arises only when man is *complete* and *both* of his fundamental drives have developed" (AL 144, translation altered). As if he were signaling his departure from Kant, Schiller continues to state that "freedom will, therefore, be lacking as long as he is incomplete, as long as one of the two drives is excluded" (AL 144).

Let us be clear. Schiller is not always entirely clear about his departure from Kant.[43] It is clearly the case that Schiller proposes the aesthetic condition as the resolution of the origin of political conflict, which is the perceived opposition between the moral-intelligible and the sensible. However, there is an equivocation in Schiller regarding the exact positioning of the aesthetic operation. That is, Schiller will at times view the aesthetic as enabling the transition from sensible, particular life to the moral domain; at other times, he decidedly takes the position that the aesthetic condition is not the transition from sensibility to morality, but rather the resolution of the conflict of the two and thus the resolution of the origin of political conflict. This equivocation is clearly on view in the remainder of the Twentieth Letter. In that letter Schiller provides a developmental, anthropological treatment of the training of the human being, a training wherein "The sensuous drive, therefore, comes into operation earlier than the rational, because sensation precedes consciousness, and in this *priority* of the sensuous drive we find the clue to the entire history of human freedom" (AL 144). That history is to include the Kantian notion of freedom and morality, and Schiller has in a previous letter first called for a moral education, albeit one that is only the preparatory ground for aesthetic education. In the Sixteenth Letter Schiller will write that moral education consists of a reflection upon what we do when we perform moral actions, the kind of reflection in which Kant engages in the *Grundlegung*; this is a reflection that is mirrored in the kind of knowledge exacted from the world of nature and that Kant takes as the task of *The Critique of Pure Reason*. Thus Schiller writes that "To refer these experiences back to those abstractions—to replace morals by morality, the facts of knowledge by knowledge itself, happy events by happiness—that is the business of physical and moral education (*Bildung*)" (AL 133). Aesthetic education is formally similar to both of these in that "the task of aesthetic education is to make the beautiful out of the multiplicity of beautiful things" (AL 133). And, while a reflection focused on beautiful things might well make the transition from our sensible nature to our moral nature thematic, thus allowing to have the morally problematic nature of the political domain in view, this does not mean the appearance of morality within that domain is without subjugation or that the reappearance of sensible life within the political domain is no longer guided in the heat of the moment by moral demands. For those reasons, our sensible and moral natures still yet requires the guidance of an aesthetic education, that is, an education whose more abstract nature will provide the insights for recognizing the subjugation of one domain over the other and provide for the possible unity of the two domains in a world of indeterminacy.

This equivocation is what seemingly gives rise to Schiller's two types of beauty that make up the aesthetic, the energizing and melting, the opposing natures of which are then extinguished (*auslöscht*) "in the unity of ideal beauty" (AL 134). Schiller does not argue in the following manner, but I would argue that the text of Schiller makes the most sense if the transitional nature of the aesthetic, which on its own would result in the Kantian schema, is more fully realized in the ideal form of beauty that is treated in the Twentieth Letter. Appealing, once again, to Schiller's developmental account of human nature, we can realize the following: the resolution of the opposition between the sensible and the intelligible that is so characteristic of the political order and made so apparent to Schiller in the French Revolution gives rise to an essential insight regarding what was initially proposed as the transition between the two orders. That is, the proposed transition was not really a transition at all or, if it were, the transition was provided as the effacement of the sensible order by means of the Kantian moral order. The insight, then, is not simply the critical one regarding Kantian moral subjugation, but that the will and freedom reside, not within the domain of Kantian *Vernunft*, but rather "the will," which as Schiller writes, "maintains perfect freedom between the two drives (*beiden*)" (AL 142). He continues, "It is, then, the will that acts as a *power* (*as the ground of all reality*) relating both drives, but neither of these can of itself act as a power against the other" (AL 142). The will, then, as such a power and freedom, as the ground of all reality, functions, says Schiller in the Twentieth Letter, as a middle disposition. Sounding like a Heidegger to come, the will functions as a middle *Stimmung*, what Schiller also calls a "free disposition [*freie Stimmung*]" (AL 145). Why free? Because it is "subject neither to physical nor to moral constraint," and "one must call this condition of real and active determinability the *aesthetic*" (AL 145). As such a free disposition, the aesthetic condition would operate as an essential openness because constrained by neither of the two orders perceived to be in opposition. In the language of Derrida, the aesthetic condition as such an openness operates according to only one law, which is that it never be reduced to the present for, as Schiller states in a long note to the Twentieth Letter, "the laws according to which the psyche [*Gemüt*] then behaves *do not become apparent*, and since they encounter no resistance, never appear as constraint" (AL 146).

This being the case, then, if what we call politics is the ordering of the δῆμος then what we would call political aesthetics is its disruption, or what Schiller should call for as the effect of aesthetic education. Such a disruption would arise as an infinite task inasmuch as the call for freedom from the metaphysical distribution of forces that have come to determine the being of political life, returning that life, even if for only the briefest moment, to its open determinability or the equality between the forces of singular and universal life. For this reason, and consistent with Benjamin, the aesthetic condition is beyond fascist appropriation, for it would give rise to an art that serves to disrupt fascism or the reproducible usability of a political aesthetics. Such an aesthetic is the resistance against the demand for any law whatsoever, even a law impossible to fulfill such as the demand for a universal liking characteristic of Kant's aesthetics. This, then, is an art become political, a political art, and not an aesthetic politics. One example of such an art suggested by Benjamin is Dadaism along with the one requirement that would seem to be generalizable for political art: "to outrage the public."[44] The various critiques of the politics to which Schiller is said to have given rise would be no more than the reversal of this thesis, which would be, not the disruption of the political order as the exercise of equality (pace Rancière), but rather the determination of that order such that it conceals the inequality of its appearance; or, stated differently, such that the exercise of equality is perceived as the disruption of order.

Notes

1. Walter Benjamin, "The Work of Art in the Age of Its Technological Reproducibility," in *Selected Writings*, vol. 3: *1935-1938*, eds. Michael W. Jennings and

Howard Eiland, trans. Edmund Jephcott and Harry Zohn (Cambridge, MA: Harvard University Press, 2002), 122.

2. Ibid., 121.

3. See Peter Fenves, "Is There an Answer to the Aestheticizing of the Political?" in *Walter Benjamin and Art*, ed. Andrew Benjamin (New York: Bloomsbury, 2005) 60–72; Fenves there begins his essay by saying "For in response to the question 'is there a solution to the aestheticizing of the political?' I say 'no' " (60). Alexander Garcia Düttmann, "Language and Destruction" in *Walter Benjamin's Philosophy: Destruction and Experience*, ed. Andrew Benjamin (New York: Routledge, 2013); for Düttmann, this impossibility is derived from the destruction of tradition inherent in the two conditions of historical materialism, the base and superstructure (what Düttmann calls the infrastructure and superstructure), and this destruction is ultimately the destruction of this distinction between these very two conditions, which then results in the following: "The language of destruction only says destruction, it has nothing to say, it communicates nothing" (54).

4. Martin Heidegger, *Kant and the Problem of Metaphysics*, trans. Richard Taft (Bloomington: Indiana University Press, 1990), 77.

5. Immanuel Kant, *Kritik der Urteilskraft* (Hamburg: Felix Meiner, 1993), §59. In English, *Critique of the Power of Judgment*, trans. Paul Guyer and Eric Matthews (New York: Cambridge University Press, 2000).

6. Paul Guyer, *Kant and the Claims of Taste* (Cambridge, MA: Harvard University Press, 1979), 374.

7. Kant, *Kritik der Urteilskraft*, §59.

8. Ibid., §59.

9. Ibid.

10. Guyer, *Kant and the Claims of Taste*, 376.

11. Kant, *Kritik der Urteilskraft*, §17.

12. This might well be an opportunity to draw Heidegger into relation to Kant for Derridean reasons having to do with animality, for it is here that an essential distinction is made between the rational being—man—and the non-rational animal. The Derridean source for doing so would, of course, begin with *Of Spirit*.

13. Ibid., §17.

14. Of note in this regard is a 1936 letter to Benjamin from Adorno. What I have called historical conditions, Adorno has correctly viewed as a dialectical operation concerning the self-negation of myth in the dialectical formation of the technology of art. In the letter, Adorno writes: "My ardent interest and my complete approval attach to that aspect of your study which appears to me to carry out your intention—the dialectical construction of the relationship between myth and history—within the intellectual field of the materialistic dialectic: namely, the dialectical self-dissolution of myth, which is here viewed as the disenfranchisement of art." In *Aesthetics and Politics* (Brooklyn, NY: Verso, 2007), 120.

15. Benjamin, *Work of Art*, 121.

16. Ibid., 121.

17. Ibid., 121.

18. Ibid., 104.

19. Ibid., 104–05.

20. Theodor Adorno, ""Paralipomena" in *Aesthetic Theory*, ed. and trans. Robert Hullot-Kentor (Minneapolis: University of Minnesota Press, 1997), 274–75.

21. Benjamin, *Work of Art*, 105.

22. I could certainly go into further detail in characterizing what Benjamin means by aura. One of his clearest expressions for it is provided in a fragment from around the same time as the art essay, a fragment called "The Significance of Beautiful Semblance." There we find that that "strange tissue of space and time" is the veil of distance through which the beautiful appears, and without it the beautiful fails to appear. Citing his own essay, "Goethe's Elective Affinities," Benjamin writes: "'The beautiful is neither the veil nor the veiled object but rather the object in its veil'—this is the quintessence of the ancient aesthetic. Through its veil, which is nothing other than the aura, the beautiful appears [*scheint*]. Wherever it ceases to appear, its ceases to be beautiful" (Benjamin, *Work of Art*, 137).

23. Benjamin, *Work of Art*, 105.

24. Nevertheless, we should note here that Benjamin entertains the opposite in his earlier *Trauerspiel* book, albeit mainly by means of a citation, and an odd citation at that, for he cites of all people, Wilamowitz-Moellendorf. The text is as follows: "As far as the philologist is concerned 'there is no basis in the cult for the tragic chorus." Walter Benjamin, *The Origin of German Tragic Drama*, trans. John Osborne (New York: Verso, 1998), 104.

25. As is well known, Adorno was always suspicious of the influence Brecht had over Benjamin. This suspicion seems warranted, relative to other possible influences, but for the most part Benjamin really seemed to be his own man, perhaps even a model for what Kant meant by his use of *sapere aude*! According to Howard Eiland and Michael W. Jennings, "The Author as Producer" is a return to earlier concerns first expounded in Benjamin's "Little History of Photography" (where Benjamin first takes up the discussion of aura), and with regard to the later essay "the positive model of an effective artistic practice is provided by Brecht's notion of 're-functioning' or functional transformation (*Umfunktionerung*): the idea that cultural materials and practices that had heretofore served the status quo could be 'refunctioned' so as not to supply but actually to change the apparatus of production." See Howard Eiland and Michael W. Jennings *Walter Benjamin: A Critical Life* (Cambridge, MA: Harvard University Press, 2014), 441.

26. Walter Benjamin, "Conversations with Brecht," in *Aesthetics and Politics*, 86.

27. For a more recent foray into the transformation of the notion of property in the technological age, see Michael Hardt's "The Common in Communism," in *The Idea of Communism*, eds. Costas Douzinas and Slavoj Žižek (New York: Verso, 2010), 131–44.

28. Benjamin, *Work of Art*, 105. Benjamin's emphasis.

29. Ibid., 103. Benjamin's emphasis.

30. Aside from what follows concerning aura and technology, Benjamin also shows a degree of ambivalence concerning the total destruction of aura, an ambivalence that has not always been heeded in the secondary literature. This is the straw man version of Benjamin presented by Robert Kaufman in "Aura Still" in *Walter Benjamin and Art*, ed. Andrew Benjamin (New York: Continuum, 2005), 121–47. See especially pages 126–27.

31. Walter Benjamin, "The Little History of Photography," in *Selected Writings*, vol. 2, part 2, eds. Michael W. Jennings, Howard Eiland, and Gary Smith. Trans. Edmund Jephcott and Kingsley Shorter (Cambridge, MA: Harvard University Press, 1999), 510.

32. Benjamin, *Work of Art*, 116.

33. This is not to deny or designate as illegitimate a recourse to identity politics, although it is to allow for only a strategic recourse to such . . . for the purpose of disrupting any and all attempts at its consolidation. Thus a more traditional appeal to identity seems perfectly legitimate, but only for strategic purposes, and not as an ontological determination.

34. Ibid., 106.

35. Immanuel Kant, "Perpetual Peace," in *On History*, ed. and trans. Lewis White Beck (Indianapolis, IN: Bobbs-Merrill Company, Inc., 1963), 119.

36. Ibid.

37. Ibid.

38. Karl Marx, *The German Ideology*, in *The Marx-Engels Reader*, ed. Robert C. Tucker (New York: W. W. Norton & Company, Inc., 1978), 159.

39. Friedrich Schiller, *On the Aesthetic Education of Man in a Series of Letters*, trans. Elizabeth M. Wilkinson and L. A. Willoughby (New York: Oxford University Press, 1982), 45. The Seventh Letter. Hereafter referred to as AL followed by the letter number.

40. See Henri Lefebvre, *Dialectical Materialism*, trans. John Sturrock (London: Jonathan Cape Ltd., 1968), especially "Part I: The Dialectical Contradiction."

41. Fourteenth Letter. The translation has here been altered. The German reads: *Dieses Wechselverhältnis beider Triebe ist zwar bloss eine Aufgabe der Vernunft*. The task denoted by the German *Aufgabe* is translated slightly differently as "exercise" in its pronominal form in the next citation for it is not as a task to be performed but as the exercise of a task offered up by reason.

42. One can also see the possible influence of Schiller in the variously attributed "The Oldest Program toward a System in German Idealism." Regarding this text, see David Farrell Krell's commentary in chapter 1 of his *The Tragic Absolute: German Idealism and the Languishing God* (Bloomington: Indiana University Press, 2005), 16–44.

43. Frederick Beiser, in his *Schiller as Philosopher: A Re-Examination* (New York: Oxford University Press, 2005), seems more confident than I, although he has marshalled all the evidence required for that confidence especially as it regards the dispute concerning morality. See especially chapter 5, "Dispute with Kant," (169–90).

44. Benjamin, *Work of Art*, 119.

10

Aesthetic *Dispositifs* and Sensible Forms of Emancipation

María Luciana Cadahia

Dispositif has become a key concept for exploring the modus operandi of power today. At present, thinkers like Agamben, Esposito, and the TIQUUN collective have adopted the term *dispositif* to refer to one of their key theoretical concepts. Nonetheless, they have neglected a fundamental aspect, i.e., the link between this term and crucial theoretical proposals of modernity. Although Agamben does establish a bridge between the term *dispositif* and the notion of positivity as used by the young Hegel, he never inquires as to Hegel's source for this expression. In this text we are going to show that the term had already been used by Schiller before it was adopted by Hegel.[1] Moreover, we will start to illustrate how the concept of positivity in Schiller's *Letters on the Aesthetic Education of Man* may help to explore an aspect of the *dispositif* that few scholars have undertaken until now, namely, its sensible dimension. This sensible dimension will help to establish a different interpretation of the term *dispositif* in our reading of Schiller. Far from considering it as a stigmatized form of power, we are interested in thinking it as a form of aesthetic-political mediation.

However, in order to understand what is at stake in this new interpretation, it is necessary to contextualize the different ways in which the term *dispositif* has been used. Broadly speaking, we are going to explore the two most common approaches. The first is characterized by a pejorative reading of the term, introduced among others by the authors cited above. The second, which is more subtle and less frequently encountered in contemporary debates, helps to develop a more dialectical notion of *dispositif*. In this regard we will consider De Certau's and Martín-Barbero's works along with a reinterpretation of the term found in the work of Deleuze. If the interpretation encountered in the writings of the young Hegel established a pejorative reading of *positivity*, Schiller's approach to the term in his *Aesthetic Letters* is an attempt to connect the notion to a more dialectical interpretation. This, in turn, will help us develop an understanding that is slightly different from the young Hegel's notion of positivity proposed by Agamben.

I.

To investigate the origins of the terms *dispositif* and its uses in contemporary philosophy, we need to go back to the works of Michel Foucault. In the mid-1970s, Foucault became somewhat dissatisfied with the term *episteme* and decided to replace it with *dispositif* in order to overcome the strictly epistemological and discursive dimension of his early research.[3] This change of terms allowed him to account for two aspects that had been overlooked until then, namely, the role of nondiscursive practices and the function of power within said practices.[4] It is probably the very ambiguity of the term *dispositif* that gives it its operational force and the possibility of being assimilated into other schools of thought. If we consider the place it occupies in the work of authors such as Giorgio Agamben, Roberto Esposito, and the TIQUUN collective, for instance, *dispositif* is ultimately identified with power, to the point of becoming a mechanism for organizing the world. In *Che cos'è un dispositivo?*[5] Agamben establishes two different genealogies for the concept of *dispositif*. He begins by establishing a link between the notion of positivity in the young Hegel and the term *dispositif* in Foucault. Broadly speaking, he tells us that, thanks to Hyppolite's studies of Hegel's early writings, Foucault was able to connect these two terms.[6] Nevertheless, Agamben soon abandoned this interpretation and attempted instead to establish a novel link between the term *dispositif* and the Heideggerian notion of *Gestell*.

Hyppolite studies the role of positivity in Hegel's early writings in the light of the dialectics between history and reason. This framework allows him to speak of positivity as a historic element that acts upon the rational development of humankind. It is thanks to this historic element that reason loses its abstract character and is concretely incorporated into the lives of men. Thus,

Hyppolite's great discovery consisted of showing the twofold meaning of this historic element:

> In other terms, as often occurs with Hegelian concepts, there is a double meaning of positivity: one pejorative, the other affirmative. Positivity is like memory, as something living and organic, the past is always present; while as something inorganic and separate, the past is nothing more than an inauthentic present.[7]

While Agamben very lucidly establishes this subterranean link between Hegel and Foucault by discovering a common matrix (i.e., the link between power and life), it is remarkable that instead of taking this double dimension of positivity into consideration, he prefers to limit it to the pejorative pole. In his book titled *Due. La macchina della teologia politica e il posto del pensiero*,[8] Roberto Esposito resumes the discussion of *dispositif* and gives it a linguistic turn of his own.[9] The strategy underlying his entire book is not only to show how the *dispositif* of the person has developed, but to dislocate it as well through a "philosophy of the impersonal."

Despite these differences between Agamben and Esposito, both interpret the term *dispositif* in a pejorative way. This is because they identify *dispositif* with a form of Western power permeated by an estrangement that penetrates our experience, separating it from itself and producing a splitting of life into two different spheres: *bios/zoé*[10] in the case of Agamben, and body/person in the case of Esposito.

In contrast, the TIQQUN collective introduces the question of *dispositifs* or apparatuses in a different register. In the text titled "Ceci n'est pas un programme comme science des dispositifs,"[11] the TIQQUN collective recovers one of the most original ideas from Ernesto de Martino's *El mundo mágico*: the taboo Western culture experiences in order to assume the fragility of presence in the world. TIQQUN takes up the approaches developed by De Martino and extends them to the magic rituals of capitalism and the failure of Marxism to deal with them. The purpose of their science of *dispositifs* is to subvert the economy of presence and destroy *dispositifs*. They despise *dispositifs* because they try to guarantee the economy of presence, and it considers that "the essence of all dispositifs is to impose an authoritarian division of the sensible where everything that reaches presence must face the blackmail of its opposite."[12] It is paradoxical that these authors declare themselves heir to Deleuze's famous essay titled *Qu'est-ce qu'un dispositif?* since Deleuze seems to be vindicating in this essay a dimension of *dispositifs* or apparatuses that is overlooked in all of the former proposals, namely, the possibility of a different use. In the above-mentioned text Deleuze tells us:

> Thus, dispositifs have as components lines of visibility, of enunciation, lines of forces, lines of subjectivation, lines of caesura, of fissure, of fracture, that are intertwined and mixed, some stopping others or generating new ones through variations or even mutations by appropiation.[13]

Here Deleuze speaks to us of *dispositifs* as a regime of the visible and of the enunciable that also includes the processes of subjectivation. But far from considering them exclusively in a pejorative sense, as something we should rid ourselves of, he tells us that "we belong to dispositifs and we act in them."[14] By pointing out that *we act*, he makes it evident that a reorientation of the relations of forces can take place within a *dispositif*. Therefore, Deleuze invites the inference of a possibility of "mutations by appropriation," the *reversibility* of *dispositifs*.

This reversible nature is something that authors like De Certeau and Martín-Barbero had already delimited in their classic books *L'invention du quotidien* and *De los medios a las mediaciones*, respectively. Both texts were published prior to Deleuze's essay,[15] the first in 1980 and the second in 1987. Although they do not belong to the contemporary philosophical debate, since they are closer to areas of sociology and communication studies, it is important to observe the originality with which they explore the notion of *dispositif*. In a sort of approximation to and distancing from Foucaultian studies, both authors have the virtue of illustrating a dimension of *dispositifs* that Foucault himself had overlooked. Specifically, they study that other side of *dispositifs* Deleuze is indicating, that is, the uses that escape the *dispositifs* of subjection. We are especially interested in Martín-Barbero's proposal since it explores a dimension of *dispositifs* that few have studied, their sensible dimension. Furthermore, working on the sensible dimension means introducing the question within the register of aesthetics. The question that I am interested in asking in what follows is thus: is it possible to think of emancipatory aesthetic *dispositifs*? This would entail reactivating the path opened up by Hyppolite when he suggested a double interpretation of the term *positivity*. To answer this question we are going to undertake a cross-analysis that is somewhat heterodox. I shall refer to the work of two thinkers who are very far apart in time, but who provide the keys for developing a tentative answer: namely, Schiller and Martín-Barbero.

II.

Jesús Martín-Barbero's *De los Medios a las Mediaciones* is one of the fullest and most interesting developments, in my opinion, of the double dimension of *dispositif*, understood as an instrument of both domination and emancipation.[16] This twofold use of the term *dispositif* is the result of Martín Barbero's move toward the abandoning of a deterministic reading of culture in terms of mass culture, and his subsequent vindication of the term "popular" within this field. In this respect, Martín-Barbero began to study the manipulation of power in mass media, but soon realized that this image of power loses sight of the resistances that are implicit in all *dispositifs*. Hence he proposed inverting the strategy. The anecdote that explains his change in strategy merits presentation. One afternoon he decided to go to the local movie theater attended by all the female domestic workers of the area. A film starring Vicente Ferrer was being projected on the screen. Even though he thought the movie was awful, when it ended and the lights were turned on he realized that all the women in the audience had really liked it. At first he was surprised to discover the abyss existing between his schema of sensibility and theirs. There was a force in play of which he was ignorant and should try to understand. Critical thinking and its theoretical models were useless to him if they did not provide him with the tools needed to approach that sensibility and allow it to challenge him. After all, in his previous work he had criticized the master from the discourse of the master. Thus, instead of prioritizing how power configures its strategies of domination, he had preferred to study the different reappropriations people made of the so-called mass culture. That is to say, "to see from the other side" how certain uses escape the rituals of domination. In his text *De los medios a las mediaciones*, Martín-Barbero explores this "other side" by studying the unnoticed social uses that popular or grassroots sectors make of the *dispositifs* of the cultural industry. His main objective is to recover a notion of the popular that challenges the unilateral reading of mass culture:

> There remains the denomination of the popular attributed to mass culture operating as a *dispositif* of historical mystification, but also considering for the first time the possibility of regarding what happens culturally to the masses in a positive manner. And this constitutes a challenge thrown at the "critics" in two directions: the need to include in the study of the popular not only what the masses produce culturally, but also what they consume, what

they eat; and to think of the popular in culture not as something limited to what has to do with their past—and a rural past—, but also and mainly of the popular linked to modernity, racial mixing and the complexity of the urban.[17]

This study thus confronted him with Adorno and his reflections on mass culture. In the passages that deal with Adorno, Martín-Barbero recovers the lucidity with which Adorno analyzes the dangers of culture industry. Nonetheless, he also points to the limitations of the analysis. When it abandons its sacred sphere under the influence of the marketplace, art becomes tied to the mercantile economy. Hence for Adorno it is only by explicitly pointing out this contradiction that art can be safeguarded against becoming identified with the market. Thus art, from Adorno's viewpoint, is a form of negativity that impedes any type of reconciliation and, therefore, positivity. For Martín-Barbero, this exercise of distancing and estrangement of the practice of art proposed by Adorno is flawed by a deep disdain for any cultural practice that fails to meet this criterion, leading to the dismissal of all such practices as mere entertainment. That is to say, any mode of cultural production that entails a mode of *approach to* and activation of the emotions and collective experiences would be doomed to failure as a sort of *pastiche* and reiteration of positivity in the sphere of the sensible. Martín-Barbero thus identifies this as an "aristocratic" reading of culture on the part of Adorno, in which it is necessary to scorn its different manifestations as a safeguard to protect an uncontaminated sphere. Adorno's insistence on the urgent need to prevent the positivization of art, Martín-Barbero tells us, eventually "reduces all other possible forms to sarcasm and makes of sentiment a clumsy and sinister ally of vulgarity."[18] Martín-Barbero thus criticizes Adorno for the fact that his proposal of aesthetic emancipation must be accompanied by disdain for popular sentiments, which he considers to be a form of vulgar alienation. To the contrary, he prefers to follow the path opened up by Benjamin. Unlike Adorno, who rejected the new forms of artistic manifestation in music, cinema, and photography, Benjamin devoted his undivided attention to these above all because, as Martín-Barbero tells us, that is where "the transformations of the *sensorium* of the modes of perception, of social experience" are expressed.[19] It could be said that Benjamin's attitude situates him in better conditions than Adorno for thinking the transformations of contemporary sensibility and their forms of mediation. In the words of Martín-Barbero:

> Hence the paradox. Adorno and Habermas accuse him [Benjamin] of not giving an account of mediations, of leaping from economics

to literature and from there to politics in a fragmentary manner. And they accuse Benjamin of this, who was the pioneer in discerning the fundamental mediation that makes it possible to think historically about the relation of transformation of the conditions of production to changes in the cultural sphere, i.e., transformations of the *sensorium* of modes of perception, of social experience. But for enlightened reason, experience is what is dark, constitutively opaque, unthinkable. For Benjamin, on the contrary, thinking about experience is the way to gain access to what bursts into history with the masses and technology.[20]

While Adorno's aristocratic attitude involves an aesthetic distancing that separates us from art forms that establish forms of sensible approach and a common sense regarding all the contradictions and dangers that this implies, Benjamin's attitude enables us to comprehend this phenomenon in all of its historical and political complexity. These new forms, according to Martín-Barbero, are the material expression of new modes of collective perception.

> The new sensibility of the masses is that of a *nearness*, namely, that which for Adorno was the grim sign of their need for engulfment and their resentment, and for Benjamin a sign, not of an aura-like consciousness, but rather of a long social transformation, of the conquest of sense for that which is equal in the world. And it is that sense, it is that new *sensorium* that is expressed and materialized in technologies like photography or cinema that violate, that desecrate the sacredness of the aura—"the inimitable manifestation of a remoteness"—, making possible another type of existence of things and another mode of access to them.[21]

Having identified these two lines, Martín-Barbero continues his research on the dialectics inherent to *dipositifs* by orienting it toward the tension between mass culture and popular culture. However, he does not expand upon the other problem raised by Adorno, namely, the link between positivity and sensibility elaborated in his study on aesthetics. The question we ask ourselves here is whether the deactivation of positivity cannot be accompanied by this notion of nearness that Benjamin so acutely pointed out and that Martín-Barbero recovered. For them it is vital to know whether we can find this tension between positivity and sensibility within the philosophic tradition from the perspective of aesthetics.

III.

When we think about the problem of positivity and sensibility, the texts of the young Hegel and the interpretations of Hyppolite immediately come to mind. This is something that, as we pointed out at the beginning of this text, Agamben himself emphasized in his text "What is an apparatus?". Nevertheless, it is necessary to take one step back since Schiller was really the first to consider this problem. This will allow us to venture the hypothesis that Hegel's notion of positivity is connected to Schiller's use of the positive element in his *Letters on the Aesthetic Education of Man*. Also, and through Schiller, incorporating the aesthetic dimension allows for the exploration of the *sensible dimension of dispositifs*.

Schiller refers to the term *positive* in the *Aesthetic Letters* on two occasions. On one hand, he uses it to refer to positive society (*positive Gesellschaft*), understood as the place where forms of life are defined at a given moment.[22] On the other hand, he uses it to refer to art, understood as a territory that is capable of transforming that place precisely because it is free from the positive element:

> Art, like science, is absolved from positive constraint and from all conventions introduced by man; both rejoice in absolute immunity from human arbitrariness. The political legislator may put their territory out of bounds; he cannot rule within it. (AL 108)

Here the term *positive* does not necessarily acquire a pejorative sense since it refers to the concrete form assumed by politics, laws, and institutions in a given epoch. That said, according to Schiller, in an epoch in which the force of abstract understanding has become the lord and master (*Herr*) of the forces of sensibility, the positive element is reflected in the form of a double violence. The first violence takes place within the individual and is the result of the tyrannical relationship between understanding and sensibility. This tyranny, Schiller argues, produces a tearing asunder of the internal unity of human nature (see AL 101). The second violence is a reflection of the first and is produced when the formal nature of the State becomes alien to the feelings of its citizens. "Thus little by little the concrete life of the individual is destroyed in order that the abstract idea of the whole may drag out its sorry existence, and the state remains forever a stranger to its citizens since at no point does it ever make contact with their feeling" (AL 101). When this separation between the

State and sensibility occurs, Schiller tells us, the State ends up acting exclusively from the viewpoint of understanding since "[t]his disorganization, which was first started within man by civilization and learning, was made complete and universal by the new spirit of government" (AL 99). Schiller thus establishes a line of continuity between the violence that is exercised within the individual and that which is exercised in the sphere of politics. Aware of the importance of feeling in the configuration of politics, Schiller's critique is aimed at the Enlightenment. By having specialized in the cultivation of understanding vis-à-vis sensibility, it dissociated the spiritual forces that live within men. He therefore writes: "[w]e see not merely individuals, but whole classes of men, developing but one part of their potentialities, while of the rest, as in stunted growths, only vestigial traces remain" (AL 98).

In this direction, authors like Paul de Man have denounced the ideological and authoritarian nature of Schiller's aesthetic proposal.[23] However taking the problem of affection into account does not necessarily lead to authoritarian politics. It might be worthwhile to pay more attention to the link between sensibility and politics proposed by Schiller before reproducing the dangers interpreted by other thinkers. It is quite likely that this link is the key to thinking about the role affection and sensibility can play in the construction of political subjectivities today. Isn't it possible that the aesthetic experience that Schiller speaks of functions as a space of *mediation* between the rigidity of the laws and the conflictive nature of politics? Schiller establishes a distinction between a purely rational nature and a *sensible rational* one capable of assimilating (*aufgehoben*) the unresolved tension between rationality and sensibility. In aesthetic experience, he writes, "beauty links the two opposite conditions of feeling and thinking" (AL 137). But, Schiller warns us, this does not imply reaching any "middle term" that would annul the previous ones (see AL 137–39). On the one hand, beauty "unites two conditions that *are diametrically opposed* and can never become one" (AL 137). On the other hand, however, "beauty *unites* [*verbinden*] these two opposed conditions and thus overcomes [*aufhebt*] the opposition" (AL 137–38).[24] That is to say, it is not a dialectics of common sense starting from two contradictory moments that configures here a transcendent synthesis between them. Aesthetics involve a tension between a quest for the unity of both extremes and the recognition of the fact that said unity is impossible. Schiller uses the term *aufheben* to refer to the type of union that aesthetics can achieve: "both conditions remain everlastingly opposed to each other, there is no other way of uniting them except by overcoming them (*aufgehoben*)" (AL 138). That is to say, the task consists of simultaneously suppressing (*vernichten*) and preserving (*beizubehalten*) the determination of the State: "they cancel each other out as determining forces, and bring about a negation by means of an opposition" (AL 145). Being familiar with the Kantian distinction between understanding (*Verstand*) and reason (*Vernunft*), Schiller not only seems to anticipate the speculative thinking that Hegel would propose in the *Wissenschaft der Logik* by saying that "nature (sense and intuition) [*der Sinn*] always unites, intellect [*Verstand*] always divides; but reason [*Vernunft*] unites once more" (AL 139). He also seems to insist on the fact that sensibility forms an essential part of this movement. Like Hegel, Schiller refers to a positive reason that preserves and cancels out the two previous moments. This reason has the distinctive feature of being a *sensible reason*, i.e., an aesthetic one. Schiller therefore tells us that the man who has not yet begun to philosophize is closer to the truth than the philosopher is and that "we can, without further examination, declare a philosophical argument to be false if, in its results, it has the general feeling [*gemeine Empfindung*] against it" (AL 139). This priority is reiterated in the *Ältestes Systemprogramm*, where it is stated that "the supreme act of reason" is "an aesthetic act" and that it is therefore necessary "to transform philosophers into sensible philosophers,"[25] i.e., capable of connecting with the sensibility of the people. Otherwise, philosophy will do nothing but deepen the breach between enlightened reason and popular sensibility.[26]

It is within the framework of this unresolved tension between the abstract power of understanding and the atrophy of sensibility that Schiller poses the problem of the positive. Moreover, Schiller's critique is addressed to the *disposition* that understanding *experiences* toward the positive. Thus, from the viewpoint of a culture of understanding, the laws, institutions and rules that a given epoch grants to itself become something rigid, an external imposition whether it be moral or political. In contrast, aesthetic experience, without abandoning the tension experienced between sensibility and understanding, seems to establish another type of *disposition* toward the *positive*. Thus, aesthetics is a *disposition* that is not only differentiated from other types of disposition—such as the physical, the moral, or that of knowledge—but one that also takes them into account at the moment of acting. In this respect, Schiller tells us,

> [a] thing can relate directly to our sensual condition (to our being and well-being): that is its *physical* character. Or it can relate to our intellect, and afford us knowledge [*Verstand*]: that is its *logical* character. Or it can relate to our will, and be considered as an

object of choice for a rational being: that is its *moral* character. (AL 145 46)

He goes on to say that "finally, it can relate to the totality of our various functions without being a definite object for any single one of them: that is its *aesthetic* character" (AL 146). This is because in the aesthetic disposition, we are affected by our sensibility, our understanding, and our moral condition, but none of these conditions determine our way of being. On the contrary, the aesthetic disposition allows for this tension among the different dispositions to become *visible* without implying a form of coercion. When Schiller writes that the aesthetic disposition is free from coercion, he is not presupposing a state of indeterminability or of absolute indetermination, understood as a celebration of anomie and of the ideal of an empty infinity. He is rather proposing that

> our psyche in the aesthetic state does indeed act freely, is in the highest degree free from all compulsion, but is in no wise free from laws, and that this aesthetic freedom is distinguishable from logical necessity in thinking, or moral necessity in willing, only by the fact that the laws according to which the psyche then behaves *do not become apparent* [are not set before it][27] as such, and since they encounter no resistance, never appear as a constraint. (AL 146)

Let us dwell for a moment upon this passage. Unlike the genealogy traced by Agamben and Esposito, where the term *dispositif* is associated with that of *Gestell* (from the German verb *stellen*),[28] Schiller doesn't seem to create a necessary link between the aesthetic disposition and *vorstellen*. This move allows us to refer to the term *dispositif* in another way. The word he chooses to express the idea of disposition is *Stimmung* not *stellen*. From this perspective, *dispositif* does not refer to a given position or imposition (*stellen*), and to a much lesser extent to a repetition of something previously given (*vorstellen*). It rather refers to a state of mind or to the way we determine our way of being (*Stimmung*) (see AL 147–48). It makes visible, therefore, the dual and intertwined operation of reason and sensibility. Furthermore, the distinctive feature of the aesthetic disposition is that it is free from imposition. The aesthetic disposition is not the representation (*Vorstellung*) of something given *a priori*, but rather the presentation (*Darstellung*) of a disposition or state of mind for acting in the world.[29] That is to say, the aesthetic disposition, by not re-presenting itself, by not reiterating itself as a mechanism of repetition of the given, problematizes the area of re-presentation that other types of disposition simply take for granted:

> Our psyche passes, then, from sensation to thought via a middle disposition in which sense and reason are both active *at the same time*. Precisely for this reason, however, they cancel each other out as determining forces, and bring about a negation by means of an opposition, This middle disposition, in which the psyche is subject neither to physical nor to moral constraint, and yet is active in both these ways, preeminently deserves to be called a free disposition; and if we are to call the condition of sensuous determination the physical, and the condition of rational determination the logical or moral, then we must call this condition of real and active determinability the *aesthetic*. (AL 144 45)

From this perspective, a *dispositif* functions less as an ensnaring web than as a sensible experience produced by the articulation of different ways of seeing, saying, and thinking. It is not so much a way of escaping from *dispositifs* and returning to a space of anomie of the living being, i.e., an originary space. It is much more a way of examining the different types of sensible experience that produce *dispositifs*. In other words, the aesthetic disposition, by not re-presenting, by not reiterating itself as a means of repetition of the given, examines the sphere of re-presentation that other types of disposition take for granted. While from the perspective of understanding, denounced by Schiller throughout the *Aesthetic Letters*, the legal disposition or the moral disposition tend to impose the realm of representation, i.e., a reification of positive society, the aesthetic disposition tends to set this same process in motion. And this is made possible through the notions of play-drive and the appearance game. Schiller writes:

> The dynamic state can merely make society possible, by letting one nature be curbed by another; the ethical state can merely make it (morally) necessary, by subjecting the individual will to the general; the aesthetic state alone can make it real, because it consummates the will of the whole through the nature of the individual. Though it may be his needs that drive man into society, and reason that implants within him the principles of social behavior, beauty alone can confer upon him a *social character* [*geselligen Charakter*]. (AL 176)

However, this aesthetic disposition does not function as an alternative that must eliminate the others. On the contrary, it operates together with them, opening up the game of politics. The aesthetic disposition makes it possible to see law and morals as spheres that are necessary, but which can set its principles in motion. Vis-à-vis the abstract *dispositif of understanding* that seems to reign in the epoch of the Enlightenment, Schiller juxtaposes the *aesthetic dispositif*, understood as another type of disposition toward that which exists. It is the distance that the aesthetic dispositif establishes with respect to the field of representation that allows for a repolitization of what is presented as given. In other words, the aesthetic dispositif deactivates the reification function of positive society and gives us a dialectical *image* of it in return. By making visible the field of forces in dispute that are configuring the fragile present, that which exists ceases to be the crushing weight of a dead tradition and a reality organized on the bases of that same rigid past.

IV.

The split Schiller poses between sensibility and understanding is also characterized as a split between form and life. This reminds us of the problem raised by Agamben and Esposito regarding the role of *dispositifs*—which is to produce a division that establishes a dominant relation of politics over life. As we have shown in previous sections, the alternative proposed by both thinkers was to examine the origin of this schism, showing how it gave rise to the relations of power that have shackled the Western world. However, if we consider the way Schiller explains this split, we can see that it does not necessarily produce a form of domination. In Schiller, this contraposition between life and form is presented as the relationship between two opposite drives or demands, namely, a formal demand determined through laws and a sensible demand determined as material life. As two opposite drives, one tends to annul or dominate the other, but they also need each other at the same time, since "as long as we merely think about his form, it is lifeless, a mere abstraction; as long as we merely feel his life, it is formless, a mere impression" (AL 128). The affirmation of these two drives as a living form does not imply a reconciliation that risks making the conflict between the two invisible. It also does not necessarily establish a relation of domination of one over the other. Living form is rather the result of an ongoing conflictual tension between the two drives.

Meanwhile, the play-drive also escapes the logic of sacrificing one part for the other. This, as we saw, was another risk entailed in Agamben and Esposito's accounts of *dispositifs*. In Schiller, however, the play-drive is not based on a sacrifice of life as the only mechanism for its own preservation. The contradictory relationship between the drives is not, in Schiller's case, the finished expression of a contradiction between preexisting elements, each of which is identical to itself and opposed to the other (form vs. life). If we were to follow this logic, we would indeed have to think in terms of sacrifice. Furthermore Schiller criticizes this form of opposition as one resulting exclusively from the formal violence of understanding. The kind of antagonistic relationship Schiller wants to propose has to do with the affirmative difference that results from a mediation process between life and form. He writes: "Only when his form lives in our feeling and his life takes on form in our understanding, does he become living form" (AL 128). Or, again, "his form would have to be life, and his life form" (AL 128). The relationship of opposition between the drives is thus impure, and cannot be thought as an "uncontaminated" and "unproblematic" relation. The opposition is not merely one between opposite determinations in something that is external to them as their foundation, but rather the conflict itself. It is the movement between the two opposite drives that gives rise to the play between life and form. If Schiller shows us anything, it is that the conflictual aspect that produces this split opens up the game of politics. As Foucault reminds us, there is a substantial difference between relations of power and relations of domination. In relations of power, the game is always open since the conflict is made explicit and spaces of negotiation and transformation are left open also as a result. In relations of domination, however, there is almost no margin for action and the links become stratified. Thus the point is not so much about deducing that there is a will to dominate behind every split, an acute consciousness that points to the fact that behind every split there is a will to dominate, but rather *to pose a different way of conceiving opposition*, which is something that the living form permits. If the genealogy traced by Agamben and Esposito is characterized by making the notion of *dispositif* coincide with that of the German term *Gestell*, the genealogical proposal based on Schiller's texts places us in the opposite position. Not only because it is possible to speak of different types of *dispositifs* or *dispositions* toward that which exists, but also because the aesthetic *dispositif* involves a type of disposition that examines and transforms the organizational mode that results from the instrumental rationality of understanding. Thus, the aesthetic notion or approach to the questions of *dispositifs* as developed by Schiller enables us to draw up a genealogy regarding the problem of positivity and sensibility in a different direction from that developed by Adorno: a genealogy that allows us to build new bridges for exploring the question of *dispositifs* in the configuration of contemporary sensibilities.

Notes

1. Hyppolite studied the role of positivity in the writings of the young Hegel, and was reading them in light of the dialectics between history and reason. This permitted him to speak of positivity as a historic element that acts on the rational development of men. It is thanks to this historic element that reason loses its abstract character and is concretely incorporated into the lives of men. While Agamben very lucidly manages to establish this subterranean link between Hegel and Foucault by discovering a common matrix (i.e., the link between power and life), it is remarkable that—instead of taking this double dimension of positivity into consideration—he preferred to limit it to the pejorative pole. Thus, the link between the historic element (positivity) and men (living beings) would be understood as a form of domination of one over the other, but only by overlooking the affirmative pole.

2. For more information about the link between *episteme* and *dispositif*, see the following texts: Judith Revel, *Le vocabulaire de Foucault* (Paris: Ellipses, 2002), 24-25; and Sandro Ghignola, "Sobre o dispositivo. Foucault, Agamben, Deleuze," *Cuadernos IHU Ideias* 12 (2014): 3-24.

3. We are referring here to *Les mots et les choses. Une archéologie des sciences humaines* (Paris: Gallimard, 1966) and *L'archéologie du savoir* (Paris: Gallimard, 1969).

4. The text where Foucault deals most systematically with the concept of *dispositif* is *Histoire de la sexualité. La volonté de savoir Vol. I* (Paris: Gallimard, 1976). He also made an effort to define the concept in an interview titled "Michel Foucault's game" in which he stated that *dispositifs* are considered: (a) heterogeneous sets; (b) links among these heterogeneities; (c) a strategic function of said links. See: Michale Foucault "El juego de Michel Foucault" in *Saber y verdad* (Madrid: La Piqueta, 1985), 127-62.

5. Giorgio Agamben, *Che cos'è un dispositivo?* (Roma: Nottetempo, 2006). See in English "What is an Apparatus" in *What is an Apparatus? and other Essays*, trans. David Kishik and Stefan Pedatella (Sanford, CA: Stanford University Press, 2009) 1-24.

6. For a better development of the implications of this approach proposed by Agamben and a possible alternative to the link between positivity and *dispositif*, see: Luciana Cadahia, "¿Espiritualización de la zoé y biologización del espíritu?: bíos y positividad en la historia," *Bajo palabra* 7 (2012): 325-35.

7. Jean Hyppolite, *Introduction à la philosophie de l'histoire de Hegel* (Paris: Seuil, 1983), 46.

8. Roberto Esposito, *Due. La macchina della teología política e il posto del pensiero* (Einaudi: Torino, 2013).

9. For further reference regarding my research on Agamben's and Esposito's use of the term *dispositif*, see: Luciana Cadahia, "Hacia una nueva crítica del dispositivo," *Revista Internacional de Filosofía Iberoamericana y Teoría Social: Utopía y Praxis* 66 (2014): 95-108.

10. While these two issues were first raised by Agamben in *Homo sacer I*, he returned to them time and again in the different volumes of the *Homo sacer* saga.

11. TIQQUN, "Podría surgir una metafísica crítica como ciencia de los dispositivos," in *Contribución a la guerra en curso* (Madrid: Errata Naturae, 2012), 27–118.

12. TIQQUN, "Podría surgir una metafísica crítica," 101.

13. Gilles Deleuze, "Qué es un dispositivo," in *Contribución a la guerra en curso* (Madrid: Errata Naturae, 2012), 16.

14. Ibid., 21.

15. This essay was prepared for the international colloquium on the philosophy of Michel Foucault, organized in 1988 by the *Association pour le centre Michel Foucault*, which was then in charge of collecting the philosopher's unpublished texts and promoting the publication of the lecture courses he had given at the *Collège de France*.

16. See Jesús Martín-Barbero, *De los medios a las mediaciones. Comunicación, cultura y hegemonía* (Mexico: Gili, 1991), 61.

17. Ibid., 47.

18. Ibid., 55.

19. Ibid., 56.

20. See ibid., 56–57.

21. Ibid., 58.

22. "On the Aesthetic Education of Man," trans. Elizabeth M. Wilkinson and L. A. Willoughby (1976), repr. in *Friedrich Schiller: Essays*, ed. Walter Hinderer and Daniel Dahlstrom (New York: Continuum, 2001), 101. Following referred to as AL.

23. See Paul De Man, *The Rhetoric of Romanticism* (New York: Columbia University Press, 1984), 289.

24. The English translation uses the verb *destroy* for the expression *aufgehoben*, but this is not really appropriate since it fails to convey the twofold idea of conserving and cancelling contained in the original German. We use here "overcoming" as an alternative, abet also not an ideal one.

25. Georg Wilhelm Friedrich Hegel, *Escritos de juventud* (Mexico: FCE, 2003), 219. Even though the attribution of the *Älteste Systemprogram* fragment to Hegel remains problematic, I am confident that at least the position exhibited there is coherent with Hegel's early writings. The text has been published in Spanish always in connection to Hegel's writings.

26. María Acosta has also developed how close Schiller and Hegel are on this point and in relation to a particular notion of reason and its historical consequences. See her text in this volume on both authors' criticisms to the French Revolution.

27. The translator has used the word "apparent," but we prefer the translation "set before itself."

28. See Roberto Esposito, *Due. La Macchina della teologia politica*, 18–24; Giorgio Agamben, *El Reino y la Gloria. Por una genealogía teológica de la economía y del gobierno* (Valencia: Pre-Textos, 2008), 271–72.

29. See Martha B. Helfer, *The Retreat of Representation. The Concept of Darstellung in German Critical Discourse* (Albany, NY: State University of New York Press, 1996), 128.

Friedrich Schiller's Works Cited

ÄB   "Über die ästhetische Erziehung des Menschen in einer Reihe von Briefen," in *Schillers Werke: Nationalausgabe*, i.A. des Goethe und Schiller-Archivs, des Schiller-Nationalmuseums und der Deutschen Akademie, ed. Julius Petersen et al. (Weimar: Herrman Böhlaus Nachfolger, 1943–2010), vol. 20: Philosophische Schriften 1, 309–412.

AL   "On the Aesthetic Education of Man," trans. Elizabeth M. Wilkinson and L. A. Willoughby (1976), repr. in *Friedrich Schiller: Essays*, ed. Walter Hinderer and Daniel Dahlstrom (New York: Continuum, 2001), 86–178.

AuW   "Über Anmuth und Würde," in *Schillers Werke: Nationalausgabe*, i.A. des Goethe und Schiller-Archivs, des Schiller-Nationalmuseums und der Deutschen Akademie, ed. Julius Petersen et al. (Weimar: Hermann Böhlaus Nachfolger, 1943–2010), vol. 20/1: Philosophische Schriften 1, 251–308.

GD   "On Grace and Dignity," trans. Jane V. Curran in *Schiller's "On Grace and Dignity" in Its Cultural Context*, eds. Jane V. Curran and Christophe Fricker (Rochester, NY: Camden House, 2005), 123–70.

CS   "Concerning the Sublime," trans. Daniel Dahlstrom, in *Friedrich Schiller: Essays*, ed. Walter Hinderer and Daniel Dahlstrom (New York: Continuum, 2001), 70–85.

KB   "Kallias oder über die Schönheit," in *Schillers Werke: Nationalausgabe*, i.A. des Goethe und Schiller-Archivs, des Schiller-Nationalmuseums und der Deutschen Akademie, ed. Julius Petersen et al. (Weimar: Herrman Böhlaus Nachfolger, 1943, 2010), vol. 26, scattered among letters to Körner.

KL "*Kallias* or Concerning Beauty: Letters to Gottfried Körner," in *Classic and Romantics German Aesthetics*, ed. Jay M. Bernstein (Cambridge: Cambridge University Press, 2003): 145–84.

NA *Schillers Werke: Nationalausgabe*, i.A. des Goethe und Schiller-Archivs, des Schiller-Nationalmuseums und und der Deutschen Akademie, ed. Julius Petersen et al. (Weimar: Herrman Böhlaus Nachfolger, 1943, 2010)

NSD "Über naïve und sentimentalische Dichtung," in *Schillers Werke: Nationalausgabe*, i.A. des Goethe und Schiller-Archivs, des Schiller-Nationalmuseums und der Deutschen Akademie, ed. Julius Petersen et al. (Weimar: Herrman Böhlaus Nachfolger, 1943, 2010), Band 20, hrsg. Benno von Wiese (Weimar: Böhlau, 1962):

NSP "On Naive and Sentimental Poetry," trans. Daniel Dahlstrom, in *Friedrich Schiller: Essays*, ed. Walter Hinderer and Daniel Dahlstrom (New York: Continuum, 2001): 179–260.

Bibliography

Primary Sources

Schiller, Friedrich. "Concerning the Sublime," trans. Daniel Dahlstrom, in *Friedrich Schiller: Essays*, ed. Walter Hinderer and Daniel Dahlstrom (New York: Continuum, 2001), 70-85.

Schiller, Friedrich. "Connection between Animal and Spiritual Nature in Man." In Schiller, *Nationalausgabe*, 37-75.

Schiller, Friedrich. "Don Carlos, Infant von Spanien," in *Sämtliche Werke*, Bd. 2, eds. Gerhard Fricke, Herbert G. Göpfert (München: Bertelsman, 1981).

Schiller, Friedrich. "Kallias oder über die Schönheit," in *Schillers Werke: Nationalausgabe*, i.A. des Goethe und Schiller-Archivs, des Schiller-Nationalmuseums und der Deutschen Akademie, ed. Julius Petersen et al. (Weimar: Herrman Böhlaus Nachfolger, 1943-2010), vol. 26, scattered among letters to Körner.

Schiller, Friedrich, "Kallias, oder Über doe Schönheit," in *Theoretische Schriften*, ed. Rolf-Peter Janz (Frankfurt am Main: Deutscher Klassiker Verlag, 2008).

Schiller, Friedrich. "*Kallias* or Concerning Beauty: Letters to Gottfried Körner," in *Classic and Romantics German Aesthetics*, ed. Jay M. Bernstein (Cambridge: Cambridge University Press, 2003): 145-84.

Schiller, Friedrich. *Kallias; Cartas sobre la educación estética del hombre*, trans. Jaime Feijoo (Bilingual edition), Anthropos: Barcelona, 1997.

Schiller, Friedrich. *Nationalausgabe*, eds. Helmut Koopman and Benno von Wiese. Weimar: Böhlaus, 1962.

Schiller, Friedrich. "On the Aesthetic Education of Man," trans. Elizabeth M. Wilkinson and L. A. Willoughby (1976), repr. in *Friedrich Schiller: Essays*, ed. Walter Hinderer and Daniel Dahlstrom (New York: Continuum, 2001), 86–178.

Schiller, Friedrich. "On Grace and Dignity," trans. Jane V. Curran in *Schiller's "On Grace and Dignity" in Its Cultural Context*, eds. Jane V. Curran and Christophe Fricker (Rochester, NY: Camden House, 2005), 123-70.

Schiller, Friedrich. "On Naive and Sentimental Poetry," trans. Daniel Dahlstrom, in *Friedrich Schiller: Essays*, ed. Walter Hinderer and Daniel Dahlstrom (New York: Continuum, 2001): 179–260.

Schiller, Friedrich, "*Die Polizei*." In Schiller, *Sämtliche Werke*, eds. Gerhard Fricke, and Herbert G. Göpfert. München: Bertelsman, 1981, Bd. 3.

Schiller, Friedrich. *Sämtliche Werke*. Edited by Gerhard Fricke and Herbert G. Göpfert. München: Bertelsman, 1981.

Schiller, Friedrich. *Schillers Werke: Nationalausgabe*, i.A. des Goethe und Schiller-Archivs, des Schiller-Nationalmuseums und und der Deutschen Akademie, ed. Julius Petersen et al. (Weimar: Herrman Böhlaus Nachfolger, 1943–2010).

Schiller, Friedrich. *Theoretische Schriften*. Edited by Rolf-Peter Janz with assistance from Hans Richard Brittmacher, Gerd Kleiner, and Fabian Störmer. Frankfurt: Deutscher Klassiker Verlag, 1992.

Schiller, Friedrich. "Über Anmuth und Würde," in *Schillers Werke: Nationalausgabe*, i.A. des Goethe und Schiller-Archivs, des Schiller-Nationalmuseums und der Deutschen Akademie, ed. Julius Petersen et al. (Weimar: Hermann Böhlaus Nachfolger, 1943–2010), vol. 20/1: Philosophische Schriften 1, 251–308.

Schiller, Friedrich, "Über Anmut und Würde." In Schiller, *Theoretische Schriften*, Edited by Rolf-Peter Janz with assistance from Hans Richard Brittmacher, Gerd Kleiner, and Fabian Störmer. Frankfurt: Deutscher Klassiker Verlag, 1992.

Schiller, Friedrich, "Über die ästhetische Erziehung des Menschen in einer Reihe von Briefen," in *Schillers Werke: Nationalausgabe*, i.A. des Goethe und Schiller-Archivs, des Schiller-Nationalmuseums und der Deutschen Akademie, ed. Julius Petersen et al. (Weimar: Herrman Böhlaus Nachfolger, 1943–2010), vol. 20: Philosophische Schriften 1, 309–412.

Schiller, Friedrich. "Über die ästhetische Erziehung des Menschen in einer Reihe von Briefen," in Schiller, *Sämtliche Werke*. Edited by Gerhard Fricke and Herbert G. Göpfert. München: Bertelsman, 1981.

Schiller, Friedrich. "Über die Ästhetische Erziehung des Menschen in einer Reihe von Briefen." In Schiller, *Theoretische Schriften*, 635–36.

Schiller, Friedrich. "Über naïve und sentimentalische Dichtung." In *Schillers Werke: Nationalausgabe*, i.A. des Goethe und Schiller-Archivs, des Schiller-Nationalmuseums und der Deutschen Akademie, ed. Julius Petersen et al. (Weimar: Herrman Böhlaus Nachfolger, 1943–2010), Band 20, hrsg. Benno von Wiese (Weimar: Böhlau, 1962).

Schiller, Friedrich. "Über die notwendigen Grenzen beim Gebrauch Schönen Formen." In Schiller, *Werke: Nationalausgabe*, V. 21: 3–27.

Schiller, Friedrich, "Über Matthissons Gedichte." In Schiller, *Theoretische Schriften*, ed. Rolf-Peter Janz (Frankfurt am Main: Deutscher Klassiker Verlag, 2008).

Schiller, Friedrich. "Aus Vorlesungen zur Ästhetik." In Schiller *Theoretische Schriften*, ed. Rolf-Peter Janz (Frankfurt am Main: Deutscher Klassiker Verlag, 2008).

Schiller, Friedrich. *Werke und Briefe in zwölf Bänden*. Edited by Otto Dann et al. Frankfurt/Main: Suhrkamp, 1988–2004.

Other Sources

Acosta, María del Rosario, "On the Poetical Nature of Philosophical Writing: A Controversy over Style between Schiller and Fichte." In *Philosophy and its Poets*, eds. Charles Bambach and Theodore George. Albany, NY: State University of New York Press, forthcoming.
Acosta, María del Rosario. *Narrativas de la comunidad: de Hegel a los pensadores impolíticos*. Madrid: Abada, forthcoming.
Acosta, María del Rosario, "La violencia de la razón: Schiller y Hegel sobre la Revolución Francesa," *Philosophical Readings*, 9:2 (2017): 141–50.
Acosta, María del Rosario, "Banquo's Ghost: Hegel on Law, Violence and Memory." *New Centennial Review* 14, no. 2 (2014): 29–48.
Acosta, María del Rosario, "Making Other People's Feelings our Own: From the Aesthetic to the Political in Schiller's *Aesthetic Letters*." In High, Martin, and Oellers, *Who is this Schiller now?* 187–203.
Acosta, María del Rosario, ed. *Friedrich Schiller: estética y libertad*. Bogotá: Universidad Nacional de Colombia. Facultad de Ciencias Humanas, 2008.
Acosta, María del Rosario. *La tragedia como conjuro: el problema de lo sublime en Friedrich Schiller* Bogotá: Universidad de los Andes and Universidad Nacional de Colombia, 2008.
Acosta, María del Rosario, "¿Una superación estética del deber? La crítica de Schiller a Kant." *Episteme* 28, no. 2 (2008): 1–24; 5n.
Adorno, Theodor et al. *Aesthetics and Politics*. Brooklyn, NY: Verso, 2007.
Adorno, Theodor. *Mahler: A Musical Physiognomy*. Translated by Edmund Jephcott. Chicago: University of Chicago Press, 1992.
Adorno, Theodor, ""Paralipomena." In *Aesthetic Theory*, edited and translated by Robert Hullot-Kentor, 274–75. Minneapolis: University of Minnesota Press, 1997.
Agamben, Giorgio. *Che cos'è un dispositivo?* Rome: Nottetempo, 2006.
Agamben, Giorgio. *El Reino y la Gloria. Por una genealogía teológica de la economía y del gobierno*. Valencia: Pre-Textos, 2008.
Agamben, Giorgio *Homo sacer I. El poder soberano y la nuda vida*. Valencia: Pre-Textos, 2003.
Agamben, Giorgio. *Means Without End: Notes on Politics*. Translated by Vincenzo Benetti and Cesare Casarino. Minneapolis: University of Minnesota Press, 2000.
Agamben, Giorgio. *What is an Apparatus? and other Essays*. Translated by David Kishik and Stefan Pedatella. Stanford, CA: Stanford University Press, 2009.
Agamben, Giorgio. *L'uso dei corpi*. Milan: Neri Pozza, 2014.

Babel, Reinhardt, and Horst Nitschack. *La actualidad de Friedrich Schiller. Para una crítica cultural al inicio del siglo XXI*. Santiago: LOM, 2010.
Bahnsen, Julius. *Schiller. Eine Gedächtnissrede gehalten den 10ten November 1859 im Gymnasium zu Anclam*. Anclam: Fr. Krüger, 1859.
Bahnsen, Julius. *Das Tragische als Weltgesetz und der Humor als ästhetische Gestalt des Metaphysischen*. Lauenberg: F. Ferley, 1877.
Baxley, Ann Margaret. *Kant's Theory of Virtue. The Value of Autocracy*. Cambridge: Cambridge University Press, 2010.
Beiser, Frederick. "Un lamento: sobre la actualidad del pensamiento de Schiller." In *Friedrich Schiller: estética y libertad*. Edited by María del Rosario Acosta, 131–51. Bogota: Universidad Nacional de Colombia, 2008.
Beiser, Frederick. *Schiller as Philosopher. A Re-Examination*. Oxford: Oxford University Press, 2005.
Benjamin, Walter. "Conversations with Brecht." Translated by Anya Bostock. In *Aesthetics and Politics*, edited by Ernst Bloch, 86–96. New York: Verso, 1980.
Benjamin, Walter. "The Little History of Photography." Vol. 2, part 2, *Selected Writings*. Edited by Michael W. Jennings, Howard Eiland, and Gary Smith, translated by Edmund Jephcott and Kingsley Shorter. Cambridge, MA: Harvard University Press, 1999.
Benjamin, Walter. *The Origin of German Tragic Drama*. Translated by John Osborne. New York: Verso, 1998.
Benjamin, Walter. "The Work of Art in the Age of Its Technological Reproducibility." In *Selected Writings: 1935–1938*, Vol. 3. Edited by Michael W. Jennings and Howard Eiland, translated by Edmund Jephcott and Harry Zohn. Cambridge, MA: Harvard University Press, 2002.
Bollenbeck, Georg, and Lothas Ehrlich, eds. *Friedrich Schiller. Der unterschätzte Theoretiker*. Köln: Böhlau, 2007.
Burke, Edmund. *Reflections on the Revolution in France, and on the Proceedings of Certain Societies in London Relative to That Event. In a Letter Intended to Have Been Sent to a Gentleman in Paris*. London, 1791. Reprinted as *Reflections on the Revolution in France*. New York: Oxford University Press, 1999.
Burtscher, Cordula. "*Die gesunde und schöne Natur braucht [. . .] keine Gottheit*. Schillers Weg von der Religionskritik zur Ästhetik," in *Schiller im philosophischen Kontext*, Würzburg: Königshausen & Neumann, 2011.
Burtscher, Cordula. *Glaube und Furcht. Religion und Religionskritik bei Schiller*. Würzburg: Königshausen & Neumann, 2014.
Burtscher Cordula, and Markus Hien, eds., *Schiller im philosophischen Kontext*. Würzburg: Königshausen & Neumann, 2011.
Cadahia, Luciana. "¿Espiritualización de la zoé y biologización del espíritu?: bíos y positividad en la historia." *Bajo palabra* 7 (2012): 325–35.
Cadahia, Luciana. "Hacia una nueva crítica del dispositivo." *Revista Internacional de Filosofía Iberoamericana y Teoría Social: Utopía y Praxis* 66 (2014): 95–108.

Chignola, Sandro. "Sobre o dispositivo. Foucault, Agamben, Deleuze," *Cuadernos IHU Ideias* 12 (2014): 3-24.
Comay, Rebecca. "Dead Right: Hegel and the Terror." *The South Atlantic Quarterly* 103, no. 2/3 (2004): 375-95.
Comay, Rebecca. *Mourning Sickness*. Stanford, CA: Stanford University Press, 2010.
Cramer, Konrad. *Nicht-reine synthetische Urteile a priori der Transzendentalphilosophie Immanuel Kants*. Heidelberg: Carl Winter, 1985.
Darras, Giles. *L'âme suspecte. L'anthropologie littéraire dans les premiers oeuvres de Schiller*. Paris: Editions Connaissances et Savoirs, 2005.
De Certeau, Michel. *La invención de lo cotidiano*. México DF: Universidad Iberoamericana, 2000.
Dehrmann, Mark-Georg. "*Moralische Empfindung, Vernunft, Offenbarung. Das Problem der Moralbegründung bei Gellert, Spalding, Chladenius und Mendelssohn.*" In *Gellert und die empfindsame Aufklärung. Vermittlungs-, Austausch- und Rezeptionsprozesse in Wissenschaft, Kunst und Kultur*, edited by S. Schönborn and V. Viehöver, 53-65. Berlin: Schmidt Verlag, 2009.
Deleuze, Gilles. "Qué es un dispositivo." In *Contribución a la guerra en curso*. Madrid: Errata Naturae, 2012.
Deligiorgi, Katerina. "The Proper Telos of Life: Schiller, Kant and Having Autonomy as an End." *Inquiry*, 5:54 (2011): 494-511.
De Man, Paul. "Kant and Schiller." In *The Aesthetic Ideology*, edited Andrzej Warminski, 129-62. Minneapolis: University of Minneapolis Press, 1996.
De Man, Paul. *The Rhetoric of Romanticism*. New York: Columbia University Press, 1984.
Derrida, Jacques. *Marges de la philosophie*. Paris: Les editions de minuit, 1972.
D'Hondt, Jacques. *Hegel: Biographie*. Paris: Calmann-Lévy, 1998.
Düttmann, Alexander Garcia. "Language and Destruction." In *Walter Benjamin's Philosophy: Destruction and Experience*, edited by Andrew Benjamin. New York: Routledge, 2013, 32-58.
Eiland, Howard, and Michael W. Jennings. *Walter Benjamin: A Critical Life*. Cambridge, MA: Harvard University Press, 2014.
Esposito, Roberto. *Due. La macchina della teología política e il posto del pensiero*. Torino: Einaudi, 2013.
Esposito, Roberto. *El dispositivo de la Persona*. Madrid-Buenos Aires: Amorrortu, 2011.
Esposito, Roberto. *Terza Persona. Politica della vita e filosofia dell impersonale*. Torino: Einaudi, 2007.
Fenves, Peter "Is There an Answer to the Aestheticizing of the Political?" In *Walter Benjamin and Art*, edited by Andrew Benjamin, 60-72. New York: Bloomsbury, 2005.
Fichte, Johann Gottlieb. "Einige Vorlesungen über die Bestimmung des Gelehrten." In *Werke*, edited by Immanuel Hermann Fichte. Berlin: Theater der Zeit, 1971.
Fichte, Johann Gottlieb, "Some Lectures Concerning the Scholar's Vocation." In *Early Philosophical Writings*, translated by D. Breazeale. Ithaca, NY: Cornell, 1988, 137-84.

Foucault, Michael. *L'archéologie du savoir*. Paris: Gallimard, 1969.
Foucault, Michael. *Les mots et les choses. Une archéologie des sciences humaines*. Paris: Gallimard, 1966.
Foucault, Michael. "El juego de Michel Foucault" in *Saber y verdad*, 127–62. Madrid: La Piqueta, 1985.
Foucault, Michael. *Histoire de la sexualité. La volonté de savoir Vol. I*. Paris: Gallimard, 1976.
Frauenstädt, Julius. *Aesthetische Fragen*. Dessau: Gebrüder Katz, 1853.
Gadamer, Hans-Georg. *Truth and Method*. London: Continuum, 1975.
Gadamer, Hans-George. *Truth and Method*. Translated by J. Weinsheimer and D. G. Marshall. New York: Crossroad, 1989.
Gadamer, Hans Georg., *Wahrheit und Methode: Grundzüge einer philosophischen Hermeneutik*, 2nd revised ed. Tübingen: Mohr-Siebeck, 1965.
Ghignola, Sandro. "Sobre o dispositivo. Foucault, Agamben, Deleuze." *Cuadernos IHU Ideias* 12 (2014): 3–24.
Griffin, Martin. *Latitudinarianism in the Seventeenth-Century Church of England*. Annotated by R. H. Popkin. Edited by L. Freedman. Leiden: Brill, 1992.
Goethe, Johann Wolfgang. "Einfache Nachahmung der Natur, Manier, Stil." Edited by Christian Beutler. In *Gedenkausgabe der Werke, Briefe und Gespräche*. Zürich: Artemis, 1954, 13: 66–71.
Goethe, Johann Wolfgang. *Gedenkausgabe der Werke, Briefe und Gespräche*, Vol. 24. Edited by Ernst Beutler. Zürich: Artemis, 1948.
Guyer, Paul. *Kant and the Claims of Taste*. Cambridge, MA: Harvard University Press, 1979.
Hamburger, K. "Schillers Fragment 'Der Menschenfeind' und die Idee der Kalokagathie." *Deutsche Vierteljahrsschrift für Literaturwissenschaft und Geistesgeschichte*, no. 30 (1956): 367–400.
Hardt Michael. "The Common in Communism." In *The Idea of Communism*, edited by Costas Douzinas and Slavoj Žižek, 131–44. New York: Verso, 2010.
Harris, H. S. *Hegel's Development: Toward the Sunlight 1770–1801*. New York: Oxford University Press, 1972.
Hart, Gail K. *Friedrich Schiller: Crime, Aesthetics, and the Poetics of Punishment*. Cranbury, NJ: Rosemont, 2005.
Hegel, Georg Wilhelm Friedrich. *Ästhetik*. Edited by Friedrich Basssenge with introductory essay by Georg Lukács. Berlin: Aufbau-Verlag, 1955.
Hegel, Georg Wilhelm Fredrich. *Early Theological Writings*. Translated by T. M. Knox. New York: Harper, 1961.
Hegel, Georg Wilhelm Friedrich. *Escritos de juventud*. México DF: FCE, 2003.
Hegel, Georg Wilhelm Friedrich. *Elements of the Philosophy of Right*. Edited by Allen W. Wood, translated by H. B. Nisbet. New York: Cambridge University Press, 1991.
Hegel, Georg Wilhelm Friedrich. *Escritos de Juventud*. Madrid: FCE, 2003.

Hegel, Georg Wilhelm Friedrich. *Hegels theologische Jugendschriften*, ed. Hermann Nohl. (J. C. B. Mohr: Tübingen, 1907).
Hegel, Georg Wilhelm Friedrich. *Phenomenology of Spirit.* Translated by Terry Pinkard. New York: Cambridge University Press, 2018.
Hegel, Georg Wilhelm Friedrich. "The Spirit of Christianity and its Fate" (1798). In *Early Theological Writings.*
Hegel, Georg Wilhelm Friedrich. *Werke.* Edited by Eva Moldenhauer and Karl Markus Michel. Frankfurt/Main: Suhrkamp, 1979.
Heidegger, Martin. *Kant and the Problem of Metaphysics.* Translated by Richard Taft. Bloomington: Indiana University Press, 1990.
Heidegger, Martin. *Sein und Zeit.* Tübingen: Niemeyer, 1972.
Heinz, Jutta. "*Philosophischpoetische Visionen Schiller als philosophischer Dilettant.*" In *Dilettantismus um 1800,* edited by. S. Blechschmidt and A. Heinz, 185-2014. Heidelberg: Winter Verlag, 2007.
Helfer, Martha B. *The Retreat of Representation. The Concept of Darstellung in German Critical Discourse.* Albany, NY: SUNY Press, 1996.
Henrich, Dieter. "Der Begriff der Schönheit in Schillers Ästhetik" in *Zeitschrift für philosophische Forschung* (Frankfurt am Main: Vittorio Klosterman, 1957), VI: 527-47.
High, Jeffrey Nicholas Martin, and Norbert Oellers, eds. *Who is this Schiller now?* London: Camden House, 2011.
High, Jeffrey. *Schillers Rebellionskonzept und die Französische Revolution* (Lewiston–Queenston–Lampeter: Mellen, 2004).
Hinderer, Walter, and Daniel Dahlstrom, eds. *Friedrich Schiller: Essays.* Translated by Daniel Dahlstrom. New York: Continuum, 2001.
Hölderlin, Friedrich. "Farewell." In *Poems and Fragments,* translated by Michael Hamburger. London: Anvil Press Poetry Ltd., 2004.
Husserl, Edumund. *Ideas I.* Translated by Daniel O. Dahlstrom. Indianapolis, IN: Hackett Publishing Co., 2014.
Hyppolite, Jean. *Introduction à la philosophie de l'histoire de Hegel.* Paris: Seuil, 1983.
Jirku, B. E., and J. Rodríguez Gonzáles, eds. *El pensamiento filosófico de Friedrich Schiller.* Valencia: Universitat de València, 2009.
Jones, M. T. "Schiller Trouble: The Tottering Legacy of German Aesthetic Humanism." *Goethe-Yearbook,* 10 (2001): 222-45.
Kant, Immanuel. *Critique of Judgment.* Translated by Werner S. Pluhar. Indianapolis, IN: Hackett Publishing Co., 1987.
Kant, Immanuel. *Critique of the Power of Judgment.* Translated by Paul Guyer and Eric Matthews. Cambridge: Cambridge University Press, 2000, 2001.
Kant, Immanuel. *Critique of Practical Reason.* Edited by. M. Gregor. Introduction by A. Reath. Cambridge: Cambridge University Press, 1997.
Kant, Immanuel. *Critique of Pure Reason.* Translated by Norman Kemp Smith. New York: Palgrave Macmillan, 2007.

Kant, Immanuel. *Kritik der Urteilskraft.* Hamburg: Meiner, 1974, 1993.
Kant, Immanuel. *Kritik der Urteilskraft.* Edited by Wilhelm Weischedel. Frankfurt: Suhrkamp, 1996.
Kant, Immanuel. *The Metaphysics of Morals.* Edited by M. Gregor. Introduction by R. J. Sullivan. Cambridge: Cambridge University Press, 1996.
Kant, Immanuel. *On History.* Edited and translated by Lewis White Beck. Indianapolis, IN: Bobbs-Merrill Company, Inc., 1963.
Kant, Immanuel. "Perpetual Peace." In *On History*, edited and translated by Lewis White Beck. Indianapolis, IN: Bobbs-Merrill Company, Inc., 1963.
Kant, Immanuel. "Die Religion innerhalb der Grenzen der blossen Vernunft." In *Gesammelte Schriften*, edited by the *Königlich Preußische Akademie der Wissenschaften*. Berlin: de Gruyter, VI.
Kant, Immanuel. *Religion within the Boundaries of Mere Reason and Other Writings.* Translated and edited by A. Wood and G. di Giovanni. Cambridge: Cambridge University Press, 1998.
Kaufman, Robert. "Aura Still." In *Walter Benjamin and Art*, edited by Andrew Benjamin, 121–47. New York: Continuum, 2005.
Krell, David Farrell. *The Tragic Absolute: German Idealism and the Languishing God.* Bloomington: Indiana University Press, 2005.
Kulenkampf, Jens. *Materialien zu Kants "Kritik der Urteilskraft."* Frankfurt: Suhrkamp, 1974.
Lacoue-Labarthe, Phillipe, and Jean-Luc Nancy. *The Literary Absolute.* Translated by Philip Barnard and Cheryl Lester. Albany: SUNY Press, 1998.
Lacoue-Labarthe, Philippe and Jean-Luc Nancy. "The Nazi Myth," trans. Brian Holmes, *Critical Inquiry* 16, no. 2 (1990): 291–312.
Leibniz, Gottfried Wilhelm. "Discourse on Metaphysics." In *Philosophical Papers and Letters*, edited and translated by Leroy E. Loemker. Boston: D. Reidel Publishing Co., 1976.
Leibniz, Gottfried Wilhelm. *Philosophische Schriften*, Vol. 1. Frankfurt: Suhrkamp Verlag, 1996.
Lefebvre, Henri. *Dialectical Materialism.* Translated by John Sturrock. London: Jonathan Cape Ltd., 1968.
Louden, R. B. "Moralische Stärke: Tugend al seine Pflicht gegen sich selbst." In *Moralische Motivation. Kant und die Alternativen*, edited by H. Klemme, M. Kühn, and D. Schöneker, 79–95. Hamburg: Meiner, 2006.
Lozano, V. Rocco. "*Los cambios de paradigma de la 'Schiller-Forschung,'*" *Daimon Revista Internacional de Filosofia* 46 (2009): 205–13.
Lyotard, Jean-François. "After the Sublime, the State of Aesthetics." In *The Inhuman*, translated by Geoffery Bennington and Rachel Bowlby, 135–43. Stanford, CA: Stanford University Press, 1991.
Lyotard, Jean-François. "Anima Minima." In *Moralité Postmodernes*, 199–210. Paris: Galilée, 1993.

Macor, L. "The Bankruptcy of Love. Schiller's Early Ethics." *Publications of the English Goethe Society* 86 (2017), forthcoming.

Macor, L. "Introducing the New Schiller," *Philosophical Readings*, Volume 5 (2013): 3-6.

Macor, L. *Der morastige Zirkel der menschlichen Bestimmung. Friedrich Schillers Weg von der Aufklärung zu Kant, von der Verfasserin aus dem Italienischen übersetzt, auf den neuesten Stand gebracht und erweitert.* Würzburg: Königshausen & Neumann, 2010.

Macor, L. *Die Moralphilosophie des jungen Schiller. Ein "Kantianer ante litteram,"* in High, Martin, and Oellers (eds.), *Who Is This Schiller Now?* 99-115.

Mainland, W. "Introduction," in *On Naïve and Sentimental Poetry*. Edited with introduction and annotation by William F. Mainland. Oxford: Blackwell, 1957.

Mannheim Karl. "Conservatism: its concept and its nature." In *Conservatism. A Contribution to the Sociology of Knowledge*. London: Routledge, 1997, 72-110.

Martín-Barbero, Jesús. *De los medios a las mediaciones. Comunicación, cultura y hegemonía.* Naucalpan: Gili, 1991.

Marx, Karl. "The German Ideology." In *The Marx-Engels Reader*. Edited by Robert C. Tucker. New York: W. W. Norton & Company, Inc., 1978, 146-200.

Mendelssohn, Moses. "On the sublime and naive in fine sciences." In *Philosophical Writings*, edited and translated by D. O. Dahlstrom. Cambridge: Cambridge University Press, 1997.

Menke, Christoph. "Die Depotenzierung des Souveräns im Gesang. Claudio Monteverdis *Die Krönung der Poppea* und die Demokratie." In *Literatur als Philosophie—Philosophie als Literatur*, edited by Eva Horn, Bettine Menke, and Christoph Minke, 281-96. München: Gallica, 2005.

Menke, Christoph. *Die Gegenwart der Tragödie. Versuch über Urteil und Spiel.* Frankfurt: Suhrkamp Verlag, 2005.

Menke, Christoph,"Praxis und Spiel. Bemerkungen zur Dialektik eines postavantgardistischen Theaters," in *AufBrüche. Theaterarbeit zwischen Text und Situation*, edited by. Patrick Primavesi and Olaf A. Schmitt, 27-35. Berlin: Theater der Zeit, 2004.

Menke, Christoph "The Presence of Tragedy." *Critical Horizons* 5, no. 1 (2004): 201-25.

Misch, M. "Schiller und die Religion." In *Schiller-Handbuch*, edited by Helmut Koopmann, 198-215. Stuttgart: Kroner, 1998.

Mr. Smith Goes to Washington, directed by Frank Capra. 1939. Los Angeles, Columbia Pictures.

My Fair Lady, directed by George Cukor. 1964. Burbank, CA: Warner Home Video.

Nancy, Jean-Luc, "The Inoperative Community." In The Inoperative Community, translated by Peter Connor, Lisa Garbus, Michael Holland, and Simona Sawhney, 1-42. Minneapolis: University of Minnesota Press, 1991.

Nancy, Jean-Luc. *La Remarque spéculative (Un bon mot de Hegel).* Paris: Galilée, 1973.

Nancy, Jean-Luc and Phillipe Lacoue-Labarthe. *The Literary Absolute*. Translated by Philip Barnard and Cheryl Lester. Albany, NY: SUNY Press, 1998.

Nietzsche, Friedrich. *Human, All Too Human: A Book for Free Spirits*. Translated by R. J. Hollingdale. New York: Cambridge University Press, 1986.

Nietzsche, Friedrich. *Sämtliche Werke. Kritische Studienausgabe in 15 Bänden.* Edited by Giorgio Colli and Mazzino Montinari. Munich: Walter de Gruyter 1999.

Nilges, Yvonne. "Schiller und die Demokratie." In High, Martin, and Oellers, *Who is this Schiller now?* 205-16.

Nilges, Yvonne. *Schiller und das Recht.* Göttingen: Wallstein, 2012.

Norris, Andrew. "The Disappearance of the French Revolution in Hegel's *Phenomenology of Spirit.*" *The Owl of Minerva* 44, no 1/2 (2012-2013): 37-66.

Novalis. *Schriften.* Vol. II. Edited by Richard Samuel, Hans-Joachim Mähl, and Gerhard Schulz. Stuttgart: Kohlhammer, 1965.

Nuzzo, Angelia. "Arbitrariness and Freedom: Hegel on Rousseau and Revolution." In *Rousseau and Revolution*, edited by R. Lauristen and M. Thorup, 64-82. London: Continuum, 2011.

Peperzak, Adrian. *Le Jeune Hegel et la vision morale du monde.* The Hague: Martinus Nijhoff, 1969.

Rancière, Jacques. *Aesthetics and its Discontents.* Translated by Steven Corcoran. Malden, MA: Polity, 2009.

Rancière, Jacques. «Aesthetics as Politics,» in Rancière, *Aesthetics and its Discontents*, 19–44.

Rancière, Jacques. "Les antinomies du modernisme," in, Rancière, *Malaise dans l'esthétique.* Paris: Editions Galilée, 2004.

Rancière, Jacques. "The antinomies of Modernism," in Rancière, *Aesthetics and its Discontents*,

Rancière, Jacques. "L'esthétique comme politique," in Rancière, *Malaise dans l'esthétique*, 31-64.

Rancière, Jacques. *Malaise dans l'esthétique.* Paris: Galilée, 2004.

Rancière, Jacques. *Le partage du sensible. Esthétique et politique.* Paris: Wilhelm Fink, 2000.

Rancière, Jacques. *The Politics of Aesthetics: The Distribution of the Sensible.* Translated by Gabriel Rockhill. New York: Continuum International Publishing Group, 2004.

Revel, Judith. *Le vocabulaire de Foucault.* Paris: Ellipses, 2002.

Riedel, W. *Abschied von der Ewigkeit*, in *Gedichte von Friedrich Schiller. Interpretationen.* Edited by N. Oellers. Stuttgart: Reclam, 1996.

Riedel, W. *Die Anthropologie des jungen Schiller. Zur Ideengeschichte der medizinischen Schriften und der "Philosophischen Briefe."* Würzburg: Königshausen & Neumann, 1985.

Riedel, W. "Theorie der Übertragung. Empirische Psychologie und Ästhetik der schönen Natur bei Schiller." In *Kunst und Wissen. Beziehungen zwischen Ästhetik und Erkenntnistheorie im 18. und 19. Jahrhundert*, edited by A. Bauereisen, S. Pabst, and A. Vesper, 121-38. Würzburg: Königshausen & Neumann, 2009.

Riedel, W. "Philosophie des Schönen als politische Anthropologie. Schillers 'Augustenburger Briefe' und die 'Briefe über die ästhetische Erziehung des Menschen,'"in "Reading Schiller. Ethics, Asthetics, and Religion," ed. L. A. Macor, special issue, *Philosophical Readings*, no 5 (2013): 118-71.

Riedel, W. "*Um ein Naturprinzip der Sittlichkeit. Motive der Mitleidsdiskussion im 18. Jahrhundert.*" In *Ethik und Ästhetik des Mitleids*, edited by N. Gülcher and I. van der Lühe, 15-31. Freiburg/Berlin: Rombach, 2007.

Robert, J. *Vor der Klassik. Die Ästhetik Schillers zwischen Karlsschule und Kant-Rezeption.* New York: de Gruyter, 2011.

Rousseau, Jean Jacques. *Du contrat social, ou Principes du droit politique*, Vol. 5 of *Œuvres de Jean-Jacques Rousseau*, Paris: E. A. Lequien, 1821-23.

Rousseau, Jean Jacques. *Correspondance complète de Jean Jacques Rousseau*, Vol. 3. Edited by the Institute et Musée Voltaire and the Voltaire Foundation (Geneva/Oxford 1965-1998).

Rousseau, Jean Jaqcues. "Of the Social Contract," in *The Social and other later political writings*, edited and translated by Victor Gourevitch. New York: Cambridge University Press, 1997.

Sánchez, A. Quero. "Der Einfluß der Kantischen Philosophie auf Schiller und der fragmentarische Zustand des 'Geistersehers' und der 'Philosophischen Briefe,'" *Literaturwissenschaftliches Jahrbuch, NF*, no 45 (2004): 71-98.

Sartre, Jean-Paul. *L'être et le néant: Essai d'ontologie phénoménologique.* Paris: Gallimard, 1943.

Schelling, Friedrich Wilhelm Joseph. *Materialen zu Schellings philosophisches Anfängen.* Edited by M. Frank. Frankfurt: Suhrkamp, 1975.

Schelling, Friedrich Wilhelm Joseph. *Sämmtliche Werke*, Division I, Vol. 3. Edited by K. F. A. Schelling. Stuttgart: J.G. Cotta, 1856-64.

Schings, H. J. *Der mitleidigste Mensch ist der beste Mensch. Poetik des Mitleids von Lessing bis Büchner.* Munchen: Beck, 1980.

Schlegel, Friedrich. *Kritische Ausgabe seiner Werke*, Vol. XVIII. Edited by Ernst Behler. München: Ferdinand Schöningh, 1975.

Schopenhauer, Arthur. *Gesammelte Briefe*. Edited by Arthur Hübscher. Bonn: Bouvier, 1978.

Schopenhauer, Arthur. *Sämtliche Werke.* Edited by Wolfgang Freiherr von Löhneysen. Stuttgart: Cotta-Insel, 1968.

Sharpe, Lesley. *Schiller: Drama, Thought and Politics.* Cambridge: Cambridge University Press, 1991.

Sharpe, Lesley. *Schiller's Aesthetic Essays: Two Centuries of Criticisms.* Columbia, SC: Camden House, 1995.

TIQQUN, "Podría surgir una metafísica crítica como ciencia de los dispositivos." In *Contribución a la guerra en curso*, 27-118. Madrid: Errata Naturae, 2012.

Von Hartmann, Eduard. "Aphorismen über das Drama" in *Gesammelte Studien und Aufsätze Gemeinverständliche Inhalts*, 251-307. 1870. Reprint Berlin: Duncker, 1876.

Von Wiese, Benno. *Schiller.* Stuttgart: Metzler, 1963.

Wilhelm, Fredrich, and Joseph Schelling. *Materialen zu Schellings philosophisches Anfängen.* Edited by M. Frank. Frankfurt: Suhrkamp, 1975.

Witte, William. "The Reflective Poet." In *Schiller*, 53-68. Oxford: Clarendon Press, 1949.

Contributors

María del Rosario Acosta López is currently Associate Professor of Philosophy at DePaul University, Chicago. She is the author of several monographs in Spanish, including *La tragedia como conjuro: el problema de lo sublime en Friedrich Schiller* [Tragedy's Spell: On the Sublime and the Political in Friedrich Schiller] (Universidad Nacional de Colombia/Universidad de los Andes, 2008), and has coedited and organized special volumes in English on *Law and Violence* (New Centennial Review, 2014), *Philosophy in Colombia* (Philosophical Readings, 2018), *Collective Temporalities* (diacritics, 2019), and *Critique in German Philosophy* (SUNY, 2019).

Frederick Beiser is currently Professor of Philosophy at Syracuse University, Syracuse, New York. He is the author of many books, of which the most recent are *The German Historicist Tradition* (OUP, 2011), *Late German Idealism* (OUP, 2013), *After Hegel* (Princeton, 2014) and *The Genesis of Neo-Kantianism* (2014).

María Luciana Cadahia is currently Assistant Professor at Pontificia Universidad Javeriana, Bogotá, Colombia. She holds a European PhD in Philosophy from the Universidad Autónoma de Madrid (2012) and has been a Professor at Universidad Autónoma de Madrid and FLACSO-Ecuador and visiting Researcher and Professor at Friedrich Schiller-Universität Jena, Université Paris I (Sorbonne), University of Brighton, and Universidad de Los Andes. She has published numerous papers, essays and edited collections, and she is the author of the monograph *Sensibility Mediation. Towards a Critique of Dispositive*s (Fondo de Cultura Económica, 2017).

Daniel O. Dahlstrom, John R. Silber Professor of Philosophy at Boston University, is the author of *Philosophical Legacies* (Catholic University of America Press,

2008), *The Heidegger Dictionary* (Bloomsbury, 2013) and *Identity, Authenticity, and Humility* (Marquette, 2017). His translations include Friedrich Schiller's *Aesthetic Writings* (Continuum, 1993).

Manfred Frank, Professor of Philosophy Emeritus at Eberhard Karls University of Tübingen, Germany, is the author of a great many books and essays. His many works in English include *What is Neostructuralism?* (Univeristy of Minnesota, 1989), *The Subject and the Text. Essays on Literary Theory and Philosophy* (Cambridge University Press, 1997), *The Philosophical Foundations of Early German Romanticism* (SUNY, 2005), and the forthcoming *An Introduction to Early Romantic Aesthetics* (Columbia University Press).

Laura Anna Macor is currently Assistant Professor of the History of Philosophy at the University of Florence. Her research interests lie in German eighteenth- and nineteenth-century culture, with a particular emphasis on interdisciplinary issues. She is the author of four scholarly monographs, and particularly: *Der morastige Zirkel der menschlichen Bestimmung. Friedrich Schillers Weg von der Aufklärung zu Kant* (Würzburg: Königshausen & Neumann, 2010); *Die Bestimmung des Menschen (1748–1800). Eine Begriffsgeschichte* (Stuttgart-Bad Cannstatt: frommann-holzboog, 2013).

Christoph Menke is Professor at the Goethe Universität Frankfurt am Main, in the Department of Philosophy. He is the author of several publications, including in English *The Sovereignty of Art. Aesthetic Negativity after Adorno and Derrida* (MIT Press, 1998); *Reflections of Equality* (Stanford UP, 2006); *Tragic Play. Tragedy. Irony and Theater from Sophocles to Beckett* (Columbia UP, 2009); *Force. A fundamental Concept of Aesthetic Anthropology* (Fordham UP, 2012); and *Law and Violence. Christoph Menke in Dialogue* (Manchester: Manchester Univ. Press, 2018).

Yvonne Nilges received her Doctorate in German and English philology from the University of Heidelberg (Germany) in 2006. From 2006 to 2007 she was Visiting Fellow at Harvard University and from 2007 to 2010 she was Powys Roberts Fellow at the University of Oxford (UK). She currently works at the Catholic University of Eichstätt-Ingolstadt (Germany) and the University of Heidelberg and has been Visiting Professor at both the University of Canterbury (Christchurch, New Zealand) and the University of Osnabrück (Germany). Her publications focus on German and Comparative literature and culture from the eighteenth to the twentieth century. Her books include monographs on Richard Wagner's aesthetic response to Shakespeare (2007), Schiller and law (2012), and religious themes in the works of Thomas Mann (forthcoming).

Jeffrey L. Powell is Professor of Philosophy at Marshall University. He is editor of *Heidegger and Language* (Indiana University Press, 2013), and co-translator (with Will McNeill) of Martin Heidegger's *The History of Beyng* (Indiana University Press, 2015). He has published essays concerning Husserl, Levinas, Heidegger, Blanchot, Foucault, and others.

Jacques Rancière is Professor of Philosophy Emeritus at the University of Paris-VIII. He is the author of many texts translated into English, including *The Ignorant Schoolmaster* (Stanford University Press, 1991), *Dis-agreement: Politics and Philosophy* (University of Minnesota, 1999), *The Philosopher and His Poor* (Duke University Press, 2004), *Aesthetics and Its Discontents* (Polity Press, 2009), *Dissensus: On Politics and Aesthetics* (Continuum, 2010), and *Aisthesis: Scenes from the Aesthetic Regime of Art* (Verso, 2013).

Index

Adorno, Theodor, 130, 134, 140–41, 160–61, 171n14, 172n25, 180–81, 188
aesthetic autonomy, 126, 129, 131, 140, 143
aesthetic idea, 41, 47
aesthetic education, 11–19, 63–64, 66, 95, 132–33, 136–49, 169–70
aesthetic experience, 49, 123–24, 130–31, 183–84
aesthetic law, 143
aesthetic path, 66, 76
aesthetic regimes, 130, 144, 148
aesthetic state, 5, 18–21, 81n42, 94, 124, 133–34, 143, 185–86
Agamben, Giorgio, 60, 175–77, 182, 185, 187–89
alienation, 16, 135, 180
analytic of beautiful, the, 129
Ancient Greeks, 52, 84, 108, 112, 131
Aristotle, 52, 85, 103
art of the beautiful, 125
artificial, the, 103
aura, 160–65, 172n22, 173n30, 181
autonomy, 129–31
   Kant's conception of, 5, 149
   Rousseau's conception of, 69
avant-garde, the, 129, 132, 140, 146

Bahnsen, Julius, 83–84, 86

Balibar, Etienne, 165
barbarian, 75, 141–42
Bataille, Georges, 149
Beautiful Soul [*die schöne Seele*], 30–31, 53
beautiful action, 30
beauty, 40–53, 183
   as the appearance of freedom, 44, 93
   as the symbol of the morally good, 45, 154–58, 165
   ideal form, and, 164
   Kantian Ideal of, 158
Beiser, Frederick, 78n9
Benjamin, Andrew, 171n3
Benjamin, Walter, 153–55, 158–70, 161, 162, 181–82
bios, 177
Brecht, Bertolt, 139–40, 161, 172n25
Burke, Edmund, 12, 20n6, 198

Calderón de la Barca, Pedro, 86
Capra, Frank, 117n12
Cervantes, Miguel de, 110
character, 27–29, 31, 102, 184–85
Che cos'è un dispositivo?, 175
cinema, 180–81
cognition
   Kant's two-stem theory of, 38–56
   Schiller's theory of, 52–56
collective perception, 181

Comay, Rebecca, 78n7, 81n39
community, 124, 129–30, 132–33, 146
constitutional law, 11
critique
    of epistemological turn, 67
    of metaphysics, 60
    of violence, 60–61
Critique of Judgment (1790), 32, 37–56, 126, 154–58, 164, 166
Critique of Practical Reason (1788), 24, 32, 164
Critique of Pure Reason (1781), 24–25, 38, 169
culture, 126–28
    Ancient Greek, 94, 108
    evils of, 108
    moral role of, 28, 32

D'Hondt, Jacques, 78n5
Dadaism, 170
darstellende Schriftsteller, 67
Darstellung, 185
De Certeau, Michel, 178
De Man, Paul, 5, 7 183
De Martino, Ernesto, 177
    El mundo mágico, 177
Delgiorgi, Katerina, 36n14
democracy, 60
    monarchical, 157
    representative, 19–20
demos, 170
Derrida, Jacques, 115, 170
Descartes, René, 38
destiny. *See* fate
dialectic of enlightenment, 17
dispositif, 175–88
    sensible dimension of, 182
dissensus, 129, 132, 135
distribution of the sensible, 125, 127–28, 139–41, 146, 161
divine creation, 88
domination, 126–29, 140–48

drive, 25, 28, 30, 70, 75, 126, 143, 145, 167–69, 186–88. *See also under* play
Düttman, Alexander, 154, 171n3
duty, 27–33, 88, 95, 126
    Schiller's critique of, 31–33

elegy, 110, 118
Elements of the Philosophy of Right (1821), 16, 75
Emile, or On Education (1762), 14
emotion
    education of, 27–29
    role in moral life, 23–33
Enlightenment, the, 60–76, 87, 187
    Schiller's critique of, 183
entelechy, Aristotle's model of, 52
episteme, 176
Esposito, Roberto, 60, 77, 175–77, 185–88
    Due. La macchina della teologia politica e il posto del pensiero, 177
Ethical Ascetics, Kant's conception of, 32
Euclid
    axioms, 55

fascism, 153–54, 159–61, 165, 167, 170
fate, 84, 87, 92, 147
Fenves, Peter, 154
Ferrer, Vicente, 179
Fichte, Johann Gottlieb, 54–55, 145
Fielding, Henry, 110
Flaubert, Gustave, 129
Forberg, Karl, 54
form
    drive, 126, 131
    relation to content, 133, 156
Foucault, Michel, 176–78, 188
foundationalism, 55–56
Frauenstädt, Julius, 85–86
free play. *See* play

freedom
appearance of, 44, 93
in Schillerian tragedy, 91–93
Kant's conception of, 41, 44–46, 168
self-mirroring of, 53
French Revolution, The, 11–12, 14, 17–18, 38, 59–76, 79n11, 124, 127–28, 165–66, 169
Futurism, 159–60

Gadamer, Hans-Georg
Truth and Method, 42
genius, 101, 105–109, 130
gender and, 106
naïveté of, 107, 117n14, 117n15
German Idealism idealism, 38, 54–55, 63, 132, 160
German Romanticism, 1–2, 63, 168
Goethe, Johann Wolfgang von, 58n21, 84, 86, 102, 116n4g
good heart, 26
grace [*Gnade*], 50, 94, 106
Greek polity, 16
Guyer, Paul, 155–56

Hardenberg, Friedrich von. *See* Novalis
harmony, 27, 94, 102, 110–11, 119n24, 129, 158, 167
of the faculties, 93
Hartmann, Eduard von, 84
Hegel, G. W. F., 16, 37, 51, 56, 59–76, 81n47, 82n48, 132–34, 140–41, 161, 175–77, 182, 184, 189n1
absolute freedom, conception of, 63, 74–75
civil society, conception of, 64
immediacy, conception of, 70
Heidegger, Martin, 59, 114, 119n27, 155, 170, 176
authenticity, conception of, 114
Dasein, 119n27
Henrich, Dieter, 45

historicity of philosophy, 65
Hölderlin, Friedrich, 44, 48–51, 132
Farewell, 48
Hyperion, 44
letter to Neuffer (1794), 51
Homer, 102
Horace, 110
Husserl, Edmund, 113–15, 119n27
hypotyposis, 155–56
Hyppolite, Jean, 176–78, 182, 189n1

idyll, 110–11, 118n20
industrial revolution, 153, 161
imagination, 37–56, 75, 135, 143, 162
impersonal, philosophy of, 199
inclination [*Neigung*], 26, 27, 29, 31, 49, 51, 94–95
indifference, 53. *See also* zero condition
intellectual intuition, 39, 55
intellectus archetypus. *See* intellectual intuition

Jacobin dictatorship, 64, 68
Johnson, Samuel, 85
Juno Ludovisi statue, 124, 125, 130, 139
justice, 86, 89, 90–91, 147
Juvenal, 110

Kant and the Problem of Metaphysics, 155
Kant, Immanuel, 37–56, 153–70
beauty as the symbol of the morally good, 44–45
ethics, 11, 25–27, 31, 33
genius, 106
ideal of beauty, 158
practical philosophy, 23–33
schematism, 155
sublime, theory of, 129
symbolic presentations, 41, 156
Klopstock, Friedrich Gottlieb, 110

Körner, Christian Gottfried, 15, 24, 29, 34n4, 44, 116n5
Krell, David Farrell, 173n42

Lacoue-Labarthe, Philippe, 77
latitudinarian, 27, 35n10
law
  hatred of, 32
  love of, 32
Lebenskunst, 139
Lectures on Aesthetics, 133
Lefebvre, Henri, 167
Leibniz, Gottfried Wilhelm, 38–39, 87
Leibnizian-Wolffian School. *See* Wolffian School
Leibnizianism, 55
living form, 187–88
Locke, John, 157
love, 26, 48–52, 87
Lukàcs, Georg, 141, 146
Lyotard, Jean-Francois, 129, 135

Mahler, Gustave, 134
Maimon, Salomon, 38
Mainländer, Philipp, 84
Mallarmé, Stéphane, 129
Manner [*Manier*], 102, 116n5
Mannheim, Karl, 77n4
Marinetti, Filippo Tommaso Emilio, 153, 159
Martín-Barbero, Jésus, 176, 178–81
Marx, Karl, 16, 62, 132, 141, 161, 165
Marxism, 177
Marxist avant-garde, 132
Matthisson, Friedrich, 46
mass culture, 179–80
Mendelssohn, Moses, 116n7
Metaphysics of Morals (1797), 32
Milton, John, 110
mimesis, 127
monogram of the soul, 48
Montesquieu, 91

mood [*Stimmung*], 40, 112, 170, 185
moral constitution, 105
moral feeling, 25, 32–33
moral freedom, 29, 129, 166
moral judgments, 157–58
moral nostalgia, 108
moral pleasure, 103–107, 114, 117n15
moral respect. *See* respect
moral sense, Scottish theory of, 23
moral state, 70, 74, 81n42
Mosaic Law, 135
music, 162, 180
musician, 124–25, 134
myth, 77n2, 132, 159, 171n14

naïve poetry, 101–15
naïveté, 104–109, 112, 115–17
Nancy, Jean-Luc, 60, 77n2
naturalness, paradox of, 112
nature, 87
  longing for, 107
  poetry's relation to, 101–15
Naturstaat. *See* state of nature
nearness, 181
negation, 72, 76, 140, 160–62, 167, 184, 186
neutralization, 114, 131
Nietzsche, Friedrich, 17, 140, 160
Notstaat. *See* State of Nature
Novalis, 39, 47–48, 54–56
null state. *See* zero condition
Nuzzo, Angelica, 79n12

Oedipus complex, 146–47
Oldest System-Program of German Idealism 54, 132–33, 173n42, 184
On Perpetual Peace, 158, 164
original sin, 85, 134
Ovid, 49, 119n24

Paradise Lost, 110
pessimism, 83–96

phenomena
    givenness of, 113
phenomenology
    poetic, 111–15
    Schillerian, 101–15
    twentieth-century 112
Phenomenology of Spirit, The, 63, 65, 67–68, 71–72, 74
philosophical language, 67
photography, 162, 180–81
phyein [φύειν], 52
Plato, 50, 54, 127, 141, 147, 165
play [*Spiel*], 41, 45–46, 53, 66, 95, 110, 119, 123–29, 132, 138–49, 188
    drive, 127, 129, 143, 186–87
    of rule and exception, 127
poetic justice, 85–86, 147
poetic spirit, 102
poetry
    ancient vs. modern, 102, 108, 112
    Greek, 104
police regime, 147
politician, the, 154
politics
    aestheticization of, 5–7, 159–70
    game of, 187–88
Pope Adrian VI, 105
positivity
    Hegel's early conception of, 175, 182
    Schiller's conception of, 175–82
postmodern, the, 140, 148
postmodernity, 138
practical reason, 31, 41–49, 66, 164
private sphere, 148
proletariat, the, 159, 166–67
providential order, 88

quietism, 95

Rancière, Jacques, 137–49, 161, 170
Rapp, Gottlieb Heinrich, 25

reason [*Vernunft*]
    and sensibility, 92–93, 185
    demands of, 43, 88
    egoism of, 75
    self-positing of, 70
    sovereignty of, 32, 60, 146
    violence of, 59–76
recollection [*Erinnerung*], 110
reflection, Husserl's conception of, 113, 115
Reflections on the Revolution in France, 12
Reign of Terror, 11, 61–63, 68. See also French Revolution
Reinhold, Karl Leonhard, 38, 42, 55–56
Religion within the Boundaries of Mere Reason (1794), 32
representation. See *Darstellung* and *Vorstellung*
repeatability, 154
reproducibility, 154, 162, 165
respect [*Achtung*], 25, 29–31, 49–53, 95, 135, 158. See also moral feeling
Rousseau, Jean-Jacques, 11–20, 119n24
    amour de soi, 13
    civilization, theory of, 13, 19
    Emile, or On Education (1762), 14
    general will [*volonté générale*], 11–12, 15–19, 68–71, 75
    inalienable, conception of, 14
    Julie, or the New Heloise [*Julie ou la Nouvelle Héloïse*], 15
    legal and political philosophy, 11
    Of the Social Contract, [*Du Contrat social*] (1762), 15, 69, 82n47
    social contract theory, 14–17, 68–70

Sartre, Jean-Paul
    good faith, conception of, 114
satire, 110, 119n22
Schelling, Friedrich, 37–56, 132–33
    identity philosophy, 56

Schelling, Friedrich *(continued)*
    System of Transcendental Idealism
        (1800), 133
Schiller, Friedrich
    account of moral agency, 24, 31, 33
    critique of duty, 32
    freedom, conception of, 52
    ideas, conception of, 71
    positivity, conception of, 175–78, 182
    theory of cognition, 46–52
    theory of poetry, 101–15

    works:

    "Artists, The," 21n16
    Augustenburger Briefe, 20n7, 24–25
    Bride of Messina, The, 83, 85, 90–91
    *Connection between Animal and
        Spiritual Nature in Man*, 79
    Don Carlos, 85–86, 91–92, 137–47
    Freigeisterei der Leidenschaften, 88
    Kallias Letters, or On Beauty, 42
    Legislation of Lycurgus and Solon, The,
        11, 79n11
    Letters to Prince Friedrich von Schleswig,
        79n10
    *Moral Utility of Aesthetic Manners,
        The*, 25, 27–28
    Natur und Schule, 118n16
    *On the Aesthetic Education of Man
        in a Series of Letters*, 11–20, 27,
        63–69, 101, 103, 123–24, 138–39,
        145, 164, 175, 182
    On the Art of Tragedy, 92
    On the Danger of Aesthetic Manners,
        25
    On Grace and Dignity, 25, 27, 30, 32,
        34, 48, 50, 81n42, 93–94
    On Matthison's Poetry, 46, 58n22
    On Naïve and Sentimental Poetry, 94,
        101–15
    On the Sublime (1801), 56
    Philosophical Letters, 34n8, 39, 88–89

    Philosophische Egoist, Der, 118n16
    Philosophy of Physiology, 39
    Police, The, 147–48
    "Relationship of the Beautiful to
        Reason," 49
    "Resignation," 25, 34n8, 86, 88
    Robbers, The, 35n9, 85, 90–91
    Spaziergang unter den Linden, 87
    Spielende Knabe, Der, 118n16
    Stage as a Moral Institution, The, 20n3
    Wallenstein, 85
Schlegel, Friedrich, 56, 139
Schopenhauer, Arthur, 83–96
    Letter to Frauenstädt, 85
    tragedy, theory of, 85–86, 90–93
    *World as Will and Representation, The
        [Die Welt als Wille und Vorstellung]*
        (1st ed., 1819), 84–86, 96
Scottish Enlightenment, 87
sentimental poetry, 101–15
    self-conscious character of, 109
    three types of, 110–11, 118n20
self-feeling, 42
sensibility [*Sinnlichkeit*], 12, 14, 16,
    27–31, 38–43, 46–49, 37–53,
    65–66, 75–76, 92–93, 124–26,
    139–42, 145, 154, 168, 179–88
    culture of, 27
    education of, 28–29, 31
sensitivity, 13
sensus communis [common sense], 126,
    157
Shakespeare, William, 85–86, 102
Shaw, George Bernard
    Pygmalion, 117
Sorrows of Young Werther, The, 102
Sophocles, 83, 86
sovereign, the, 150n24
spectator, the. *See* spectatorship
spectatorship, 62, 84–85, 93, 124,
    129–30, 144
speculative idealism
    Hegelian, 51

speculative thinking, 67, 73, 184
spirit [*Geist*]
    Schiller's conception of, 52
Spirit of Christianity and its Fate, The, 78n6, 82n47
State, the, 11–13, 16–18, 75, 105, 128, 132, 146, 157, 165–66, 182–84
    as machine, 12
    as work of art, 12
state of nature, the, 13–14, 21n9, 132
statesman, the, 165
subjectivity, 46, 74, 113, 141–48, 166
    free, 141–43
    political, 146
sublime, the [*Erhabene*], 56, 76, 107, 129, 135

tacit consent, 69
Taylorism, 134
technē, 154
Thalia, 88
theater, 134, 179
    moral role of, 89–90
theodicy, 89
Thrasymachus, 165
TIQUUN Collective, 175–76
totalitarianism, 77
tragedy, 15, 84–96, 118n21, 153, 160
    cosmic justice in, 90
    Greek, 153, 160

tragic hero, 84–85, 92–93
transcendental philosophy, 18

understanding [*Verstand*], 38–49, 65–67, 76, 123–26, 129, 139–43, 155, 182–88
unity of reason, 39, 46

violence, 30, 59–76, 182–83
    cycles of, 76
    of reason, 59–76
    of understanding, 182–83
virtue, 23–27, 31–33, 85, 89–90, 94–95, 117n14, 137–38, 132, 145–48, 150n24
    inner necessity of, 25
vocation of man, 29, 94
Voltaire, 21
Vorstellung, 73, 185

war, 153–54, 159–61, 167
will, 170, 188
Wolff, Christian, 38–39
Wolffian school, 23, 87
"Work of Art in the Age of Mechanical Reproduction, The," 170

zero condition 53, 143. *See also* Indifference
zoé, 177